THE MASTERS
GOLF'S MOST PRESTIGIOUS TRADITION

DAWSON TAYLOR

CONTEMPORARY
BOOKS, INC.
CHICAGO ▪ NEW YORK

Library of Congress Cataloging-in-Publication Data

Taylor, Dawson.
     The Masters : golf's most prestigious tradition.

     1. Masters Golf Tournament—History.   2. Augusta
National Golf Club—History.   I. Title.
GV970.T393   1986   796.352'7   86-16553
ISBN 0-8092-4889-1

To the memory of two of the greatest gentlemen golfers of all time, the late Mr. Robert Tyre Jones, Jr., and the late Mr. Clifford Roberts, whose good taste and intelligence made the Masters what it is today, the finest golf tournament in the world.

Photographs, except as otherwise noted on page x, by Peter Dazeley.

Copyright © 1986 by Dawson Taylor
All rights reserved
Published by Contemporary Books, Inc.
180 North Michigan Avenue, Chicago, Illinois 60601
Fourth Edition
Manufactured in the United States of America
Library of Congress Catalog Card Number: 86-16553
International Standard Book Number: 0-8092-4889-1

Published simultaneously in Canada by Beaverbooks, Ltd.
195 Allstate Parkway, Valleywood Business Park
Markham, Ontario L3R 4T8 Canada

CONTENTS

PREFACE

I am a true golf fanatic. I love the game of golf, and I love great golf courses. I have been playing "the gentlemen's game" for more than fifty years with more or less success. My game is a respectable one with scores usually in the mid-seventies, so that when I play an especially difficult course such as Pine Valley or the Augusta National Golf Club, I try to break 80 (and sometimes I don't!).

For a long time, I have played what I call "imaginary golf" when I could not actually play a particular course. I remember walking famous Oakmont outside of Pittsburgh one year in February when there was an inch of snow on the ground. It didn't really matter. I knew, in my mind's eye, where my drives would go, what trouble I would get into, and how I would birdie the short uphill 4-par seventeenth hole to "save the round."

In 1964, I was fortunate enough to be invited to join a fine group of golfers, gentlemen all, who were going on a jaunt to Scotland and Ireland. We played many of the famous courses—Turnberry, Troon, Carnoustie, St. Andrews, Portmarnock, and others equally as renowned. One of our players, Mr. Herbert Trapp, had the thrill of an ace or hole-in-one at Dollymount or Royal Dublin. I arranged for a photograph of the group with Herb holding up the hole-in-one ball in triumph. The photographer was Mr. David Cowie of the *Dundee Courier and Inquirer*. I asked Mr. Cowie if he would follow my round of golf the next day at St. Andrews and photograph my shots from some of the famous "hallowed" places. He would. He came the next day and the result was an unusual album of sequential photographs of myself and some of the rest of our party playing the Old Course at St. Andrews. In particular, there were some very unusual sequences taken of searches in the gorse and heather, of striking the newly found ball and then searching for it again a few feet ahead where it had once more disappeared from view. There was one interesting photograph of my own explosion shot from "Shell" bunker over "Strath" bunker at the famous eleventh hole where the great "Bobby" Jones "picked up," certain that he had blown himself out of the

1921 British Open tournament with a bad 6 or 7 on that hole after a first-nine score of 41 strokes.

These photographs proved to be a great consolation and pleasure to me later on, especially in the wintertime, when they could be reviewed and the game replayed mentally. I began to call this pastime "imaginary golf."

Those golfer-readers who wish to play "Imaginary Golf at the Masters" can do so by studying the hole-by-hole drawings in plan layout and in "profile" layout, and by following in Chapter 59 the pictures and account of my own round, in which I attempt to unlock the secrets that would enable almost any reasonably good golfer to break 90 at Augusta National.

In 1966, I was privileged to be invited to attend the Masters tournament at Augusta National Golf Club in Augusta, Georgia. This was arranged by the late John Walter, great sportswriter of the *Detroit News*, who knew Mr. Clifford Roberts, Tournament Chairman and one of the founders of the club along with Mr. Robert T. Jones, Jr.

In the meantime, I had spoken to a book publisher that specialized in sports about my idea of writing a book that would show in pictures and words how the average golfer would play the Augusta National course. He liked the idea, and so I proceeded to get permission from Clifford Roberts, Chairman of the Augusta National Golf Club.

Mr. Roberts kindly gave me access to all the past tournament records. I was allowed to go into the locker rooms, trophy rooms, and places on the golf course where gallery members may never go. More than three hundred photographs were taken in one day. In Mr. Roberts' files, I found copies of the only tournament programs ever issued, those of 1934 and 1935. There was a wealth of information in them alone, particularly the comments of Dr. Alister MacKenzie regarding the construction of the course and the similarity of several Augusta holes to famous holes in Great Britain and Scotland. In the photographer's files were many

historical black-and-white photographs as well as another three hundred color transparencies of the play in earlier Masters tournaments. It became obvious that the book should be a complete tournament record of all the Masters tournaments, embellished by historical photographs and by color drawings of the holes on the golf course. Fortunately, a recent topographical survey of the terrain had been made. This was made available to me, and subsequently Robert Yaskell drew the beautiful hole-by-hole layouts that you find in this book.

Countless hours of research and study were spent in the microfilm library of *The New York Times* in my attempt to recreate the scene and the drama of the many past Masters tournaments. This I hope I have been able to do in the "capsule histories" of the Masters.

I have now attended twenty of the past twenty-one Masters tournaments. Every time I enter the clubhouse grounds down "Magnolia Lane" I get another thrill of excitement from being at the Augusta National course as another Masters tournament begins. Invariably I come to the course early on the first day and head for a vantage point behind the first green. It is quite a climb down into the deep valley in front of the first tee and then back up the hill to the beautiful fresh doubly-cut green more than 400 yards away. Soon the honorary starters, this year Gene Sarazen and Sam Snead, will tee off and then the rest of the field will come along playing in twosomes at ten-minute intervals.

Unless you have been there, you cannot appreciate the incredible beauty of that golf scene on opening day. The weather is usually magnificent, a little on the cool side. The birds are singing their hearts out in the woods nearby—cardinals, mockingbirds, blue jays, and flickers. There is not a sound, not even a whisper from the huge gallery that now extends all the way down the fairway toward the green several hundred yards. The first tee shots arch over the valley and come to rest on the fairway or sometimes in the large bunker. Someone with field glasses will yell "There it is" as a drive lands and runs along. Another Masters is underway, the greatest, most prestigious tournament in the world of golf.

The flower scene is beyond description; it is so beautiful, with literally thousands of azaleas everywhere, especially along the 500-yard-long thirteenth hole that winds around Rae's creek.

John Betjeman, the late poet laureate of England, once wrote a poem called "Seaside Golf." He expressed the Masters scene perfectly when he ended saying, "The splendour, the splendour of it all."

ACKNOWLEDGMENTS

This book would not have been possible without the kind permission and cooperation of Clifford Roberts, the late Chairman of the Augusta National Golf Club. It was he who ordered that the club records be opened to me and arranged for me to play this wonderful course, the dream of this golfer's lifetime.

I would like to express my sincere appreciation, too, to the following persons, publishers, and photographers: To Doubleday and Co. for their permission to reprint excerpts from the writings of Robert T. Jones, Jr.; to Prentice-Hall for their permission to reprint excerpts from *Advanced Golf* by Cary Middlecoff; to Tom Flaherty for permission to use excerpts from his book *THE MASTERS*; to Herbert Warren Wind for his inspiring golf reporting in *The New Yorker* magazine; to *The New York Times* and *Sports Illustrated* for their wonderful golf reporting; to Marion Benton for the historical photos of the early days of the Masters, its champions and its contestants; and to Robert Yaskell for his hole-by-hole drawings.

Photographic Credits

Smith, Hogan, Demaret picture: C. E. Englebrecht, Sparta, New Jersey.

Henry Picard picture: Bert and Richard Morgan Studio, Palm Beach, Florida.

Ben Hogan, Robert T. Jones, Jr., Clifford Roberts: P.G.A. of America.

Sam Snead, 1949 Masters: Augusta National Golf Club, George Schaeffer, Augusta, Georgia.

Palmer and Jones, Watson, Zoeller, Bembridge pictures: United Press International Photos.

Palmer, Venturi, and Jones, Player, Watson, Palmer, Ballesteros pictures: Wide World Photos.

Photos on pages 2, 3, 38 (bottom), 36, 49, 61 (top), 64 (bottom), 66, and 70: Marian Benton.

Jack Nicklaus photo, page 202: John Tacono for *Sports Illustrated* © Time, Inc.

Nick Price photos, page 209: Jeff McBride, PGA of America.

Nick Price scorecard, page 210: Jacqueline Duvoisin for *Sports Illustrated* © Time, Inc.

Color drawings, Chapter 59: Robert Yaskell.

1986 Masters photos, pages 204–205: Judy Ondrey, *Augusta Chronicle*.

Photos on pages 42–43, 58–59, 92–93, and 124–125: Stephen Szurlej.

Other photography: Peter Dazeley.

COMMENTS OF FORMER CHAMPIONS

Arnold Palmer: "As far as I am concerned there will never be another tournament to equal it."

Gary Player: "There is a certain atmosphere that a player does not experience in any other tournament. The golf course is the finest conditioned and most challenging I've ever played."

Jack Nicklaus: "Augusta National is my favorite course and the Masters my favorite golf tournament."

Bob Goalby: "To win on this challenging, superbly conditioned, and beautiful course was truly the thrill of my golfing lifetime."

Horton Smith: "To me the Augusta National has character, individuality, and personality. It is one of the few courses that really presents two games on almost every hole: a game of reaching the greens and another of figuring the ever-challenging contours after reaching the greens. In my opinion, contour is the best feature of the course . . . the golfer must place his tee shots in the best spots to simplify the shots to the green and figure the slopes and speed of the large and undulating putting surfaces."

Byron Nelson: "The course itself is the most beautiful one we play, and it requires our best efforts in both skill and judgment. Each hole presents an entirely different picture . . . and a different problem."

Ben Hogan: "Dignity is the keynote of the Masters Tournament, where the game of golf is elevated to the high position it deserves."

Sam Snead: "It is a course you enjoy playing even when 'Old Man Par' is giving you a going over. The Masters is the best tournament of all to watch. It is the most beautiful course of all, with all those azaleas and other beautiful flowers. Over the years the course has been built up so that spectators can watch two or three holes at a time instead of one. That's the way any great tournament should operate.

"Besides, they take good care of the players. They even have a special room where the past champions change their shoes."

Beautiful Augusta National opened its doors in 1932.

1
THE BEGINNING

In 1930, Robert T. Jones, Jr., in the eyes of the American public held a place of esteem second only to the immortal Babe Ruth. In fact, it might be said that Bobby Jones (all his life Bob Jones hated that diminutive nickname, and his friends never used it) brought the game of golf to the attention of millions of persons who either had never heard of the game before or, having heard of it, dismissed it as an effete game for rich men's sons.

Jones had had a remarkable career in golf. Even as a youngster of fourteen he had qualified for the United States Open—the toughest tournament in U.S. golf. He had won everything there was to win in golf by late 1929, so when he won all four of the important championships in 1930—the British Amateur, the British Open, the United States Open, and finally the United States Amateur—he had accomplished what came to be called "The Grand Slam of Golf." When he returned to America after winning the last British championship, he was given a ticker-tape procession down New York City's Fifth Avenue—the welcome of an Eisenhower returning triumphant from the war.

Bob Jones had done everything he had set his mind and body to do in the world of competitive golf, but he was tired from fourteen years of the battle—tired of the sinking feeling in the pit of his stomach as he stepped onto the next first tee of a championship course; tired of not eating because he couldn't eat during important matches; tired of the adulation of the crowds who would not allow him a private game of golf for his own pleasure.

So in 1930 Bob Jones announced that he would no longer engage in competitive golf but would retire to his law practice and business at his home in Atlanta. The American public was amazed at his decision, but as time went on, it began to see how right the decision had been. Perhaps Babe Ruth should have quit baseball immediately after hitting his record sixty home runs in one season. Later on, didn't Joe DiMaggio model his own career after that of Bob Jones?

In 1930, Bobby Jones accomplished what came to be called "The Grand Slam of Golf" by winning the British Amateur, the British Open, the United States Open, and the United States Amateur. He retired later that year and took on his next challenge—designing and building a golf course.

So Bob Jones did quit the competitive trail and played "friendly golf" with people whose company he enjoyed. He could now give instructions in golf, something he had dared not do as an amateur. The finest golf instructional movies came from Warner Brothers Films as a result of Bob Jones's knowledge and love of the game. He looked into the problem of better club design. His own set had been a conglomerate clutch of all different clubs, with weights and balances that did not agree with one another. Jones was sure that he could help design a better golf club, and he did. The A. C. Spalding Company brought out a set of Jones-designed golf clubs and sold them by the millions to the golfers of America. After all, hadn't the great Bobby Jones designed them?

Finally it came time for another venture Bob Jones had had in mind for many years. He wanted to help design and build a golf course with all the delights and challenges, the pleasures and travails, of the many fine courses he had played in his long career. He would find a choice piece of rolling countryside in Atlanta or near to it, and there he would build a golfer's paradise for himself and for his friends to enjoy. At last he would be able to play that private friendly game without the mob being on his heels, beseeching him for autographs at each successive tee.

At this point in Bob Jones's life there occurred a most marvelous melding of his great talents and experience with those of a successful Wall Street banker named Clifford Roberts. The two men had met several years before at a golf tournament. Roberts occasionally visited Augusta, Georgia, where Bob Jones's wife had been born. Cliff Roberts was aware of 365 acres of beautiful rolling Georgia pinelands that might fit into Bob Jones's golf-course-building plans. The property had been in the hands of a famous horticulturist and nursery owner, a Belgian baron named Prosper Jules Alphonse Berckmans. Although we are getting ahead of the story a bit, later on when the beautiful Augusta National opened its doors in 1932,

"The Manor House" at Augusta National Golf Club.

P. J. A. Berckmans's son (whose name was the same as his father's) was general manager of the club and his brother Alphonse Berckmans was its treasurer.

The Berckmans family had moved to Augusta in 1857, after having left Europe for political reasons. P. J. A. Berckmans, Sr., was a scholar, a horticulturist, a landscape architect, a botanist, and a nursery man. In Augusta he established the foremost nursery in the United States of America. In recognition of his remarkable work in horticulture, Mr. Berckmans was honored by many societies in Europe and America. The University of Georgia bestowed on him a Master of Science degree. He originated and disseminated hundreds of species of flowers, shrubs, and trees. It is very probable that without his imagination and talent the American South as we know it now would not have been so beautiful with azaleas and camellias, with peach and jasmine

trees. In the catalogue of Berckmans's nursery for 1861, there were 1,300 varieties of pears, 900 of apples, 300 of grapes, and more than 100 each of azaleas and camellias.

It was to this magnificent spot that Robert T. Jones and Clifford Roberts came. Accompanying them was Alfred Bourne of the Singer Sewing Maching Company, who had a winter home in Augusta. (Incidentally, the explanation for one's having a winter home in Augusta is that Atlanta is 1,050 feet above sea level to Augusta's 162. Winters are cold in Atlanta, less severe in Augusta.)

Jones has recorded in the following words what he felt as he turned off the highway and rode down the long archway of magnolias to the manor house: "I stood at the top of the hill before that fine old house and looked at the wide stretch of land rolling down the slope before me. It was cleared land for the

The program for the first Masters of 1934 read "First Annual Invitation Tournament."

most part, and you could take in the whole vista all the way down to Rae's Creek. I knew instantly it was the kind of terrain I had always hoped to find. I had been told, of course, about the marvelous trees and plants, but I was still unprepared for the great bonus of beauty Fruitlands offered. Frankly, I was overwhelmed by the exciting possibilities of a golf course set in the midst of such a nursery."

Next, the organization of the new golf club membership was established. Clifford Roberts and Robert Jones had many friends throughout the country, true golfers—that is, gentlemen who would appreciate and enjoy the kind of golf course and golf club membership the two entrepreneurs were envisioning. They sought and obtained a cosmopolitan group of members.

The program published in 1934 for the "First Annual Invitation Tournament" had a section devoted to "some of the members of Augusta National Golf Club" along with their portraits. Among the names were Edward F. Hutton, the stockbroker, of New York City; Eugene G. Grace of the steelmakers in Bethlehem, Pennsylvania; L. B. Maytag, industrialist, of Newton, Iowa; the sportswriter Grantland Rice; and many other equally prominent gentlemen and substantial businessmen. Only thirty members were to be allowed from Augusta itself. Truly, this club would be a national golf club in every sense of the word.

Robert T. Jones, Jr., had always admired the golf architecture of the famous Scot, Dr. Alister MacKenzie. Dr. MacKenzie was the overwhelming choice to design the new course and, after accepting the challenge, set about laying out the course in the spring of 1931.

Both Jones and MacKenzie wanted to construct a challenging golf course that would take the greatest possible advantage of the natural terrain and the natural beauty of the nursery acreage. Jones and MacKenzie were great believers in the principle of strategic design of a golf course. That is, let the player judge his own capabilities on any given day and give him one or even two alternate routes or methods of attack on par. If the player felt strong, he should be encouraged to cut the dogleg and be rewarded, after a successful shot, with a simpler shot to birdie territory than, say, the player who skirted trouble, played it safe, and thus would be left with a longer, more difficult shot onto the green. Here were two golf experts—MacKenzie by training and experience, Jones with less formal training but even greater golf playing experience and basic intuition concerning the rightness and wrongness of a golf hole layout. They decided to reward the player in proportion to the type of golf shot required of him and how well that shot was played.

Jones planned the Augusta course as a wide open one, because he wanted to accommodate the average golfer. So, to make things more difficult for the good golfer, the hole itself was made more difficult. This was done by placing the flagsticks in more difficult and demanding positions—perhaps just over an upslope on a green, perhaps tucked in neatly behind a front guarding bunker. In addition, the speed of the greens was increased by cutting them closely with the mowers. The cups were then narrowed, and sometimes it was said that the only opening to the hole was in the dead center of the cup. The greens, too, were maintained in a firm condition so that the approach shot that did not have underspin on it might hit once on the green and then continue to roll and roll, even off the green at the rear.

The greens at Augusta National were designed to be large and to feature large and small undulations. The combination of speed in putting and the subtle slopes proved to be very difficult for all but those with the keenest putting touch. Truly it could be said that only a master would win a tournament at this golf course.

2
JONES ON THE DESIGN OF THE COURSE

The following article is from the book *Golf Is My Game* by Robert Tyre Jones, Jr., copyright © 1959, 1960 by Robert Tyre Jones, Jr., and published by Doubleday & Company, Inc.

The Augusta National Golf Club itself was born of very modest aspirations to begin with. Clifford Roberts had been coming to Augusta for some years as a seasonally regular winter visitor. He and I were close friends of Walton H. Marshall of the Vanderbilt Hotel in New York City, who also operated the Bon Air Vanderbilt in Augusta during the winter season. We were also patrons of both Marshall hotels.

Living in Atlanta only a short distance away, I had come to Augusta often over a period of years for friendly golf and an occasional charity match. I also played in the Southeastern Open Tournament over the country club and Forest Hills courses in Augusta during the early part of 1930. I had always been impressed by the fact that, especially during the winter season, golf courses around Augusta were considerably better conditioned than courses near Atlanta, and since at that time we were doomed to coarse Bermuda grass for putting greens in the summer, it was in winter golf that our best hope lay.

In any event, when Cliff came to Atlanta during the late fall of 1930 to suggest to me that I join him in organizing a club and building a golf course near Augusta, I found myself in a very receptive frame of mind.

The attractive aspects of the proposal were somewhat as follows: Augusta was well known to me as a resort area and a pleasant setting for golf during the winter months. Cliff and I had a number of friends among the permanent and winter residents there who could be counted on to form a nucleus around which to build our club. I felt that the financing of such a project would be infinitely more likely to succeed in Augusta than in Atlanta.

Secondly, I was acutely aware of the fact that my native Southland, especially my own neighborhood, had very few, if any, golf

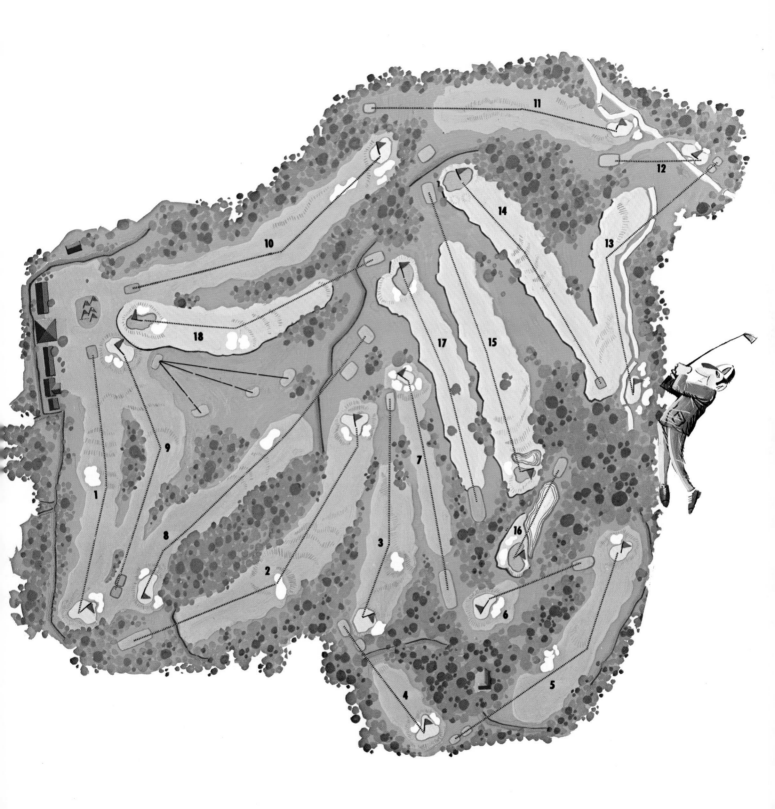

Layout of the Augusta National Golf Club.

An aerial view of the Augusta National Golf Club, looking southwest.

courses of championship quality. The prospect of building a course according to the high standards of excellence I would set, based on what I considered to be a very wide experience in the game, was most intriguing. I truly regarded it as an opportunity to make a contribution to golf in my own section of the country, as well as to give expression to my own very definite ideas about golf-course design.

Thirdly, the piece of ground available, as described by Cliff and as later confirmed by me in a personal visit, seemed ideally suited to the purpose Cliff was suggesting. In brief, the dream was completely enthralling, especially at a time when I was, I suppose, flushed with success and already deeply involved in enough golfing projects to preclude, at least for many years, my taking any serious interest in other activities.

As the name implies, the new club was set up on a national basis. We planned to have only a small group of local members upon whom we could rely for help in the day-to-day administration of the club's affairs. Our aim was to develop a golf course and a retreat of such nature, and of such excellence, that men of some means and devoted to the game of golf might find the club worthwhile as an extra luxury where they might visit and play with kindred spirits from other parts of the nation. This policy has never been changed, and I am happy to be able to say that the club apparently has adequately fulfilled this mission.

In this view, of course, the all-important thing was to be the golf course. I shall never forget my first visit to the property that is now the Augusta National. The long lane of magnolias through which we approached was beautiful. The old manor house with its cupola and walls of masonry two feet thick was charming. The rare trees and shrubs of the old nursery were enchanting. But walking out on the grass terrace under the big trees behind the house and looking down over the property was an unforgettable experience. It seemed that this land had been lying here for years just waiting for someone to lay a golf course on it. Indeed, it even looked as though it were already a golf course, and I am sure that one standing today where I stood on this first visit, on the terrace overlooking the practice putting green, sees the property almost exactly as I saw it then. The grass of the fairways and greens is greener, of course, and some of the pines are a bit larger, but the broad expanse of the main body of the property lay at my feet then just as it does now.

I still like to sit on this terrace and can do so for hours at a time, enjoying the beauty of this panorama.

With this sort of land, of a soft, gentle rather than spectacular beauty, it was especially appropriate that we chose Dr. Alister MacKenzie to design our course. It was essential that we build a course within the capacity of the average golfer to enjoy. This did not mean that the design would be insipid, for our players were expected to be sophisticated. They would demand interesting, lively golf but would not endure a course that kept them constantly straining for distance and playing out of sand.

There was much conversation at the time to the effect that MacKenzie and I expected to reproduce in their entirety holes of famous courses around the world where I had played in competitions. This was, at best, a bit naive, because to do such a thing, we would have had literally to alter the face of the earth. It was to be expected, of course, that the new layout would be strongly influenced by holes that either MacKenzie or I had admired, but it was possible only to keep certain features of these holes in mind and attempt to adapt them to the terrain with which we were working.

I think MacKenzie and I managed to work as a completely sympathetic team. Of course, there was never any question that he was the architect and I his advisor and consultant. No man learns to design a golf course simply by playing golf, no matter how well. But it happened that both of us were extravagant admirers of the Old Course at St. Andrews, and we both desired as much as possible to simulate seaside conditions insofar as the differences in turf and terrain would allow.

MacKenzie was very fond of expressing his creed as a golf-course architect by saying that he tried to build courses for the "most enjoyment for the greatest number." This happened to coincide completely with my own view. It had seemed to me that too many courses I had seen had been constructed with an eye to difficulty alone and that in the effort to construct an exacting course that would thwart the expert, the average golfer who paid the bills was entirely overlooked. Too often the worth of a layout seemed to be measured by how successfully it had withstood the efforts of professionals to better its par or to lower its record.

The first purpose of any golf course should be to give pleasure, and that to the greatest possible number of players, without respect to their capabilities. As far as possible, each golfer should be presented with an interesting problem that will test him without being so impossibly difficult that he will have little chance of success. There must be something to do, but that something must always be within the realm of reasonable accomplishment.

From the standpoint of the inexpert player, there is nothing so disheartening as the appearance of a carry that is beyond his best effort and offers no alternative route. In such a situation, there is nothing for the golfer to do, for he is given no opportunity to overcome his deficiency in length through either accuracy or judgment.

With respect to the employment of hazards off the tee and through the green, the doctor and I agreed that two things were essential. First, there must be a way for those unwilling to attempt the carry; second, a definite reward must await the man who makes it. Without the alternative route, the situation is unfair. Without the reward, it is meaningless.

There are two ways of widening the gap between a good tee shot and a bad one. One is to inflict a severe and immediate punishment on a bad shot, to place its perpetrator in a bunker or in some other trouble that will demand the sacrifice of a stroke in recovering. The other is to reward the good shot by making the second shot simpler in proportion to the excellence of the first. The reward may be of any nature, but it is more commonly one of four—a better view of the green, an easier angle from which to attack a slope, an open approach past guarding hazards, or even a better run to the tee shot itself. But the elimination of purely punitive hazards provides an opportunity for the player to regain his situation with an exceptional second shot.

A course that is constructed with these principles in view must be interesting, because it will present problems that a golfer may approach according to his ability. It will never become hopeless for the duffer or fail to concern and interest the expert. And it will be found, like old St. Andrews, to become more delightful the more it is studied and played.

We try very hard in Augusta to avoid placing meaningless bunkers on the course. Some of the natural hazards are severe, but usually so for the ambitious player. Possibly the dearth of bunkers on the course is a feature most commented on by visitors. Yet there are some that perhaps could be dispensed with, except that they are in use to protect players from more dire consequences. Occasionally a bunker may be used to stop a ball from running into a hazard of a more serious nature.

I have already said that 1931 was a very bad year in which to start a golf club. The depression got worse instead of better. The early years of the club were not easy from an operating standpoint.

The golf course, on the other hand, gave every indication of fulfilling our ambitions for it in a most gratifying way. We very soon became convinced of the soundness of the basic conceptions on which the course had been built. Most important of all to me was confirmation of my hope that during the spring months a combination of Bermuda base and Italian-rye surface could provide as good putting as was to be found anywhere. For the first time I became aware that championship golf could be played in the South.

Somewhere during the second year of the existence of the golf course in its completed form, and from somewhere within the hard core of faithful who had accepted responsibility for the direction of the club, came the suggestion that we try to get the National Open Championship for our club. We had many conversations on the subject among ourselves and with officials of the United States Golf Association.

The idea was regarded among all of us as not entirely without merit, but in the end, enough objections were found to cause us all to agree that the project was not feasible, the most important opposing reason being that the championship would have to be played during the early spring instead of, as customarily, during the month of June or the first half of July.

These conversations were really the beginnings of the Masters Tournament, because from them Clifford Roberts came up with the idea that we might stage a tournament of our own. In this way we might just as well demonstrate the virtues of the kind of golf course we had created and, at the same time, bring to Augusta and the adjoining section an annual golfing event that would give our people the opportunity to see the world's best players in action on a first-class golf course.

It was Cliff also who persuaded me that the tournament could be set apart from the rest of those springing up as fixtures on the winter circuit, by casting me in the role of host and building the tournament around this as my one appearance in competition. I must confess that the prospect of annually entertaining my old playmates and the later arrivals in the upper crust of competitive golf was quite attractive.

From the very beginning we planned the tournament on an invitational basis. As president of the club, it was to be my privilege to invite a limited number of men I considered likely to grace the tournament because of their past accomplishments in the game, their present stature, their promise, or even on my own feeling of friendship for them.

We have ever since retained the invitational character of the tournament, but it took no time at all for us to discover that on the original basis I and others in the club's official family had let ourselves in for a considerable amount of embarrassment so long as we constructed the invitation list on any such free and easy basis. Our club's facilities, which are still not spacious, were at that time stringent indeed. It was an utter impossibility to include everyone I might wish to invite for any reason and still keep the field down to manageable numbers. It became obvious that the only possible solution was the one that we followed, namely to adopt a definite set of qualifications a player must meet in order to be considered for an invitation. And obviously, too, this set of qualifications, after its adoption for any one tournament, had to be so rigid that even I was not able to deviate from it.

The first tournament was called the Augusta National Invitation Tournament, but, even before its playing, Cliff had begun to think and talk of it as the Masters. I have occasionally forgotten this fact, but having had my memory refreshed, I remember very well that I resisted for a time the application of this name to our tournament. When Cliff suggested it, I vetoed it on the basis that it was a title entirely too presumptuous for us to apply to a tournament of our creation. I am not so certain that our ends have not been served best by this reluctance. I think the tournament is now quite well entitled to be called the Masters, because it has continued to assemble those who are entitled to be called masters of the game.

3
A DISCUSSION OF THE AUGUSTA NATIONAL COURSE

By DR. ALISTER MACKENZIE

In writing of the course I designed at Augusta, Georgia, for the Augusta National Golf Club, I want to emphasize the importance of the part played by Robert T. Jones, Jr., in working out the plans. Bob is a student not only of golf, but of golf courses as well, and while I had known him for years, I was amazed at his knowledge and clear recollection of almost all of the particularly famous golf holes in England and Scotland, as well as in America. Partly by reason of his college training in engineering, his suggestions were not only unique and original but also practical.

As president of the Augusta National Golf Club, Robert T. Jones, Jr., has been an active leader in all matters pertaining to design, construction, and organization. He has assumed the major responsibility in this effort, which we call an attempt to build the ideal golf course.

What is the ideal golf course? Bob Jones and I found ourselves in complete agreement on these essentials:

1. A really great course must be pleasurable to the greatest possible number.
2. It must require strategy as well as skill, or it cannot be enduringly interesting.
3. It must give the average player a fair chance and at the same time require the utmost from the expert who tries for subpar scores.
4. All natural beauty should be preserved, natural hazards utilized, and a minimum of artificiality introduced.

In constructing Augusta National, we had plenty of land, towering pine forests, a large variety of other trees, beautiful shrubbery, streams of water, a mildly rolling terrain of great variety, a rich soil for growing good fairway grass, and a naturally beautiful setting from an architectural standpoint.

As you may know, the property was originally settled in 1857, by a Belgian nobleman named Prosper Jules Alphonse Berckmans. He was an ardent horticulturist, and

"It is the most beautiful course of all, with all the azaleas and other beautiful flowers."—Sam Snead

in this property he indulged his hobby to the limit of his resources. There are azaleas in abundance and a great variety of small plants, shrubbery, and hedges, even a real cork tree. There are scores of camellia bushes that are so well grown in size now that they are really trees. Most impressive of all sights is the ancient double row of magnolia trees planted before the Civil War. They are said to be the finest in the South and stand like sentinels along the driveway entrance to the golfer's paradise.

Now to get back to our golf course. It has been suggested that it was our intention at Augusta to produce copies of the most famous golf holes in the world. Any attempt of this kind could only result in failure. It may be possible to reproduce a famous pic-

ture, but the charm of a golf hole may depend on a background of sand dunes, trees, or even mountains miles away. A copy without surroundings might create an unnatural appearance and cause a feeling of irritation instead of charm. On the other hand, it is wise to have a mental picture of the world's outstanding holes and to use this knowledge in reproducing their finest features, perhaps even improving on them.

At Augusta, we tried to produce eighteen ideal holes, not copies of classical holes, but holes that embodied their finest golfing features, with other features suggested by the nature of the terrain. We hope that our accomplishments at Augusta will be of such unique character that these holes will be looked on as classics in themselves.

The Masters Tournament Augusta National Golf Club Trophy.

A small crowd watches the scores being posted on a rudimentary scoreboard in the late thirties.

4
WHAT IS TRADITION?

It has often been said that the Masters Tournament is surrounded by great tradition. This is very true. A visitor to Augusta in April who partakes of the scene for a day or more comes away filled with an understanding of how tradition can affect and increase greatly the enjoyment of the players and the gallery who are jointly participating in this remarkable tournament.

The word *tradition* itself comes from the Latin *trado*, to hand over. The meaning of the word applicable to the Masters refers to handing down "an inheritance to posterity"—a set of customs, a way of doing things, especially at the Augusta National, in a gentlemanly fashion.

It is the tradition of last year's Masters champion helping the new champion into his green Masters coat.

It is the sentiment expressed in having Gene Sarazen and Sam Snead, venerable Masters champions, always be the first two-some to begin the tournament, precisely on the stroke of the starting hour the morning of the first day.

It is the absence of commercialism in the beautifully printed starting-time schedules handed out generously and free to the guests at the Masters.

It is the lightness and easygoing nature of the Three-Par Tournament on the Wednesday before the Masters begins, a delightful warm-up for the players and spectators in more than one sense of the word.

It is Mr. Clifford Roberts himself in an electric cart with an assistant personally checking the farthest reaches of the golf course to make sure everything is running in its accustomed smooth fashion.

It is the genial caddy in spotless white overalls leaping with glee when his player sinks a birdie putt.

It is the chorus of mockingbirds along with several sweet cardinals singing for love of life in the woods around the first green, which has been freshly doubly mowed and is ready for a close approach to the cup in its apparently impregnable position of difficulty.

It is the small, elite field of golfers from

15

all over the world, every one of whom is famous either in name or by reputation to the knowledgeable spectators.

It is the young, inexperienced amateur on stage in his first major tournament with an Arnold Palmer or a Jack Nicklaus as his playing partner, dreaming of the day when he, too, will become one of the greats.

It is the standing ovation of the crowds at the fifteenth hole when an ancient and now fading champion reaches the proximity of the green and makes a commendable golf shot. It is the tipped visor and smile that follows.

It is the gasp of excitement when another red number goes up on the scoreboards for a front-running leader in the field, and the equivalent gasp of amazement and disappointment when red numbers turn to green and a well-known name comes down from the leader-board.

It is seeing a legendary international golf star such as Joe Carr of Ireland or Roberto de Vicenzo of Argentina in person, holding his own with America's best golfers.

It is the sight of the beautiful women and their well-dressed escorts sipping mint juleps at the cafe tables under the magnolia trees on the front lawn of the clubhouse overlooking the entire golfing scene below.

It is the white dogwood, the pink azaleas, the riot of flowers, the meadowlark song, the riot of color, "the splendor, splendor everywhere."

Above: The social side of the Masters. *Left:* Longtime Masters patron displays her badge collection. *Upper right:* "There will never be another tournament to equal it."—Arnold Palmer

5
UNDERSTANDING THE TERRAIN AT THE MASTERS

You enter the Augusta National Golf Club after leaving a busy highway. At once you find yourself behind boxwood hedges that emit heavenly odors. It is here that you begin to sense the quiet and peacefulness of this wonderful club and golf course.

Twenty-five feet inside the gate you pass a gatehouse, stationed in which is a uniformed watchman who will politely ask your name, phone ahead to the clubhouse to see whether your arrival is expected, and, if you are expected, direct you to proceed the 275 yards farther ahead, where the white colonial clubhouse stands behind a circular driveway.

On your left as you enter the tree-lined entrance driveway you see the practice fairway with the teeing area toward the clubhouse. At Masters Tournament time you will walk down a gravel path running parallel to the practice fairway; at the end of it you will pass a turnstile manned by more guards, who make certain that you are properly displaying your Masters badge. There are no daily tickets sold to the public for the tournament, by the way—only small

badges that entitle the bearer to see every day's action. At Masters time, the clubhouse and the grounds immediately surrounding it remain out of bounds to the general public. There are ropes and steel poles surrounding the forbidden territory, and many Pinkerton guards see to it that no one enters the clubhouse grounds without permission.

The general public enters the course along a road that passes the clubhouse, professional shop, and locker-room buildings on the left. Since the clubhouse is built on the highest point of land, and the other buildings are on the slope downward to the north, the visitor enters in a slightly down-the-hill position relative to the first tee. The monstrous scoreboard—with every player's name, place of origin, and room for hole-by-hole score for four eighteen-hole rounds—is immediately ahead on the right a little farther down the hill. To the left about 100 yards is the first tee. From its placement, it is obvious that the first hole heads north, or to the visitor's right. Directly ahead of the tee is a long, deep valley which slopes downward to a point thirty feet below the tee

The sixteenth hole is almost a level hole, there being only a two-foot differential between the tee and the green.

Above: Rae's Creek adds a real as well as psychological barrier to making a birdie four here at No. 13. *Below:* A long, straight drive is a must on this short par four dogleg left in order to reach the lower slope of the valley on No. 9.

Hubert Green hits his approach shot to the green at seven.

level and then rises rather abruptly to a plateau that is twelve feet higher than the teeing area.

We will call the bottom of the valley, or No. 1 hole, Level −30 (each numeral representing one foot above or below clubhouse level, which we will designate 0 level). It is very important that you understand the variances in the terrain levels, as a great deal of the course strategy is built on the problems of uphill or downhill play.

Let's go around the first nine, considering the problems of terrain so that you will better understand the golfer's problems in scoring well on the various holes. The prevailing wind is out of the northwest; therefore, you should also be aware of the orientation of the holes so as to know where the wind will be helping, where it will be hindering, and where it will cause a cross-wind problem. Let's examine numbers 1 to 4:

Consider No. 1 tee to be Level 0. The area

at the top of the valley down No. 1 fairway at 260 yards distance is Level 0 + 12, and the No. 1 green is Level 0 + 18. So you understand that the first hole is an uphill hole but with only a moderate upward slope of six feet from the tee-shot area to the green. Furthermore, since the hole heads due north, a northwest wind will be from the golfer's left and will be neutralizing the usual draw shot (right to left) into the green.

The second hole is from a tee slightly lower than the first green. The fairway is tree-lined and appears especially narrow from the back tee during the Masters Tournament. The hole heads west by south (240° true) and then doglegs left to 200° true for the second shot. The tee-shot area is twenty feet below the tee level, and the green itself is seventy-five feet below tee level. So, the second shot to No. 2 green goes an additional fifty-five feet downhill.

The third hole starts at Level −60. The tee is raised slightly above No. 2 green's level and heads due north for a slight dogleg to the right. The ground level below the fairway bunker in the center of the fairway is six feet higher than the teeing ground level, and the green is another eight feet higher. The result is that the hole plays uphill all the way.

The bunker in the center of the third fairway is approximately 260 yards from the tee. The entire fairway slopes left all the way from the trap area to the green, being twenty-two feet higher on the right side than on the left. When you add these variations in terrain to the fact of a very small tilted green, higher on the right than the left, it is easy to understand why the hole, although short in distance, is a troublesome one to play.

The fourth championship tee is at the same level as the third green. The hole heads northwest over a valley differential (thirty-eight to forty feet) to an elevated green 220 yards away guarded by two large traps on the right and left front of the green. The green itself is quite large but much wider than long, which necessitates proper club selection. A line of trees ends on the right-hand side of the fairway before the

No. 12—this tough, but little hole at 155 yards has cost or won many a championship in the long history of the Masters.

green is reached, and this results in very uncertain knowledge as to the strength of the wind at the green. The golfer is more or less sheltered from the wind by the trees and is therefore often misled into believing that the wind is not so strong at the green. Many shots fall short of the green here for this reason. The green itself slopes strongly from back to front and is very difficult to putt.

The fifth hole, 450 yards long, has a forty-eight-foot rise in elevation from the tee to the green area. It is a most formidable hole. Bunkers guard the left side of the fairway on the shorter line to the green, and its considerable length uphill requires a long, straight second shot. Because of the fairway mounds on the right, the dip of ground in front of the green, and the plateau effect of the green, it is a most difficult hole on which to place a second shot close to the flagstick. This hole, according to the designer, Dr. Alister MacKenzie, is of similar type to the famous seventeenth, or Road Hole, at St. Andrews, Scotland.

Having completed the fifth hole and being up high on the western side of the golf course, we now proceed to come back down via the beautiful sixth hole, which plays at 190 yards or so from an elevated tee over the valley below to a devilish green some thirty feet lower in elevation than the tee. There are several very difficult pin positions on this green, especially in the upper left- and right-hand corners. The tee shot that leaves the player more than thirty feet away from the cup on this hole will result in a three-putt green more often than not. On one occasion, in the 1970 Masters, this writer watched seventeen successive golfers attempting to two-putt to a hole cut on the upper left from positions down the slope on the front of the green. Only Billy Casper was able to get down in two strokes, and even his second putt was about five feet long.

From the seventh tee, the tee shot is downhill with a second shot to a raised green. The difference in elevation is eight feet from the teeing area to the valley in front of the green with a rise of twenty-three feet to the plateau green. Now to the eighth tee and the long climb upward to the hidden five-par green, 530 yards away. The difference in elevation is sixty feet and sets the course up for the return trip on the ninth hole from the same height (adjacent to the No. 1 green, incidentally) back down the steep slope to a plateaued, very small, well-bunkered green 420 yards away. A dangerous situation occurs on the ninth hole should the golfer's tee shot fail to carry all the way down the hill. The golfer is left with a difficult hanging lie, which requires that his pitch stop quickly on the green's surface—something almost impossible to do.

We have now come back to the top of the course for the tenth hole and will immediately start our descent into the southeastern corner of the course for the demanding downhill 470-yard tenth hole. The drive here is almost into outer space. The player cannot see the eventual landing spot of his tee shot. The total drop in elevation of this hole is ninety feet with about seventy-five feet of that amount at the tee shot area. The slope of the fairway from high right to low left also complicates the problems of this hole.

The terrain continues to drop lower and lower for the eleventh tee, back in a cathedral of pine trees, and heads downward to a green 445 yards away. The difference in elevation is fifty feet, and again the tee-shot area is in a blind spot as far as the golfer is concerned. He tries to stay to the right center of the fairway so as to catch its downward slope and gain valued yardage.

At last, we have reached the bottom of the course, No. 12. From here on, the climb will be predominantly upward on the way back to the high point of the clubhouse area and the eighteenth green.

The twelfth green is eight feet lower than the twelfth tee, so elevation is not a great problem at this hole. The winds, of course, are, for this is a gusty corner under normal conditions. This little hole at 155 yards has cost or won many a championship in the long history of the Masters.

The thirteenth fairway has a right-to-left tilt at the tee-shot landing area. This affects

The drive is an important shot on the eighteenth hole, since the green sits forty-five feet higher than the tee-shot area.

the shot into the green because the golfer frequently must play from a stance with his feet lower than the ball, which tends to cause him to pull the ball into the dangerous Rae's Creek. Of course, the creek itself has a great effect on play at this hole, adding a real as well as psychological barrier to the chance here for a birdie four.

The fourteenth hole plays at 420 yards, and since the green is eighteen feet above the tee level, it plays to a full 420 yards or more. There is a high spot eight feet above the tee level at about the 240-yard mark and then a dip back down into a shallow valley at tee level again. So, the particularly long driver is apt to face a slightly downhill second shot into the green, a situation that makes the green even harder to hold with a second shot hit with less underspin than usual.

The fifteenth hole is downhill all the way. The green is thirty feet below the tee level. The area just short of the pond in front of the green is forty-five feet below tee level, so the skillful player who does not go for the green with his second shot should attempt to get very close to the edge of the pond so as to leave himself an uphill pitch to the surface of the green.

The sixteenth hole is almost a level hole, there being only a two-foot differential between the tee and the green; the green is slightly higher.

The seventeenth hole is not unlike the fourteenth, in that it is uphill from tee to green. However, the tee-shot area on seventeen is twenty-five feet above the tee level, and the green is another ten feet higher than that.

The eighteenth green is seventy feet higher than the eighteenth tee level, but the differential appears to be much greater, because the valley in front of the tee falls away forty feet. The tee-shot area on No. 18 is twenty-five feet above the tee, which means it is necessary to play for a flagstick on the green that is forty-five feet higher than the tee-shot area. It is easy to understand now why the drive is so important on the eighteenth hole. A long blind shot to the eighteenth hole is a frightening one indeed—difficult to judge and even more difficult to execute.

We trust that this exposition of the variances in the terrain at the Augusta National Golf Club will add to your understanding of the difficulties encountered in playing the course. A more careful study of the tenth through the thirteenth holes is suggested. The reader will then fully understand how that stretch of holes came to be called the "Amen Corner."

6
MASTERS QUALIFICATIONS

1. Masters Tournament Champions (Lifetime)
2. United States Open Champions (Honorary, noncompeting after five years)
3. United States Amateur Champions (Honorary, noncompeting after two years)
4. British Open Champions (Honorary, noncompeting after five years)
5. British Amateur Champions (Honorary, noncompeting after two years)
6. P.G.A. Champions (Honorary, noncompeting after five years)
7. Ryder Cup Team
8. Walker Cup Team or World Amateur Team
9. The first twenty-four players, including ties, in the previous Masters Tournament
10. The first sixteen players, including ties, in the previous U.S. Open Championship
11. The first eight players, including ties, in the previous P.G.A. Championship
12. The semifinalists in the previous U.S. Amateur Championship
13. P.G.A. Co-sponsored Tour Tournament winners (classified by the Tournament Players Division as one of its major events) from the finish of the previous Masters Tournament to the start of the current one

Horton Smith, winner in 1934 and 1936.

7
THE MASTERS OF 1934

Horton Smith	70	72	70	72	284
Craig Wood	71	74	69	71	285
Billy Burke	72	71	70	73	286
Paul Runyan	74	71	70	71	286
Ed Dudley	74	69	71	74	288
Willie Macfarlane	74	73	70	74	291
Harold McSpaden	77	74	72	69	292
Al Espinosa	75	70	75	72	292
Jimmy Hines	70	74	74	74	292
MacDonald Smith	74	70	74	74	292

Although Robert T. ("Bobby") Jones had retired from competition in 1930, he reentered the sports world to play in his own $5,000 "First Annual Invitation Tournament" at Augusta National Golf Club. Although Jones held the practice record of 65, seven under par, it was thought that his lack of competition for several years might have dulled his edge. There were seventy-two players in the original field. For this year only, the nines were played in reverse order; that is, what is now the back nine was then the front and the front nine the back nine. Paul Runyan and Jones were quoted at six-to-one odds to win, while Craig Wood,

Horton Smith, and Willie Macfarlane were at ten to one.

At the end of the first day, Jones had fallen behind with a shaky 76 and found himself in a tie for thirty-fifth place. Horton Smith, Emmett French, and Jimmy Hines led the first day of play with 70s, while Henry Picard, John Golden, Craig Wood, and Walter Hagen had 71s.

Bobby Jones's magic did not come back on the second day as he scored a 74 to tie for twenty-eighth place at 150. Horton Smith played some erratic golf, eagled No. 17 with a six-foot putt, and made three other birdies along with some bogeys to finish at 72. The seventeenth hole, now the eighth, played at 500 yards. At the end of the second round the leaders were:

Horton Smith	70-72	142
Ed Dudley	74-69	143
Billy Burke	72-71	143
Jimmy Hines	70-74	144
R. Stonehouse	74-70	144
MacDonald Smith	74-70	144

At the end of the third round, Jones had

improved with a 72, but his total of 222 left him far behind Horton Smith, the leader, who scored a fine 70. The gallery was quite unruly as Jones played. Most of the people followed him rather than other stars. At one point, Bobby asked a cameraman to stop operating his movie camera at the short No. 3 (now No. 12), and then Jones put his ball into the pond.

Horton Smith had only two bad shots in his second-round 70, an iron on No. 9 and a bad drive on No. 6. He three-putted two greens but had uncanny shots and accurate pitches.

The third-round leaders were:

Horton Smith	142-70	212
Billy Burke	143-70	213
Ed Dudley	143-71	214
Craig Wood	145-69	214
Paul Runyan	145-70	215
Walter Hagen	147-70	217
Willie Macfarlane	147-70	217

In the final round, Horton Smith was one under par going to the fourteenth green (now No. 5), playing at 440 yards. Near the green with his second, he chipped over a hazard to four feet from the cup and then missed the putt. He then needed even par to beat Craig Wood and a one over par score to tie Wood, who had already finished his round. Smith went over par on the fifteenth (now No. 6), the short hole, when he left himself a long downhill putt. From four feet, he missed his second putt to fall behind Wood but then got his par at No. 16 with a good putt when he chipped ten feet from the hole. At the seventeenth hole (now No. 8) he again chipped short by ten feet but sank the putt for his necessary birdie.

On No. 18 he hit a tremendous drive and pitched to twenty-five feet short of the flagstick. His first putt was short by three-and-one-half feet, but he made the second successfully to win. It was Horton Smith's first major tournament victory.

Billy Burke had three hanging putts in a row on the sixteenth, seventeenth, and eighteenth holes and was the hard-luck loser when none of them would fall.

Here are Horton Smith's own words describing how he finished the 1934 Masters with a par on the eighteenth hole to win the first tournament:

"It might be interesting to tell you my own experience in winning the Masters Tournament in 1934. Craig Wood had gotten an early start, had posted a score of 285, and then had left for the East without waiting to see whether he would win or not. So, early in my round, when I was on the fourth hole, I knew that I needed a par 72 to win by one stroke, that is, provided no one else managed to come up with a sensational last round to better Wood's score. At the seventeenth tee I needed one birdie in the last two holes. Fortunately, my third shot on the seventeenth was a short pitch. I hit it to within twelve feet of the hole on a beautifully level spot on the green and quite confidently stroked the ball in for the birdie I so badly needed.

"The Augusta National course at that time was played with its present nines reversed, so the eighteenth hole that I needed only to play in par was the present ninth hole, a short four-par. The hole wasn't presenting too much difficulty, but the wind was blowing hard, and the greens were very hard, almost swept out by the wind. There was a trap guarding the short left side of the hole, and in trying to play it safe for my four, I got well over the trap and found my ball about thirty-five feet above and beyond the cup, with a slick downhill left-to-right putt coming up. Although I knew very well that I should get up to the cup so as to leave myself a short right-to-left second putt—a much easier one to hole under the circumstances—I felt that I could borrow quite a bit from the left hill and drift the ball down close for an easy second putt. I was both surprised and disappointed in myself when I borrowed too much. The ball stopped above the cup from three to three-and-one-half feet away, leaving me a fast downhill putt with a quick left-to-right break—dreaded by even the most skillful putter.

"I studied the putt, and at that moment I had one of those positive thoughts: Since the green was slippery and the break was fast, all I could do was hit the ball firmly and squarely. I was also aware that even if I didn't hole the putt, I could tie for the title and have at least an even chance to win in a play-off. So I stepped up and knocked the ball right in, to win.

"Afterward, a number of people came up to me and said, 'You certainly were confident of that last putt on eighteen, weren't you?' Although I didn't admit it then, I'll say now that it was one of the longest putts I ever holed, and I am certain that it was due to my attitude and nothing else. It was the positive thought that paid off."

8
THE MASTERS OF 1935

Gene Sarazen	68	71	73	70	282
Play-off					144
Craig Wood	69	72	68	73	282
Play-off					149
Olin Dutra	70	70	70	74	284
Henry Picard	67	68	76	75	286
Denny Shute	73	71	70	73	287
Lawson Little, Jr.	74	72	70	72	288
Paul Runyan	70	72	75	72	289
Vic Ghezzi	73	71	73	73	290
Jimmy Hines	70	70	77	74	291
Byron Nelson, Jr.	71	74	72	74	291
Bobby Cruickshank	76	70	73	72	291
Joe Turnesa	73	71	74	73	291

In beautiful weather, Henry Picard took the early lead on the first day with a sparkling 33-34, 67. Willie Goggin, Ray Mangrum, and Gene Sarazen were in at 68, Olin Dutra at 70, Bobby Jones and Horton Smith at 74. Low amateur was Lawson Little with 74.

This year the Augusta National Golf Club's "2nd Annual Invitation Tournament" had a field of sixty-three players, and the two nine-hole layouts were reversed from the play of the year before and played as they now are.

Picard shot a fine 68 on the second day for a 135 two-round total. He led Ray Mangrum and Gene Sarazen, whose 71s brought them in at 139. Amateur Charlie Yates moved into low amateur spot with a 70 for 145.

Craig Wood shot a remarkable 68, four strokes under par, in a blustery rainstorm to move into first place at the end of the third day of play. He had 209, seven under par. Olin Dutra scored his third successive 70 for an aggregate of 210. Henry Picard's game slumped. He started at the height of the rainstorm and scored a 76. There were only three strokes separating Picard, Wood, Dutra, and Sarazen as they entered the last day of play.

With the course rain-soaked and the weather near freezing, Gene Sarazen and Craig Wood tied at 282, six under par, as Sarazen scored a rare double eagle two on the 485-yard-long par-five fifteenth hole, holing out with a fairway wood. Henry Picard shot a final 38-37, 75 to finish fourth behind Olin Dutra, who had 74 for a total of 284. Lawson Little, then an amateur, scored a fine 72 for 288 and the sixth spot, ahead of such stars as Walter Hagen at 293 and

Gene Sarazen, 1935 champion.

Bobby Jones at 297. The first prize was $1,500 with $800 to the loser of the thirty-six-hole play-off.

Sarazen was actually in front when he got his par three at No. 16, where Craig Wood, playing ahead of him, had three-putted, but Craig dropped a sixteen-footer for a birdie at No. 18 where Gene got his par four.

In the play-off, again in freezing weather over the rained-drenched course, Gene Sarazen beat Craig Wood soundly with 71 against Wood's 75 in the morning round and 73 against his 74 in the afternoon round. From the eleventh hole through the thirty-fourth inclusive, Sarazen shot twenty-four consecutive pars. Gene had three birdies and three bogeys along with thirty pars. Craig Wood missed several short putts and was in the water twice at the five-par thirteenth but still salvaged a six.

Gene Sarazen's Double Eagle*

Sarazen turned away from his ball in the wet fairway grass and peered down the long slope to the fifteenth green, 220 yards away. A freezing wind disturbed the flag and ripped through his protective sweater. Around him, 1,000 eyewitnesses huddled together in a crescent that bulged behind the green and thinned out to a single line on either side of the fairway.

Before the green lay a pond. Not much of a pond, really, perhaps forty feet across at its broadest. It protected the green about as well as a moat protects a castle. Yet it was no obstacle on the road to an easy birdie for the player who could put together two excellent wood shots and was willing to gamble.

Gene Sarazen was that gambler. He reached for his favored four wood, took another quick glimpse ahead through the mist, and swung away.

He watched his ball as best he could as it sailed up into the haze and over the moat to the fifteenth green. It dropped on the apron, popped up twice on the turf, and rolled steadily toward the cup as though homing on a magnet. A thousand voices in the gallery screamed as the ball disappeared into the cup for a double-eagle two.

Gene Sarazen strode down the remaining 200 yards of fairway between the two lines of shouting fans like a king walking to his throne—the four wood held in front of him like a scepter. "I started figuring," said the man who had not cared much for schoolboy arithmetic long ago, "and it was the greatest thrill I have ever had on a golf course. I realized all I needed was par to tie."

Par was exactly what Sarazen got on the final three holes to confirm his tie with Wood and in effect clinch the tournament.

*Quoted with permission from pages 28 and 29 of *The Masters*, by Tom Flaherty, published by Holt, Rinehart and Winston (1961).

The shadows lengthen as Henry Picard and Horton Smith putt at the eighteenth in 1936, the year Horton won his second Masters.

9
THE MASTERS OF 1936

Horton Smith	74	71	68	72	285
Harry Cooper	70	69	71	76	286
Gene Sarazen	78	67	72	70	287
Bobby Cruickshank	75	69	74	72	290
Paul Runyan	76	69	70	75	290
Ray Mangrum	76	73	68	76	293
Ed Dudley	75	75	70	73	293
Ky Laffoon	75	70	75	73	293
John Dawson	77	70	70	77	294
Henry Picard	75	72	74	73	294

There were fifty-four golfers in the 1936 Augusta National "Annual Invitation Tournament." The first round was delayed until Friday because of heavy rains and cold weather.

There were twenty-seven twosomes, and the starting times ranged from 11:30 A.M. until 2:15, when Bobby Jones and Gene Sarazen played in the last twosome. The rains had been so heavy that it was feared that boats would be necessary to transport the players around the eleventh and twelfth holes. The bridge at No. 12 was completely under water. The first day of play was in near-freezing weather in biting, blustery wind. The players wore two and three layers of sweaters.

At the end of Friday's play, Harry Cooper was in the lead at 70 with Al Espinosa at 72, Horton Smith at 74, Billy Burke at 74, and Dudley, Little, Picard, and Laffoon at 75. Bobby Jones had 78.

At the end of the second day, Cooper had scored a 69 for 139 and led Denny Shute and Bobby Cruickshank by five strokes as they had 76-68 and 75-69 respectively. Espinosa, Sarazen, Laffoon, and Horton Smith were at 145 to remain in contention.

Again rain forced cancellation of the play, and thirty-six holes were scheduled for Monday. Several of the greens had miniature lakes and rivers on them.

On the final day, Horton Smith gave one of the finest exhibitions ever seen as he edged Harry Cooper out of first place by one shot, 285 to 286. Sarazen closed fast to take third, one stroke behind Cooper. Runyan and Cruickshank were fourth and fifth at 290.

The last rounds were again played in terrible weather. Smith got a break in that

he was a late starter and played the last eight holes in calmer weather, while Cooper had to battle wind and rain the entire way.

Smith did not get into the lead until the seventy-first hole. He was three strokes back of Cooper at the morning eighteen, pulled even at the seventh hole, but then fell back twice into two-stroke deficits. He was two strokes behind Cooper with five holes to play but birdied the sixty-eighth and sixty-ninth holes (No. 14 and No. 15 with three and four) to tie Cooper at that point. He went ahead by holing a long putt on No. 17 for a par where Cooper had taken a bogey five. Horton hit his second shot thirty feet below the hole on No. 18, putted to eighteen inches, and sank the putt for a finishing 72 to Cooper's 76 and the victory.

Left: Bobby Jones, the Babe Ruth of golf. *Below:* Lawson Little, Horton Smith, Harry Cooper, and Jimmy Thomson—the famous Spalding foursome.

10
THE MASTERS OF 1937

Byron Nelson	66	72	75	70	283
Ralph Guldahl	69	72	68	76	285
Ed Dudley	70	71	71	74	286
Harry Cooper	73	69	71	74	287
Ky Laffoon	73	70	74	73	290
Jimmy Thomson	71	73	74	73	291
Al Watrous	74	72	71	75	292
Tommy Armour	73	75	73	72	293
Vic Ghezzi	72	72	72	77	293
Jimmy Hines	77	72	68	77	294
Leonard Dodson	71	75	71	77	294

There was a field of forty-six players—thirty-eight professionals, seven amateurs, and host Robert T. Jones, Jr., in the 1937 "Annual Invitation Tournament." Harry Cooper, Ed Dudley, and Horton Smith were favorites to win. A new name flashed on the horizon of golf when Byron Nelson set a new course record of 66 in the opening day's play. His card read:

445 343 343 33
443 444 334 33 66

On the first day Ralph Guldahl with 69 was in second place, three strokes behind as

he set a back-nine course record of 32 on this card:

444 344 455 37
344 443 343 32 69

On Nelson's fine round, he had six one-putt greens, seven birdies, and one bogey on the short third hole, 350 yards long. Nelson drove the elevated seventh hole 340 yards away, was home in two strokes on two of the five-pars, Nos. 8 and 15.

But Ralph Guldahl was not to be counted out of it by any means. On the second day he and Nelson had 72s, while Ed Dudley with 69 and Harry Cooper with another 69 quickened the pursuit.

On the third day, Guldahl shot a fine 68 to take the lead away from Nelson, who had 75. Dudley shot 71 to move into second place at 212.

On the last day of play, after being all even with Nelson at the turn in lackluster 38s for each player, Guldahl ran into trouble on the last nine. On the short twelfth, he went into the water and ended with a double-bogey five. Again he hit the water in

HOLE	REGULAR DISTANCES	CHAMPIONSHIP DISTANCES	PAR	HANDICAP RATING	Nelson		HOLE	REGULAR DISTANCES	CHAMPIONSHIP DISTANCES	PAR	HANDICAP RATING	1937 ①
1	380	400	4	9	4		10	410	430	4	6	4
2	490	525	5	1	↙		11	390	415	4	12	4
3	335	350	4	11	3		12	130	150	3	16	3
4	175	190	3	15	3		13	455	480	5	4	4
5	425	440	4	5	4		14	405	425	4	8	4
6	160	185	3	17	3		15	465	485	5	2	4
7	320	340	4	13	3		16	120	145	3	18	3
8	475	500	5	3	4		17	380	400	4	14	3
9	390	420	4	7	3		18	395	420	4	10	4
Out	3150	3350	36		33		In	3150	3350	36		33
							Out	3150	3350	36		33
							Tot'l	6300	6700	72		66

CADDY FEE 75c

SCORER *Byron Nelson*

ATTEST *Byron Nelson*

THIS CARD OPENED MEASURES SIX INCHES (STYMIE)

HANDICAP

NET SCORES

Above: Byron Nelson set an early course record at 66 in 1937. Note the caddy fee at that time was only 75¢. *Below:* Byron Nelson, winner in 1937 and 1942.

Rae's Creek on No. 13 for another bogey to go three over par on these two holes. Nelson, on the other hand, exploded on the last nine with a course record-tying 32 against Guldahl's 38 to overtake him and win.

Nelson sank a twenty-five-foot putt for a birdie two on No. 12, chipped the ball into the hole for an eagle three on No. 13, and picked up six strokes on Guldahl in those two holes. Although Nelson did not get his birdie at No. 15, where Guldahl did get his, another bogey at No. 17 hurt Guldahl's chances to win. Byron finished with five straight pars for his 32, a 70 total, giving him 283 to Guldahl's 285. Nelson's card on the last day was:

454 344 554 38
342 345 344 32 70

Guldahl's card was:

454 352 465 38
345 644 354 38 76

Ed Dudley was third with a final 74 for 286, Harry Cooper fourth at 287, Ky Laffoon fifth at 290. Charles Yates was low amateur at 301.

11
THE MASTERS OF 1938

Henry Picard	71	72	72	70	285
Ralph Guldahl	73	70	73	71	287
Harry Cooper	68	77	71	71	287
Paul Runyan	71	73	74	70	288
Byron Nelson	73	74	70	73	290
Ed Dudley	70	69	77	75	291
Felix Serafin	72	71	78	70	291
Dick Metz	70	77	74	71	292
Jimmy Thomson	74	70	76	72	292
Jimmy Hines	75	71	75	72	293
Vic Ghezzi	75	74	70	74	293
Lawson Little, Jr.	72	75	74	72	293

Ralph Guldahl, runner-up in the 1937 Masters, takes second again to champion Henry Picard in 1938.

Rain caused cancellation of the first day's play. Eighteen holes were scheduled for Saturday, thirty-six for Sunday, and eighteen for Monday.

Harry Cooper took the early lead on a 68. Ed Dudley and Dick Metz had 70s, while Paul Runyan and Henry Picard were at 71.

There was a huge crowd of 5,000 spectators at this Masters.

Cooper fell out of the lead with a 77 on the second day as Henry Picard on 71 and 72 and Guldahl on 73 and 70 began to challenge. Ed Dudley had 70 and 69 for 216 so

Henry Picard, champion in 1938.

that going into the last round Picard led by one stroke over Cooper, Guldahl, and Dudley and by two strokes over Byron Nelson.

Guldahl came closest to catching Henry Picard in the final round. Starting out only one stroke behind, he was able to stay that close until he went into the water at No. 12. Ralph was able to pick up a birdie at No. 13, but he was never to catch Picard, who finished with a beautifully consistent 70 for 285. This gave him a two-stroke margin over Guldahl, who had 71 for 287, and Harry Cooper, also at 287 on a final 71. Paul Runyan's last round was a 70 for 288, and Byron Nelson scored a 73 for 290.

Picard won this tournament, it was said, by shooting the last three holes three successive times in two, three, four, which is birdie, birdie, par. Picard had changed his grip to an interlock from an overlap only three weeks before the tournament. His great consistency was even more remarkable in view of that fact.

Ralph Guldahl on the first tee at Augusta.

12
THE MASTERS OF 1939

Ralph Guldahl	72	68	70	69	279
Sam Snead	70	70	72	68	280
Billy Burke	69	72	71	70	282
Lawson Little, Jr.	72	72	68	70	282
Gene Sarazen	73	66	72	72	283
Craig Wood	72	73	71	68	284
Byron Nelson	71	69	72	75	287
Henry Picard	71	71	76	71	289
Ben Hogan	75	71	72	72	290
Toney Penna	72	75	72	72	291
Ed Dudley	75	75	69	72	291

Ralph Guldahl finally clinches the title in 1939.

Billy Burke, who hadn't won a major tournament since 1931 when he was the National Open champion after a marathon play-off with George Von Elm, shot a 69 to take the first-day lead over Sam Snead at 70 and Byron Nelson, Tommy Armour, and Henry Picard at 71.

In the second round, Gene Sarazen, playing in a stiff breeze that brought rain and hailstones the size of robin's eggs, tied the Byron Nelson record of two years before with a 66. Snead had another 70, Guldahl a fine 68, Nelson a 69. The field was bunched on the leader's heels.

45

On the last day, Sam Snead had already finished the tournament with 280 when Ralph Guldahl made the turn. Ralph had been beaten out of the last two tournaments but this time would not be denied. He knew he had to score a par 36 on the back nine and went out and produced it. Lawson Little had pulled into a tie with Guldahl at the tenth tee, but Guldahl's birdie three against Little's five at the tenth put Guldahl in front. Ralph made a fine tee shot at No. 12, the hole that had helped to cost him the tournament when Nelson beat him in 1937, but Ralph did not get his birdie.

He saved his par four at No. 11 with a good chip. The crucial shot for Guldahl was a side-hill three wood to the thirteenth green. He had hit a rather short drive and had a 230-yard carry over Rae's Creek. The ball just made the front of the green and rolled to within six inches of the hole for an easy and remarkable eagle three.

Guldahl needed pars in from No. 13 to win from Snead. He saved par at No. 14 with a good chip from the green and nearly eagled No. 15, so his bogey at No. 17 did not hurt too much. His three iron to the eighteenth green was strong, but he putted to within a foot of the cup and sank the putt for the victory.

13
THE MASTERS OF 1940

Jimmy Demaret	67	72	70	71	280
Lloyd Mangrum	64	75	71	74	284
Byron Nelson	69	72	74	70	285
Ed Dudley	73	72	71	71	287
Harry Cooper	69	75	73	70	287
Willie Goggin	71	72	73	71	287
Henry Picard	71	71	71	75	288
Craig Wood	70	75	67	76	288
Sam Snead	71	72	69	76	288
Toney Penna	73	73	72	72	290
Ben Hogan	73	74	69	74	290

This tournament witnessed two sensational record rounds on opening day. First, Jimmy Demaret shot a 30 on the second nine to tie the U.S.G.A. record low nine-hole score by Willie Macfarlane in the U.S. Open at Worcester Country Club in 1925 and later tied by Francis Ouimet in the National Amateur Championship against George Voight at Baltimore. Demaret's card read:

        464 343 454 37
        333 444 234 30   67

No sooner than the smoke had settled on

Demaret's remarkable round, it was eclipsed by an incredible 64 by Lloyd Mangrum. This record would stand until 1965 when Jack Nicklaus tied it on the way to winning the Masters that year.

At the end of the first day's play, Mangrum and Demaret were in front with their fine scores of 64 and 67, but right behind them were Harry Cooper and Byron Nelson at 69, while Craig Wood and Lawson Little had 70s. Demaret came back with a 72 and Mangrum a 75 to go into the third round two strokes ahead of Nelson, Henry Picard, and amateur Marvin Ward, who had scored an excellent 68 after a 74 beginning. Picard's round was unusual in that he four-putted the fourteenth hole. The cups had been put into more inaccessible places after the "easy" scoring of the first day.

Demaret continued playing sound golf. He scored a 70 on his third round to lead Mangrum by one stroke going into the last day. Snead had moved up into contention with a 69 for 212, three strokes behind Demaret. Craig Wood had brought in a 67

Jimmy Demaret shows his winning smile; he went on to claim three Masters victories—in 1940, 1947, and 1950.

The champions in their victory green jackets: Byron Nelson, Jimmy Demaret, Henry Picard, Horton Smith, Ben Hogan, Craig Wood, Claude Harmon, Gene Sarazen, and Sam Snead.

on his third round to tie Snead at 212.

On the last round, Wood, Snead, and Picard had chances to catch Demaret, but with 38s on the first nine they never got into contention. Demaret finished strongly, having putts for birdies or eagles, all within fifteen feet on the last five holes. He holed one of them for a birdie at No. 15. Just as Jimmy finished, a deluge of rain fell and caught Mangrum with a hole to go, but by then Mangrum's chances were over, as he ended with a 74 and second place, four strokes behind Demaret's total of 280.

The New York Times's veteran writer, W. D. Richardson, said that this Masters "was a somewhat drab one because of the ease with which Demaret won it."

Sam Snead took a horrible eight on the eleventh hole in his final round to slip to 76 and a tie for seventh place. He hit the water on the left of the green, took the penalty shot, dropped a new ball, and then pitched

back into the water again on the other side. He finally holed out after making the green on his sixth stroke.

Jimmy Demaret's record 30 on the second nine at Augusta National Golf Course happened this way: On No. 10, he placed a one iron three feet from the hole for a birdie three. On No. 11, he sank a thirty-foot putt for his second birdie. On No. 12, he went over the green on his tee shot but chipped back to save his par three. On No. 13, he was short of Rae's Creek with his second shot, pitched to twenty-five feet from the cup, and holed the putt for his third birdie, a four. No. 14 he played in normal par for a four. At No. 15, his second shot almost carried the pond in front of the green. The ball ended up half buried in mud and water. Demaret removed his shoes and had to stand in two feet of water in his attempt to explode out of the trouble. He blasted out successfully and sank the ensuing putt for another birdie, his fourth.

He rolled in another good putt of moderate length on the sixteenth hole, putting him now five under par on the second nine. At the seventeenth hole, his pitch to the green stopped only five feet from the flagstick, and with another one-putt he had his sixth birdie on the back nine. At the eighteenth green, he just missed holing another birdie putt. Demaret putted only twelve times on his way to this remarkable score for nine holes. The record would stand for twenty-seven years, until aging Ben Hogan tied the mark in his third round of the 1967 Masters Tournament, and it would stand again another nineteen years—until Jack Nicklaus would equal it once more in playing the last nine holes of the 1986 Masters.

This is the description of Lloyd Mangrum's course record round of 64 in the 1940 Masters by *New York Times* reporter W. D. Richardson: "In the course of his round he was never off the fairway or in bunkers, hit every green in regulation figures (or less), and three-putted on only one green."

HOLE	REGULAR DISTANCES	CHAMPIONSHIP DISTANCES	PAR	HANDICAP RATING			HOLE	REGULAR DISTANCES	CHAMPIONSHIP DISTANCES	PAR	HANDICAP RATING		
1	380	400	4	10	4		10	450	470	4	5	5	
2	490	525	5	1	4		11	390	415	4	11	4	
3	335	350	4	13	3		12	135	155	3	16	2	
4	175	190	3	15	3		13	455	480	5	4	4	
5	425	440	4	6	4		14	405	425	4	8	4	
6	160	185	3	17	3		15	465	485	5	2	4	
7	350	370	4	12	4		16	120	145	3	18	3	
8	485	510	5	3	4		17	380	400	4	14	3	
9	400	430	4	7	3		18	400	425	4	9	3	
Out	3200	3400	36		32		In	3200	3400	36		32	
							Out	3200	3400	36			
							To'l	6400	6800	72		64	

CADDY FEE $1.00

1940

LLOYD MANGRUM

SCORER

ATTEST

THIS CARD OPENED MEASURES SIX INCHES (STYMIE)

HANDICAP

NET SCORES

Lloyd Mangrum ties the Masters record round at 64.

His round hole by hole:

No. 1: 400 yards, par four—Drive and five iron to thirty feet, two putts for a par.

No. 2: 525 yards, par five—Drive and brassie to within forty feet, two putts for a birdie four.

No. 3: 350 yards, par four—Drive and seven iron to six feet, one putt for a birdie three.

No. 4: 190 yards, par three—Two iron to thirty-five feet, two putts for a par.

No. 5: 440 yards, par four—Drive and four iron to forty feet, two putts for a par.

No. 6: 185 yards, par three—Six iron to twenty feet, two putts.

No. 7: 370 yards, par four—Drive and nine iron to fifteen feet, two putts.

No. 8: 510 yards, par five— Drive and spoon to fifteen feet, two putts.

No. 9: 430 yards, par four—Drive and seven iron to fifteen feet, one putt for a birdie.

No. 10: 470 yards, par four—Drive and four wood to twenty-five feet, three putts for a bogey.

No. 11: 415 yards, par four—Drive and seven iron to twenty feet, two putts for a par.

No. 12: 155 yards, par three—Six iron to six feet, one putt for a birdie two.

No. 13: 480 yards, par five—Drive and four wood to twenty feet, two putts for a birdie four.

No. 14: 425 yards, par four—Drive and seven iron to fifteen feet, two putts for a par.

No. 15: 485 yards, par five—Drive and brassie to forty feet, two putts for a birdie four.

No. 16: 145 yards, par three—Seven iron to ten feet, two putts for a par.

No. 17: 400 yards, par four—Drive and eight iron to twenty-five feet, one putt for a birdie three.

No. 18: 425 yards, par four—Drive and seven iron to thirty feet, one putt for a birdie three.

14
THE MASTERS OF 1941

Craig Wood	66	71	71	72	280
Byron Nelson	71	69	73	70	283
Sam Byrd	73	70	68	74	285
Ben Hogan	71	72	75	68	286
Ed Dudley	73	72	75	68	288
Sam Snead	73	75	72	69	289
Vic Ghezzi	77	71	71	70	289
Lawson Little, Jr.	71	70	74	75	290
Lloyd Mangrum	71	72	72	76	291
Harold McSpaden	75	74	72	70	291
Willie Goggin	71	72	72	76	291

The time of Craig Wood, previously always the bridesmaid, had finally come. A winner of some sixteen tournaments of lesser importance, he had finished second in the U.S. Open, the British Open, and the P.G.A. Championship, by bowing either in the last holes in play-offs or in the final match. Horton Smith had stolen the 1934 Masters with his sparkling finish and it took the miracle shot of Gene Sarazen on the fifteenth hole in 1935 to force the resulting play-off. True to his golfing luck, Craig lost it.

In the 1941 Masters, Wood started out with a beautifully played 66 on the opening day of the tournament, and at nightfall found himself five strokes ahead of the field. Byron Nelson loomed ominously behind him. Nelson had beaten Wood in a play-off for the U.S. Open at Philadelphia in 1939 and might prove to be Craig's nemesis again.

Nelson's second round was a 69 and pulled him within three strokes of Wood. Wood, at 71, had saved his second day by one-putting each of the last four holes. On the third day, a surprising challenge came from ex–Yankee outfielder Sam Byrd, now turned professional golfer. Sam had a 68 to move himself two strokes past Nelson to second place. Nelson worked hard for a 73 and third place again, five strokes behind Craig Wood.

On the final day, at the end of nine holes, the five-stroke lead Craig Wood had started with had been dissipated. Nelson had shot a great 33 to Wood's 38, and it appeared that Wood was destined to lose once more.

The thirteenth hole was the crucial turning point in the hole-by-hole battle for first

Craig Wood explodes from the bunker at No. 9.

place between Wood and Nelson. Wood was playing ahead of Nelson. He reached the five-par thirteenth safely with his second shot, a wood, barely over Rae's Creek but on the edge of the green. He managed to chip well to four feet from the hole and seized the birdie with a true putt.

Nelson played the same hole a few minutes later, went wide to the right with his tee shot, and thus lengthened his distance to the green. Nelson's second, also a wood, fell just short of reaching the green, and Rae's Creek had extracted its toll from another victim: for Nelson a six, for Wood a four on the thirteenth. Wood gained confidence as the report of Nelson's trouble spread to the fifteenth hole, where Craig was attempting to nail the door shut. Wood had a birdie four at No. 15 and a birdie two at No. 16. Craig was home, Masters champion at last.

15
THE MASTERS OF 1942

Byron Nelson	68	67	72	73	280
Play-off					69
Ben Hogan	73	70	67	70	280
Play-off					70
Paul Runyan	67	73	72	71	283
Sam Byrd	68	68	75	74	285
Horton Smith	67	73	74	73	287
Jimmy Demaret	70	70	75	75	290
E. J. Harrison	74	70	71	77	292
Lawson Little, Jr.	71	74	72	75	292
Sam Snead	78	69	72	73	292
Gene Kunes	74	74	74	71	293
Chick Harbert	73	73	72	75	293

By Masters time in 1942, the United States of America had been at war for four months. The future of the tournament appeared to be dim. When invitations to eighty-eight players were sent out by the tournament committee, only forty-two were answered positively. The field was the smallest in the nine years of the tournament's history.

On the first day, Horton Smith flashed some of his old sweet swinging form and magic wand putting stroke for a 67. Paul

Byron Nelson and Ben Hogan are about to begin their memorable play-off here at the first tee. Final results—Byron 69, Ben 70.

54

A youthful Byron Nelson allows Alfred S. Bourne, one of Augusta National's founding members, to check his scorecard in 1942.

Runyan matched that score for a first-day tie. Byron Nelson and Sam Byrd were at 68, Demaret at 70, and little Ben Hogan, who was now winning everything in the money tournaments, but no important titles, scored a 73. Bob Jones had a fine par 72, only the second time he had been able to score that well in the Masters, his own course.

Nelson's second round was a fine one as he closed the gap between him and the leaders and started to make his move. He shot a 67, and his two-day total of 135 for thirty-six holes set a new thirty-six-hole record, two strokes under Wood's 137 in the 1941 Masters. Ben Hogan had a 70 for 143 and was eight strokes out of first. Sam Byrd was again making his presence known. He had scored a 68 on the first day and was back on the second day with a 69 to put him only one stroke behind Nelson. However, he would eventually shoot himself out of contention for the second year in a row.

On the third day, Hogan shot a great 67 while Nelson cooled off. The fight for the lead narrowed to just three strokes as the final day started. By the sixteenth hole of the final round, Ben had picked up one stroke on Byron and now trailed by just two strokes. Hogan parred No. 17, playing ahead of Byron, who had bogeyed. Only one stroke of the lead remained with Nelson. Ben jammed his second shot a mere three feet from the eighteenth hole, and when Nelson could not match Hogan's birdie, suddenly there was a tie and the second play-off in Masters history.

Famous sports announcer Bill Stern congratulates both Ben Hogan and Byron Nelson on their fine match in the 1942 play-off.

In the play-off, Byron Nelson started off with a shocking six. His opening drive ran under a small fir tree on the right. He chopped the ball out left-handed, put his third shot over the green, and Ben had him by two strokes. At the fourth hole, Byron found a bunker and Hogan was three strokes ahead.

The sixth hole saw a swing in the scores. Ben pulled his tee shot off the green to the left and picked up his first bogey. Nelson planted a gorgeous iron eight feet from the cup, holed the putt for a deuce, and now was only one stroke down. Nelson began to make his comeback, heartened by the change in fortune at the sixth. He almost got a birdie at No. 7 while Hogan scrambled to save his par. Then, as so often has happened in Masters history, the uphill eighth again became a turning point in an historic match. Byron was 510 yards away from the cup as he stood on the tee of the eighth hole. Two beautiful wood shots later, he was six feet away from the flagstick. Of course, he got his eagle three. Ben was getting shaky now. He had hooked on his second shot and again scrambled for a par. The lead was gone. Byron led by one stroke through the ninth.

Their play was equally good and most dramatic on the second nine. Nelson gained another stroke on Hogan at No. 10, as Ben missed making his chip and one-putt from the edge of the green. It was Byron for a two-foot birdie two at No. 12 as Ben nearly put his tee shot into the water at greenside.

Byron was now three strokes ahead and closing fast.

Both players birdied the thirteenth hole. Ben got a birdie three at No. 14 and was then only two strokes down to Byron. Ben followed it up with a birdie over the water on the dangerous fifteenth hole. Byron began to show signs of weakening as he three-putted the huge green for a par five. Now, only one stroke down to Byron at the sixteenth tee, Ben made a mistake that eventually cost him the title. His tee shot hit the bunker guarding the green on the right. Byron, shooting last, of course, could sense victory within his grasp. He stroked a crisp iron to four feet from the flagstick and, no doubt, breathed a sigh of relief. Ben could not get up and down from the bunker, settled for a bogey four, and went to the seventeenth tee with a two-stroke deficit staring him in the face.

The seventeenth was parred by both players, Nelson with ease, Hogan with difficulty after a chip and one-putt. It apparently was all over when Ben's tee shot at No. 18 hit a tree on the right-hand side of the fairway, fell short, and left him a full three wood to the hidden flagstick on the plateau green some 220 yards away. Ben almost accomplished the demanding shot but caught the sand in the front bunker instead. But Byron also hit a bunker, and not until both players had recovered to ten feet from the hole was it obvious that Byron would win. Ben sank his ten-footer, requiring Byron merely to two-putt from his ten-foot position to win. Byron Nelson did just that, took his five, and had won with a comeback 69 to Hogan's 70. A more dramatic play-off in any championship tournament would seldom be seen.

16
THE MASTERS OF 1946

Herman Keiser	69	68	71	74	282
Ben Hogan	74	70	69	70	283
Bob Hamilton	75	69	71	72	287
Ky Laffoon	74	73	70	72	289
Jimmy Demaret	75	70	71	73	289
Jim Ferrier	74	72	68	75	289
Sam Snead	74	75	70	71	290
Clayton Heafner	74	69	71	76	290
Byron Nelson	72	73	71	74	290
Chick Harbert	69	75	76	70	290

At last the war was over, and the fairways at the Augusta National could be reclaimed from the livestock that had enjoyed its lush pastureland for more than three years. The greens were once more shaved with razor-sharp mowers as fifty-one players, professionals and amateurs, began the first Masters Tournament in four years. Nelson and Hogan found themselves, as might be expected, favorites to win this Masters. Unknown Herman Keiser was also entered in this event, his invitation coming as a result of his being in ninth place among the professional golfers in money earnings that year with the tremendous sum of $3,576 to his

credit. At one time Herman had served an apprenticeship under Horton Smith at Hickory Hills in Springfield, Missouri, and somewhere along the way he had picked up Horton's smooth stroke and confident attitude.

Keiser was an early starter in the 1946 Masters, and before one o'clock of the first day he was in the clubhouse with a fine 69. So was long-hitting Melvin ("Chick") Harbert. Keiser's first round showed 26 putts. On the second day, Herman again putted like a demon and was in with an even better 68 for the day.

An unknown had taken a five-stroke lead in the Masters. And who was second? Jimmy Thomson, only a moderate threat in spite of his booming drives. Where were Ben and Byron? Seven and eight strokes behind Keiser at 145.

At the end of the third day, it was still Keiser by five strokes, although Ben Hogan had started to move closer with a 69, which included three birdies out of the last four holes. Herman, incidentally, appeared to be weakening in his third round but scored a

magnificent eagle three on the fifteenth hole to help calm his nerves.

On the final day, Keiser's game was extremely shaky, yet when he had to get the ball into the hole he was able, much of the time, to do it. Keiser played his round a half hour ahead of Ben Hogan. This was not an enviable position. Knowledge of the scores you have to match is much better than the ominous expectation of what Ben might or probably would do.

Keiser got only two pars on the first nine but, with three hard-earned birdies, cancelled most of the bogeys for a 37 start. Ben made the same nine holes in 35 strokes. The margin was now only three strokes.

Keiser managed to par eight straight

Above: Cary Middlecoff, Horton Smith, Herman Keiser, and Sam Byrd gather together for this shot at the beginning of the first Masters Tournament in four years. *Left:* Herman Keiser, the "unknown," takes the trophy in 1946.

holes on the second nine, trying desperately to keep a solid step in front of Ben. Ben, meanwhile, had been able to nail down two beautiful birdies, one at No. 12 on a fifteen-foot putt and a great downhill two-putt for a four at No. 13. Two strokes of the three-stroke lead were gone. Now Herman was at No. 18 and trying hard to get his four there. His drive ended in the left rough, but from there he played a courageous iron straight to the flagstick. The ball careened off the pole and rolled twenty-five feet away, beyond the pole, leaving Herman a danger-ous downhill sliding putt. Keiser charged for the birdie, missed, and found himself staring at a five-foot comeback putt to save par. He missed that, too, and, settling for a bogey five, was sure that Ben now could and would catch him in the three holes Hogan had yet to play. All Ben needed to win was one birdie and two pars. But those last three holes are extremely hard holes to birdie, especially when a birdie somewhere on one of them is absolutely required. Ben parred No. 16, and one birdie chance was gone. On No. 17 it appeared that he would make his move, but his putt burned the cup and stayed out. One last chance: birdie the eigh-teenth and win. Ben's drive was perfect; his second skidded to a stop only twelve feet from the hole. Just knock this putt in for the first Masters championship for Ben Hogan. Make up for that Byron Nelson beating of 1942!

Ben surveyed the twelve-footer in his in-imitable businesslike style. The cigarette had been thrown away, the white cap set even more purposefully on his head. At last he assumed his stance, rather stiff-legged and immovable. The stroke was not a good one. The slippery green had taken its toll. The ball never came close to the cup but seemed to gather momentum as it passed. It slipped farther and farther away to what was later estimated to be two feet, six inches from the hole.

Those two-and-a-half feet turned into a nightmare for Ben as he carefully lined up his stance and once more failed to hole the putt. Incredibly, Ben had three-putted from twelve feet to lose the coveted title once more. Herman Keiser, the former unknown, was the new Masters champion. Would Ben Hogan ever win?

17
THE MASTERS OF 1947

Jimmy Demaret	69	71	70	71	281
Byron Nelson	69	72	72	70	283
Frank Stranahan	73	72	70	68	283
Ben Hogan	75	68	71	70	284
Harold McSpaden	74	69	70	71	284
Henry Picard	73	70	72	71	286
Jim Ferrier	70	71	73	72	286
Ed Oliver, Jr.	70	72	74	71	287
Chandler Harper	77	72	68	70	287
Lloyd Mangrum	76	73	68	70	287
Toney Penna	71	70	75	71	287
Dick Metz	72	72	72	71	287

Jimmy Demaret had won the 1940 Masters by a comfortable four-stroke margin, but he really reached his peak in the year of 1947. He was top money-winner with $24,000 as purses became more remunerative for the postwar professional golfer. He won the Vardon Cup in 1947 for the lowest scoring average of the year, a mere 69.9 strokes per round.

Demaret was either the leader or the coleader of the 1947 Masters from start to finish and eventually won by two strokes over perennial Byron Nelson. Surprisingly,

an amateur contender, Frank Stranahan, finished with two great rounds of 70 and 68 to tie Nelson for second. Cary Middlecoff, a young dentist and fine amateur player from Memphis, had just turned professional. He made his presence known in this tournament with a great 71-69 thirty-six-hole start.

Demaret and Nelson played together the first day, Nelson having returned to the golfing scene after a six-month "retirement for good" from golf. Nelson and Demaret had good 69s for the lead as seven other players, not including Hogan, were at 70— one stroke off the pace.

Demaret was back with a 71 the second day and found himself tied with Middlecoff. Nelson was close behind with a 72, one stroke away. All the leaders had trouble scoring on the third day, but only Demaret was able to overcome the nerves everyone was showing. Jimmy drove poorly but chipped and putted his way to six out of seven saves, with one putt on each of the first seven holes, an incredible showing of getting up and down when it is necessary to

Above: One of the first large scoreboards used at the Masters. The names, not in alphabetical order, were moved around, each on its own panel. *Left:* Jimmy Demaret held on as leader or coleader of the 1947 Masters from start to finish.

do so to stay at par figures. Middlecoff soared to a 76 as Nelson remained in close contention with another 72 to remain three shots behind Jimmy going into the final eighteen holes.

Demaret won this tournament like the champion he had already proved himself to be. His fourth straight round under par, a 71, brought him in at 281 strokes, two strokes ahead of archrival Byron Nelson, who closed with an eminently satisfactory 70, and Frank Stranahan, who almost made it even closer with his 68.

Jimmy Demaret thus earned his second Masters championship award to join the illustrious company of the only other double Masters winners thus far, Horton Smith and Byron Nelson.

18
THE MASTERS OF 1948

Claude Harmon	70	70	69	70	279
Cary Middlecoff	74	71	69	70	284
Chick Harbert	71	70	70	76	287
Jim Ferrier	71	71	75	71	288
Lloyd Mangrum	69	73	75	71	288
Ed Furgol	70	72	73	74	289
Ben Hogan	70	71	77	71	289
Byron Nelson	71	73	72	74	290
Harry Todd	72	67	80	71	290
Herman Keiser	70	72	76	73	291
Bobby Locke	71	71	74	75	291
Dick Metz	71	72	75	73	291

This Masters saw the day of the club professional. Rarely is it possible for a club teaching pro to win an open, a P.G.A. Championship, a Masters. He watches too many bad swings by his club members, does not have the time to play and practice golf the way the touring professionals can, is not under the constant pressure, shot by shot, hole by hole, to produce a low score day after day.

Here in this Masters was Claude Harmon—rather short, stocky, a little rotund about the middle—playing in this great Masters tournament alongside a Hogan, a

Nelson, a Snead. How did he ever get on the guest list? It seems that Claude sneaked in the back door for this tournament. He had played at Augusta National in 1947, but his scores were poor, and he finished far down the list. It might have been expected that Claude would never be back again. But he finished exactly twentieth in the U.S. Open in 1947, and as a result received another, almost a courtesy invitation, to return again and play along with the names of golf.

Claude Harmon did just that. He played along on the first day in a very pleasant 70 strokes. He was not in front but was in a good position to make a better showing than he had made last year. The eyes of the galleries were watching Lloyd Mangrum shoot a sweet 69, flashing some of his old form once again, and the long-hitting rifle shots of Ben Hogan, who was still trying to win his first major championship. Surely this would be Ben's year to come through with his first victory at the Masters.

An unknown, Harry Todd of Dallas, breezed in on the second day with a beauti-

Finishing twentieth in the 1947 U.S. Open, Claude Harmon "sneaked in the back door" to win the 1948 Masters.

fully played 67. Regrettably, after his moment in the spotlight, he would shoot an awful 80 the next day and his day and tournament would be over. Would Claude Harmon go the same way? Not so far, at least through two rounds. Claude returned a nice 70 on his second round. That made it two 70s back to back, a very respectable start for a teaching professional.

Claude would blow up on the third day, everyone felt, and everyone was already feeling sorry for him. But no, it was Hogan who blew to a 77, Mangrum to a 75, and of course poor Todd to that 80. Claude kept plugging along, turning in steady pars, and then in the tough corner stretch rolled in a three-foot birdie three at No. 11, a six-foot deuce at No. 12, and made a four-par out of No. 13 by getting on the five-par green in two and two-putting. Suddenly it began to dawn on the increasing number of people in the gallery who were watching Claude that he might make it after all. But the last round was still to be played. They would wait and see. In the meantime, long-hitting Melvin ("Chick") Harbert had established himself as a prime contender, the touring pro who might just take over when the pressure got to the club pro. Harbert had already played three solid rounds in 71, 70, and 70 and was lying just two strokes off Harmon's pace.

On the last day, Harmon struggled at first. The galleries were now pulling for him as the underdog. When he bogeyed No. 4 and went over par for the first time, the heads nodded. "This is it. Claude is through." He managed to par the difficult fifth hole and came to the tough three-par sixth hole desperately needing a break, not only for his score but for his confidence as well. He got it. The flagstick was on the left side of the green. Claude aimed his five iron a bit to the right and gently drew the ball back toward the hole. He left himself six inches from the hole for what was practically a conceded birdie two. He tapped the ball in, and from there on nothing and nobody could or would catch Claude Harmon. He had a twelve-footer for a three at No. 7, a three wood to the eighth green, and a six-footer for an eagle three. The galleries went wild, and Claude knew he could make it now. He had gone four under par in three holes, the sixth through the eighth, and now stood three under for the round.

It was not all over, however. Claude lost two more strokes along the way on the last nine, but it didn't really matter. He was so far in front that nobody came near him on that day. Cary Middlecoff's last two rounds of 69 and 70 (which merely matched Claude's, by the way) still left Cary five strokes behind for second place. Third was Harbert, the one who did the blowing up with a final 76 for 287, nine strokes in arrears. The club professionals of America had seen Claude Harmon raise their prestige immeasurably. From then on, they would walk with their heads held a little higher and smile when anyone said "a club pro can't win one of the big ones."

19
THE MASTERS OF 1949

Sam Snead	73	75	67	67	282
Johnny Bulla	74	73	69	69	285
Lloyd Mangrum	69	74	72	70	285
Johnny Palmer	73	71	70	72	286
Jim Turnesa	73	72	71	70	286
Lew Worsham, Jr.	76	75	70	68	289
Joe Kirkwood, Jr.	73	72	70	75	290
Jimmy Demaret	76	72	73	71	292
Clayton Heafner	71	74	72	75	292
Byron Nelson	75	70	74	73	292

Sam Snead came to the 1949 Masters riding on a hot streak. He had just won open tournaments at Aiken, South Carolina, and Greensboro, North Carolina. As Aiken is only sixteen miles from Augusta, Sam was heartened by his performances on the southern fairways so early in the year. The Augusta National conditions would not be much different. After playing in the previous eight Masters Tournaments, Sam was about to lose the "can't miss" designation the galleries had attached to him. And remember, he had blown the U.S. Open twice, once with that horrendous eight on the last hole at Philadelphia Country Club in 1939

and again when he missed the thirty-and-a-half-inch putt and Lew Worsham did not miss his twenty-nine-and-a-half-incher at St. Louis in 1947. But Sam was putting well this year—at least, he was putting well for Sam Snead.

Lloyd Mangrum, with his little mustache and riverboat gambler strolling walk, got off to a great start. The winds blew, and only six out of fifty-eight players broke par. Sam Snead took 73 strokes and rested in eighth place after all the opening-day scores were on the big scoreboard.

The winds continued on the second day. Sam could do no better than 75, but Mangrum had also fallen off his brilliant pace to a 74. Herman Keiser showed that his game was still very much on as he clicked out a 68 and tied Lloyd Mangrum at 143 strokes for the halfway lead.

The third day started to tell the tale for Snead. His putter, a new one he had been using only a couple of months, was hot, and Sam showed the world he could really putt after all.

Down went a birdie four at the second;

Sam Snead dons his first Masters Tournament green jacket after winning in 1949. It was then that the Masters Champions Club was formed, and that all former Masters champions were given green jackets.

down went a twenty-two-foot putt for a two at the short fourth hole. Now an eight-footer for a birdie at No. 5 and, to top it off, a curling fourteen-footer for his fourth birdie of the nine and a 32 beginning.

While Sam did slip to a three-putt at No. 10, he managed to birdie the two five-pars, Nos. 13 and 15, and waltzed home with a 67, five under par. Now Sam was only one stroke out of first place, just behind Johnny Palmer, who had started with 73 and 71 but had tacked on a good 70 for his third round. Mangrum, with 72, was tied with Snead going into the last day's play.

Could Sam Snead win the big one with those ghosts of his blowups crowding into his imagination? He could. The fourth day Sam again putted like a demon. He got a twenty-footer on No. 1 and made a four-par birdie out of No. 2 by getting home on the 535-yard hole with an iron. He parred the third hole but scored once more with a fifteen-foot birdie deuce at No. 4. One bogey marred his card on the front nine, but he did make another routine birdie four at No. 8 to go out in 33 strokes.

Sam got a little bit off the par track as he started down into the ten, eleven, twelve corner, but by getting a ten-foot deuce at No. 12 he almost offset bogeys at Nos. 10 and 11. With the victory almost in sight and so sweet Sam Snead could savor it, he turned on more heat with great birdies at the two five-pars coming in, Nos. 13 and 15. It did not matter that he got into tree trouble on No. 18. Sam merely drilled a seven iron to within eighteen feet of the hole and dropped that putt as well for the finishing touch on a great round of exactly 67 strokes.

Sam Snead had won his first Masters in nine attempts by three strokes over Mangrum and Johnny Bulla, who had closed from nowhere with two straight 69s to share the second spot.

Sam Snead put on a new coat in front of the massed galleries surrounding the clubhouse. It was a bright green sport jacket with the Augusta National Masters symbol over its top left pocket. This was the first Masters coat to be awarded to a winner of this great tournament. A few days later the order was put out to obtain the sizes and measurements of all the past Masters champions. Every one of them would shortly receive his new green Masters coat in a belated additional recognition of his standing in the international golf scene as a master of golf.

A gathering of the Masters Club. *Top row:* Sam Snead, Henry Picard, Jimmy Demaret, Gene Sarazen, Ben Hogan, Horton Smith, and Claude Harmon. *Bottom row:* Byron Nelson, Clifford Roberts, Robert T. Jones, Jr., and Craig Wood.

20
THE MASTERS OF 1950

Jimmy Demaret	70	72	72	69	283
Jim Ferrier	70	67	73	75	285
Sam Snead	71	74	70	72	287
Ben Hogan	73	68	71	76	288
Byron Nelson	75	70	69	74	288
Lloyd Mangrum	76	74	73	68	291
Clayton Heafner	74	77	69	72	292
Cary Middlecoff	75	76	68	73	292
Lawson Little, Jr.	70	73	75	75	293
Fred Haas, Jr.	74	76	73	71	294
Gene Sarazen	80	70	72	72	294

This was the year that Jimmy Demaret once more showed the golf world what a marvelous competitor he was. He had won his first Masters in 1940 by the large margin of four strokes over Lloyd Mangrum. He had won again seven years later, this time by two strokes over Nelson. Here he was, ten years later, still spinning off consistently beautiful rounds at the Augusta National Golf Course. Consider his twelve-in-succession winning scores: 67-72-70-71 in 1940, 69-71-70-71 in 1947, and now in his customary colorful smiling fashion he methodically produced 70-72-72 and 69 in succession to win an unprecedented third Masters. That this record was made over a ten-year period adds weight to the quality of his play in retrospect.

Ben Hogan was back in the field again, following his serious car accident of a year ago. His legs were wrapped in rubber stockings, and he was constantly walking on pins and needles. He was in great pain. Ben played gamely (he had made a great physical comeback after his accident, tying for first in the Los Angeles Open in January 1950), but the strain of the physical exertion took its toll on him after three great beginning rounds of 73, 68, and 71. Ben stumbled in with a final 76 for a 288 total, five strokes behind Demaret.

This tournament was suspenseful not because Demaret won the title again, but because Jim Ferrier apparently had the victory in his grasp and then bogeyed his way into the clubhouse to let Demaret have the trophy undisputedly.

Ferrier had solved the problems of Augusta National's slick greens in his first rounds. On the first day, in a 70, Ferrier took 27 putts. That meant he was nine under putting par and yet only two under the course's par—a remarkable record of saving par.

On the second day Jim Ferrier sank six birdie putts. This time he had not been forced to scramble so much. His score, a 67, showed it.

Demaret lay five strokes back of Ferrier going into the third day. With the pressure mounting, the experienced Demaret might have been expected to gain on Ferrier in the third round. It wasn't that Ferrier was inexperienced in tournament play; it was just that Demaret, you might say, practically owned the Augusta course, and psychologically he certainly had an edge over Ferrier as the climactic last rounds came up.

On the third day Ferrier played raggedly, but once more his putter saved him from disaster. His score was a 73, but the putt total was just 29. Nor did Jimmy Demaret make much of a move to catch Ferrier. Demaret, with a 72, gained only one stroke and went into the last day four strokes away.

Incidentally, both Hogan and Sam Snead were making threatening motions at this point. They had brought in a 71 and a 70 to go up on the big scoreboard at 212 and 215 strokes respectively, only two and five strokes away from Ferrier. Demaret lay in between at 214 on his 70, 72, 72 start.

Then Jimmy Demaret made the big move. He played the first nine in a respectable 35, one under par, and picked up a birdie as usual at the five-par thirteenth, which he owned throughout the 1950 Mas-

ters. Jim had had merely birdie-eagle-eagle-birdie on the thirteenth. He was six strokes under par right there. He managed another birdie casually along the way in and, with a 69, reported in at the scoring tent back of the eighteenth green with a 283 total, the highest he had had, with a hope of winning.

But it appears that Australian Jim Ferrier scared easily. He was still far out on the course when he learned that Jimmy Demaret was in with a 283. All that meant was that Ferrier, two under par through the twelfth hole at the time, could waste four strokes and still win. From an offensive attitude, Ferrier became defensive, and his downfall was not far off.

The possible birdie hole, No. 13, was next for Ferrier. If he could get by it in par or better, he was home and dried as far as Demaret was concerned.

However, Ferrier's drive on the thirteenth hole was a wicked hook into Rae's Creek. A penalty shot and another shot short in front of the green and Ferrier lay three strokes, shooting his fourth to the tricky green. A chip too strong and two putts later, Ferrier had a bogey six. The rest of the story of Ferrier's long, hard battle in is too gruesome to relate. Suffice it to say that he managed one par out of the last six holes.

Did Jimmy Demaret back into this, his third Masters victory? I prefer to think that Jimmy won it with a great game strategy that he would shoot 70-72-72 and a final 69 and expect that score to win no matter what Hogan, Nelson, or any unknown, Ferrier or someone else, might do.

21
THE MASTERS OF 1951

Ben Hogan	70	72	70	68	280
Skee Riegel	73	68	70	71	282
Lloyd Mangrum	69	74	70	73	286
Lew Worsham, Jr.	71	71	72	72	286
Dave Douglas	74	69	72	73	288
Lawson Little, Jr.	72	73	72	72	289
Jim Ferrier	74	70	74	72	290
Johnny Bulla	71	72	73	75	291
Byron Nelson	71	73	73	74	291
Sam Snead	69	74	68	80	291

Ben Hogan had tried nine times in thirteen years to win the Masters. Perhaps he would be jinxed the way Snead was with the Open Championship and would never win no matter how well he played. But at least Ben would always prepare as perfectly as possible for the tournament. He would hit those hundreds upon hundreds of practice shots—the low ones, the high ones, the soft fades he would need at Augusta in order to set the ball down like a parachute close to that hole, close to the birdies.

Ben had not yet regained his preaccident body and leg strength. He never would, in fact; but that indomitable will was just as strong as ever, perhaps even stronger in the face of adversity. In this Masters, both George Fazio with an opening 68 and Skee Riegel with 73-68 held the first- and second-day front-running spots. But Ben Hogan was in a good place, too, after a 70-72 for 142. Ben was playing well. "The putts might drop tomorrow; they can't all stay out of the cup." Sam Snead, as always, was a threat. He had methodically put together 69 and 74 for 143 and, champion that he is, returned a cozy 68 on the third day. Now Snead and Riegel were tied heading down the stretch. Ben was just one stroke behind. Snead and Riegel could feel Ben's breath on their necks.

The only one who came close to catching Ben Hogan after a 33 first nine on the last day was Skee Riegel, who shot a creditable 71 for a 282 total, six under par for the 72 holes.

However, Ben would not be denied this time. He heard that Sam Snead was in serious trouble. Sam had taken an incredible four over par, quadruple-bogey eight, on the eleventh, the water hole, when he just

After nine attempts, Ben Hogan finally clinches the championship in 1951.

couldn't keep out of the pond there. With Sam finally dragging himself in with a frightful 80 to crash all the way down from a challenging position to eventual tenth place in the tournament, Ben could afford to play it cool and safe coming home the rest of the way.

Ben did. He played each of the two five-pars, Nos. 13 and 15, short with his second shot, yet he was able to birdie the first one and par the second. He played the uphill No. 18 cautiously short and pitched to four feet from the cup, sank the putt, and had a 68 on fourteen pars and four birdies. He had won the Masters at last. Ben couldn't believe it.

22
THE MASTERS OF 1952

Sam Snead	70	67	77	72	286
Jack Burke, Jr.	76	67	78	69	290
Al Besselink	70	76	71	74	291
Tommy Bolt	71	71	75	74	291
Jim Ferrier	72	70	77	72	291
Lloyd Mangrum	71	74	75	72	292
Julius Boros	73	73	76	71	293
Fred Hawkins	71	73	78	71	293
Ben Hogan	70	70	74	79	293
Lew Worsham, Jr.	71	75	73	74	293

Sam Snead had finished second to Ralph Guldahl in 1939 in the Masters and then had seemed to settle into an unsatisfactory rut (for Sam, that is) in 1940, 1941, 1942, and the first tournament after World War II, 1946, with scores ranging from 288 to 292, far down the list. In 1947 and 1948, Sam didn't even finish among the ten low scores. But then he crashed through with his first win in 1949 on his splendid 67–67 finishing rounds for 282 and a three-stroke margin over Johnny Bulla.

Now it was three years later, and Sam had again gone through the 287-to-291 doldrums down the list in 1950 and 1951.

Hogan remained his chief rival, and now that Hogan had broken the ice with his win in 1951, Sam had his work cut out for him if he wanted to win this, the 1952 Masters.

Hogan was methodical, as usual, and scored a sound two-under-par 70 on opening day. Sam, much less methodical but more spectacular, mixed a double bogey on the first hole and a waterlogged six on the five-par thirteenth with enough birdies to offset those errors and also had a 70 on the board.

On the second day, Hogan put another 70 back to back with his first one, and Sam merely birdied five times along the way to a front-running 67 and a 137 halfway total.

On the third day, the winds blew at more than thirty miles an hour. The greens became glassy smooth; the ball took strange bounces and did not want to go in the hole. Sam was disconsolate. He had racked up a disgraceful (not really, under the weather conditions) 77. Ben was thin-lipped as usual, the mechanical man, and while he was playing badly for Ben Hogan he still was able to gain back the three-stroke deficit from Sam, 74 to 77. The two archrivals went into

Above: Robert T. Jones, Jr. congratulates Sam Snead on his second Masters Championship in 1952 as Jack Burke, Jr., runner-up, looks on. *Below:* Sam Snead tells the Duke of Windsor "how he did it."

the final day with a dream situation for the galleries. Surely, relentless, machinelike Ben Hogan would beat Sam. Sam would skyrocket again. Hadn't he done it many times before?

Snead was scheduled to play an hour ahead of Hogan. Sam played well for eleven holes, and then it appeared that the blowup had come. On the dinky twelfth hole with the pond on its front and right, the mean bunkers around its narrow perimeter, Sam dunked his short-iron tee shot into the water. A ball over his shoulder, penalty stroke, two shooting his third shot for the green, still a delicate pitch over the same pond.

Sam almost put the ball in the water again. This time the grass at the green's edge saved him as it held the ball up, but what a lie! Now faced with his fourth shot to the flagstick, a probable two-putt, Snead was staring a six or worse in the face. And hadn't he met similar disaster last year at No. 11? Sam did his best with a very difficult shot from an awkward stance with one

foot higher than the other. He chipped the ball up onto the green, and it rolled and rolled toward the hole, never hesitating at the cup, and just plunked right in for a sweet bogey four, one of the best bogeys Sam had ever made in his life. Sam regained his composure then, settled down, played the rest of the nine in sound fashion, and hung up a remarkable 72 under great pressure. At 286 he would beat Ben Hogan, provided that Ben did not score 71 or better. But word had already crossed the course. Ben was having putting woes. Five times, Ben Hogan three-putted. He had only a single one-putt that day. The roof had fallen in on the mechanical man. He finished with a 79, seven over par, when he had needed only a par round to tie. Hogan was not unbeatable, at least in this Masters. Sam Snead was. He put on with great pleasure his second green Masters coat. Wouldn't he have loved to get Hogan in a Masters play-off again?

23
THE MASTERS OF 1953

Ben Hogan	70	69	66	69	274
Ed Oliver, Jr.	69	73	67	70	279
Lloyd Mangrum	74	68	71	69	282
Bob Hamilton	71	69	70	73	283
Tommy Bolt	71	75	68	71	285
Chick Harbert	68	73	70	74	285
Ted Kroll	71	70	73	72	286
Jack Burke, Jr.	78	69	69	71	287
Al Besselink	69	75	70	74	288
Julius Boros	73	71	75	70	289
Chandler Harper	74	72	69	74	289
Fred Hawkins	75	70	74	70	289

In 1953, Ben Hogan was almost forty-one years of age. In many sports, a man of that age would be considered to be well past his prime. Not Ben Hogan, for this was the year in which he would sweep the Masters and the professional championships of both Britain and the United States in the same year. He would win the Masters for the second time, bringing him even with his great rival, Sam Snead, another two-time winner, for that distinction. Then, with the Masters happily under his arm, he would proceed to win the United States Open at Oakmont in Pennsylvania, as well as the British Open at wickedly tough Carnoustie in Scotland.

For ten months after his unsettling failure in the last round of the 1952 Masters and a loss of the United States Open by five strokes to Julius Boros, Ben stayed away from the grueling daily tournament tour. He went back to his practice regimen of hundreds upon hundreds of balls hit every day—high, low, and exactly in between. At last he felt he had come close to controlling the ball the way he wanted to do it, with a soft final left-to-right action that caused the golf ball to sit down as if on a pillow with very little run after the green was touched.

Finally, as his fellow competitors were struggling with the Greater Greensboro Open and the Jacksonville Open during the two weeks before Masters time, where was Ben Hogan? At Augusta National Golf Course, you may be sure. He had checked in two whole weeks ahead of time and had played eleven rounds on the course by the time opening day came around. The fairways and greens were in more magnificent condition than usual. Ben was really train-

Ben Hogan obliges the photographers by demonstrating his grip.

ing his sights on the Masters this year and he didn't care who knew it. At the end of the 1953 tournament, everyone would be able to see whether he had wasted his time or not. At this point, Ben didn't think so. He thought his game was in pretty good shape.

There are often a couple of hot starters in the first rounds of the Masters, and this year the pattern remained true. Both Chick Harbert and roly-poly Ed ("Porky") Oliver were under par with a 68 and a 69 for starters. Ben was quite comfortable resting in third place with his workmanlike 70.

Hogan moved up one stroke the next day with an even more workmanlike 69 for 139 in two rounds. Oliver went to 73 and 142,

three strokes away, and Harbert matched the 73 to lie two strokes away from Ben. But Ben had already taken the lead in this tournament, which he had willed he would win. And win it he continued to do.

The next day, Ben had a mere 66 strokes, and from then on the tournament was his. Oliver tried to keep up with Ben and made a gallant try. They were paired together and played a great spectators' match. First one man and then the other would birdie; sometimes they would birdie the same holes. Ben was out in 32, Porky in 34. Ben took three putts on the five-par thirteenth as Oliver made the green with a four-iron second and sank a twenty-five-foot putt for an eagle three. Oliver made up some of the lost ground there but never really did catch Ben. The final scores on the third day were Hogan 66, Oliver 67.

On the last day rain came down during the morning, but since the leaders started later in the day, the only effect on their games was the fortunate one of helping to slow down the glassy greens to a more puttable speed. The players could actually charge the cup for a pleasant change.

Ben Hogan coasted home in another 69, his fourth straight subpar round on this difficult golf course, to win by five full strokes over Ed Oliver and the rest of the field. It must have given Ben a bit of wry satisfaction when he found that Sam Snead had finished at 292. This was eighteen strokes behind Hogan and not even among the ten top finishers; in fact, Snead was in an ignominious sixteenth spot. Now it was on to Carnoustie and Oakmont for Ben! With that determination and will, to say nothing of that mechanically repeating, grooved swing, how could anyone stop him during 1953?

24
THE MASTERS OF 1954

Sam Snead	74	73	70	72	289
Play-off					70
Ben Hogan	72	73	69	75	289
Play-off					71
Billy Joe Patton	70	74	75	71	290
E. J. Harrison	70	79	74	68	291
Lloyd Mangrum	71	75	76	69	291
Jerry Barber	74	76	71	71	292
Jack Burke, Jr.	71	77	73	71	292
Bob Rosburg	73	73	76	70	292
Al Besselink	74	74	74	72	294
Cary Middlecoff	73	76	70	75	294

This was the Masters that everyone remembers as the one that Billy Joe Patton almost won. There was great excitement among the galleries this year as Patton—a simon-pure amateur, a Walker Cup alternate player from Morganton, North Carolina—in his first Masters Tournament—fired a sweet 70 to tie for the opening-day lead with veteran player, but non–Masters winner, E. J. ("Dutch") Harrison.

Patton was a true breath of fresh air on the professional golf scene. Big, brawny, possessing a smooth but gargantuan power swing, Billy Joe became the darling of the galleries instantaneously. He would converse with the spectators, tell them what he was "a-gonna-do," and commiserate with them when he hit his infrequent bad shots. Patton was also a prodigious driver, giving no distance to Sam Snead or anybody else who thought he could drive the ball far. Whether the ball went straight was often another matter; but here, too, Billy Joe was not only courageous but also a first-class gambler. Once in the rough, if he could see an opening a yard wide between two big pines seventy-five yards away, and if that hole in the sky led to the flagstick, Billy Joe just busted the ball, blithely, matter-of-factly; and as often as not he did get through that opening.

Although Patton told the reporters he might shoot 80 the second day, he did not. In fact, he had a nice 74 and, lo, Billy Joe was leading the entire field after thirty-six holes. Ben Hogan had 72 and 73, Sam Snead 74 and 73, and E. J. Harrison a horrible 79 after his 70 beginning.

Could an amateur win it all for the first

Ben Hogan drives from the first tee as Sam Snead waits his turn during the 1954 play-off.

time in Masters history? Time would tell. In the meantime, Billy Joe kept on playing and playing pretty darn well. He slipped a little bit to a 75 on his third round, and Hogan, in typical third-round Hogan fashion, had turned in a par-breaking 69. Now the professionals would take over, it was thought, for Patton's 75 left him five big strokes behind Ben Hogan. And no amateur was going to spot little Ben five strokes on the last round of the Masters, was he? Furthermore, Hogan had more than Patton on his mind. Sam Snead was back again in an ominous position. A third-round 70 had left Sam at 217, only three strokes behind Ben's 214. Remember, Billy Joe was at 219 now, or five strokes off the pace.

Then, if ever in the Masters, the galleries went wild. It might be said that "all hell broke loose" to fit what Billy Joe Patton did for the first eleven holes of the last round of this 1954 Masters. Through the first five holes, Billy Joe matched par—good enough, but not climbing up on Snead and Hogan by any means.

Then, on the 190-yard sixth hole, knowing he badly needed a birdie, Billy Joe proceeded to knock the ball right into the hole for an ace. Actually it was an "almost" ace that wasn't. Joe Dey, of the U.S.G.A. (later czar of the Professional Golfers Association) had to jiggle the flagstick a bit to release the wedged ball and allow it to drop to the bottom of the hole, where the rules of golf require it to be to count as an ace. The roar of the galleries, it was said, was heard in Atlanta miles and miles away.

Patton—now two under par and rather encouraged, to say the least, by the turn of events—parred the seventh hole, birdied again at No. 8 with his long-ball ability, and capped the nine with another birdie at the ninth hole. He had shot a 32, had gone past Sam Snead who had shot a 37, and had pulled himself into a tie with Hogan, who would later reach the turn also in 37.

Billy Joe got through the tenth and eleventh safely in par and slipped slightly to a bogey at the twelfth, but then Rae's Creek did the amateur in. Billy Joe socked his four wood into the water. Groans from the gallery. A rueful smile from Billy Joe, but a smile nevertheless. Patton took a double-bogey seven on the thirteenth. He did not give up at this bad turn of events, however, but came right back with a birdie three at the fourteenth. Then, disaster struck again! He splashed his second shot into the pond in front of the fifteenth hole, got on the green in four, then two-putted for a bogey six.

Billy Joe parred in from there, but his day was gone, never to come again at the Masters. He finished at 290. If he had been able to par only one and bogey the other of those two five-pars, the thirteenth and the fifteenth, he still could have beaten the eventual tie of Snead and Hogan at 289. Nevertheless, it was a great day not only for Billy Joe Patton but for amateur golf all over the world. You still hear one amateur say to another, "Remember when Billy Joe Patton almost won the Masters?"

Oh, yes, Sam Snead beat Ben Hogan 70 to 71 in the play-off. The play was good but not as colorful as it would have been if Billy Joe Patton had been there.

25
THE MASTERS OF 1955

Cary Middlecoff	72	65	72	70	279
Ben Hogan	73	68	72	73	286
Sam Snead	72	71	74	70	287
Bob Rosburg	72	72	72	73	289
Mike Souchak	71	74	72	72	289
Julius Boros	71	75	72	71	289
Lloyd Mangrum	74	73	72	72	291
Harvie Ward	77	69	75	71	292
Stan Leonard	77	73	68	74	292
Dick Mayer	78	72	72	71	293
Byron Nelson	72	75	74	72	293
Arnold Palmer	76	76	72	69	293

Here is Cary Middlecoff's own description of the remarkable putt he sank on the thirteenth green in the second round of the 1955 Masters Tournament:*

In the second round of the Masters Tournament, I came to the thirteenth hole five under par. On this famous par-five hole my second shot with a three wood hit on the green about pin-high and rolled about eighty feet past the cup, way on the back of this long green. As I looked over the tremendously long putt, I could only think how nice it would be to get it close to the hole for an easy birdie and go six under par. There were several slight undulations between my ball and the cup, but otherwise it was a level putt with just a small amount of left break.

I decided that the best way to get the ball close was to try as hard as I could to hole it out. When the ball left my putter, I knew I had hit a good putt, and I watched it roll through the little dips in the happy knowledge that it would probably stop no more than a foot or two away, making for an easy birdie. The ball still had about twenty feet to go when I saw and sensed that it might go in. The gallery sensed the same thing when the ball was about fifteen feet short, and a tentative cheer went up. At five feet short, I could see that the ball was rolling at just the right speed and that it was dead in the middle of the cup. And then "plop," an eagle three.

That was about as big a thrill as I have ever got from golf, and several in the big gallery told me it was one of their biggest golf thrills. It put me seven under par, which was the way I finished the round at 65. Bobby Jones, host at this fine tournament, was kind enough to describe that round as the best ever played on that world-famous course. And it certainly helped me win the tournament.

*From the book *Advanced Golf* by Cary Middlecoff. © 1957 by Prentice-Hall, Inc., Englewood Cliffs, NJ. Reprinted with permission of the publisher.

Cary's eagle three at the thirteenth was "as big a thrill as I have ever got from golf."

Dr. Cary Middlecoff, a graduate dentist from Memphis, decided in 1947 that instead of making his career in dentistry he would prefer to play golf full-time as a professional. Even though Robert T. Jones, Jr., advised Cary not to make this move, Cary went ahead. And, from the success Cary Middlecoff has had in professional golf over the years, no one dares to say that Cary was wrong in making that choice.

At the 1948 Masters, Cary had a most respectable total of 284, a figure that would have tied or won the first, third, or fifth Masters of the twelve played up until that time. Since then Cary had won the U.S. Open Championship when that tournament was held at Medinah in Chicago in 1949, only two years and two months after he had turned professional. Since 1948, in the succeeding six tournaments at Augusta, however, Cary had finished in the top ten low scorers of the Masters only twice and then not with very impressive scores. In 1950 he had tied for seventh at 292, and in 1954 he had tied for ninth at 294.

So perhaps Cary Middlecoff was due, or even overdue, to win the 1955 Masters. This tournament started out with Jack Burke, Jr., shooting the opening day eye-opening round, a great 67. Then Burke moved out of the picture to return, as we shall see, in the 1956 Masters with a strong start and a strong finish as well.

Sam Snead opened with what appeared to be the makings of a sensational subpar round, only to take a shocking eight on the five-par thirteenth when he repeatedly hacked at a buried ball in the newly installed left bunker there. Snead's 72 might have been a 69 easily but for that bad hole. It really didn't matter in the long run, however, because this tournament was practically over and won by Cary Middlecoff on a marvelous second-round 65. Cary had started with a par 72, and his second-round eighteen-hole score gave him 137 and skyrocketed him at the halfway point into a lead that he never relinquished.

On Cary's great round, his first nine started off rather unremarkably with a birdie at No. 1 and then four straight pars. Then the lightning struck, and Cary drilled in one, two, three, four straight birdies to finish the nine at 31, a new course record.

Nos. 10, 11, and 12 fell in comfortable pars to Cary. The wicked thirteenth was next, with its threat of trouble in Rae's Creek. If Cary could just get by here in par, he might get a 67. His drive was a bit too far right. It was long enough but left a long wood second to the green—if Cary dared to try to carry over the rocky chasm with its rushing torrent of water. The gallery murmured with approbation as they saw Cary pull out a wood, his three wood. "He's going for it!"

Considering the trajectory of the wood and that the pin was placed on the very front of the green, it was very unlikely that Cary's ball would stop anywhere near the flag. The shot was struck, a good one, and to the delight of the gallery and, no doubt the relief of Cary Middlecoff, the ball just carried to the front edge of the green, but on landing it took off for the rear part of the green and finally rolled to a stop at a distance that has been estimated as between

April 8, 1955

OFFICIAL SCORE CARD

HOLE	1	2	3	4	5	6	7	8	9	Out	10	11	12	13	14	15	16	17	18	In	Totals
YARDAGE	400	555	355	220	450	190	365	520	420	3475	470	445	155	470	420	505	190	400	420	3475	6950
PAR	4	5	4	3	4	3	4	5	4	36	4	4	3	5	4	5	3	4	4	36	72
PLAYER	3	5	4	3	4	2	3	4	3	31	4	4	3	3	4	4	3	5	4	34	65

I have checked my score hole by hole.

Player Signature _Cary Middlecoff_

Attest _Hillman Robbins_

Cary's 65, only one stroke off the course record, gave him a big jump on the field, enabling him to win by seven strokes.

seventy-five and eighty-five feet from the flagstick.

Cary would have been pleased merely to take two putts and get another birdie here. He really feared a three-putt green because of the extreme distance between his ball and the hole, to say nothing of the subtle undulations in the monstrous green, one of the largest at Augusta.

Cary surveyed the long putt in his inimitable style. He hitched up his trousers again and again, adjusted the peak of his white-visored cap, and stalked the perimeter of the line to the cup in intense concentration. Cary was a great housekeeper, too, and no green ever satisfied him until he had found a piece of gravel or cut grass on his line and thrown it away dramatically.

Finally, he crouched well over the ball, head directly above it with his mallet-head putter in front of the ball, then behind it, then possibly once more in front of the ball and behind it again. At last, a slow, beautiful takeaway and the ball was on its way to the distant cup. Would the putt be long enough? The green was slick, and, though it appeared that the ball might stop short of two-putt distance, it could be seen to be coming closer and closer to the cup. As you

know from Cary's own description at the beginning of this chapter, the ball did go in.

Middlecoff's 65 put him four strokes ahead of his nearest challenger, Ben Hogan, who had brought in a fine 68 after a 73 on the first round.

Hogan and Middlecoff matched third-round 72s, and Cary was in if he could only keep plugging away at par and force Ben or anyone else to shoot a miracle round to catch him. Sam Snead and Bob Rosburg were respectively six and seven strokes behind.

All Cary did on the final day was play the front nine in 34, two under par, and stayed right there in front all the way for a 70 and a total of 279 strokes, a score second only to Ben Hogan's remarkable 274 in 1953. Cary won by a new record margin of seven strokes over the second-place finisher, Hogan, who brought in another badly putted round (for Ben, that is) of 73 strokes.

It is noteworthy that Arnold Palmer made his first appearance in the top ten finishers of the Masters in this tournament, when after a lackluster start of two 76s he came back with 72 and 69. It would be three more years before the start of the Arnold Palmer every-other-year win of the Masters.

26
THE MASTERS OF 1956

Jack Burke, Jr.	72	71	75	71	289
Ken Venturi	66	69	75	80	290
Cary Middlecoff	67	72	75	77	291
Lloyd Mangrum	72	74	72	74	292
Sam Snead	73	76	72	71	292
Jerry Barber	71	72	76	75	294
Doug Ford	70	72	75	77	294
Shelley Mayfield	68	74	80	74	296
Tommy Bolt	68	74	78	76	296
Ben Hogan	69	78	74	75	296

This was another year in which there was a serious amateur threat at the Masters. It wasn't Billy Joe Patton this time, but dark-haired, slighter Ken Venturi, only twenty-four years old and invited to this year's tournament as "a deserving player not otherwise eligible." Ken was a pupil of Byron Nelson, and, like his mentor, he hit magnificent iron shots. He had first gained recognition as a leading American amateur by making the United States Walker Cup team in 1953, had spent some time in the army, and after coming out again played well in enough tournaments to catch the attention of his peers and merit this invitation only rarely extended to an amateur.

Ken started off brilliantly the first day—playing, incidentally, with the colorful Billy Joe Patton, who undoubtedly was recalling his own day of glory in 1954. Ken was so accurate with his wood shots that he made sixteen greens in the regulation figures.

He had eight one-putt greens, too, and no bogeys to score the lowest round ever shot by an amateur in the Masters, a 66. (The record still stands, by the way, and only once has been seriously challenged, when Charlie Coe in 1959 came in with a score of 67 in the third round.)

Defending champion Cary Middlecoff was close behind Venturi with a 67. Hogan had 69. Scores were low on this calm day on which light rains helped to slow down Augusta National's normally icy greens.

The next day, strong winds blew, sometimes in gusts up to fifty miles an hour. The scores, in general, went up. Hogan took a 78, Middlecoff a 72. Ken played very well again, and by scrambling mightily saved a

APR 5 1956

OFFICIAL SCORE CARD

HOLE	1	2	3	4	5	6	7	8	9	Out	10	11	12	13	14	15	16	17	18	In	Totals
YARDAGE	400	555	355	220	450	190	365	520	420	3475	470	445	155	470	420	520	190	400	420	3490	6965
PAR	4	5	4	3	4	3	4	5	4	36	4	4	3	5	4	5	3	4	4	36	72
PLAYER	3	4	3	✓	4	3	✓	5	4	32	5	4	3	3	4	5	2	4	4	34	66

I have checked my score hole by hole.

Player Signature _Kenneth Venturi_
KENNETH VENTURI

Attest _____
R.S.J.

Ken Venturi set an amateur course record of 66 in the 1956 Masters with five birdies, one bogie, and an eagle on the thirteenth.

Jack Burke, Jr., 1956 Masters champion.

number of pars with good chipping and accurate putting. The highlight of Venturi's third round was a magnificent chip shot, his third shot to the par-five eighth hole. He was some thirty-five yards away from the hole, just off the green, but he had to negotiate two small rises in the green. The shot came off perfectly with a six iron, rolled up over the hills and dales on the thirteenth green, and dropped right into the cup for a most satisfying eagle three for Ken. He continued to hold his game together for the rest of the round and finished with a 69, four strokes ahead of Cary Middlecoff, who was in second place at 139.

With scores of 142 were Doug Ford, Shelley Mayfield, and Tommy Bolt. (Mayfield and Bolt would shoot 80 and 78 the next day, Ford a 77 on the last day.) But almost unnoticed behind the pack at 142 rested Jack Burke, Jr., with solid rounds of 72 and 71. Remember, too, that Jack Burke had always seemed to produce one or even two mediocre-to-bad rounds in each of his preceding Masters, which cost him enough strokes to hurt his chances of winning. He had had a 76 and a 78 in 1952 and lost by only four strokes to Sam Snead. He had had a 78 in 1953 and finished eighth, and a 77 in 1954, good enough for fifth place. In 1955 he had not finished in the top ten.

Jack Burke's third round was a middle-of-the-road 75, and at the end of the third day he appeared to be fighting to finish somewhere in fourth or fifth place without any chance of overhauling Venturi, now eight strokes in front of him. Nor was it thought that Ken could catch Cary Middlecoff, who had matched Venturi's third-round 75 and remained where he was when he had started the round—four strokes off the leading pace. Incidentally, Venturi had shown serious signs of blowing up midway through his third round when he took an ugly 40 on the first nine to Cary's fine 35 and had at that time gone one stroke behind Cary Middlecoff with nine holes to play. The situation changed on the back nine as Venturi regained his composure along with his putting touch while Cary lost his. Ken birdied Nos. 13, 14, and 15 in a row, came back in 35 to Cary's struggling 40, and the scene was set, everyone thought, for a showdown between the two on the last day.

It is doubtful that Burke felt that he could move into first place. He was more relaxed, having not shot as bad a third round as usual. So Jack Burke went out earlier than the leaders, played well, and hoped that his final 71, a good score but not truly great, would put him somewhere up on the list for more money than his accustomed eighth or ninth place. The 71 added to his 72-71-75 start brought Burke in at 289 strokes. This meant that Venturi, then just turning the ninth hole, would need merely 41 strokes, or five over par, to tie Burke and 40 strokes or less to win—probably. Probably, because Cary Middlecoff could not be counted out just yet. Middlecoff was playing ahead of Venturi and had shown signs of a monstrous blowup when he four-putted the fifth hole for a double-bogey six. Cary had managed to finish his nine at 38, which was a considerable consolation to Venturi when Ken took a similar 38 on his first nine; then, too, Ken still had the four-stroke lead over Cary, and Burke's 35 on the front nine had gained for Burke only three of the eight strokes he needed to get into a tie with Venturi.

Then, the famous Amen Corner started to take its toll on Venturi. He bogeyed No. 10, and one stroke of the lead was gone. He bogeyed No. 11 and two strokes of the lead were gone. Nos. 12, 14, and 15 were similar nightmares—not double bogeys, just bogeys, and five strokes were gone. Now Venturi really was in trouble. Middlecoff, ahead of him, was continuing to have his troubles.

He had three-putted the seventeenth hole after failing to get on with his second shot. Cary was now headed for more than the 289 score already posted by Jack Burke.

Ken's lead was gone entirely. He now needed straight par in, starting with the sixteenth hole, merely to tie Jack Burke. To the great relief of his huge gallery, all pulling for the obviously struggling, weary young amateur, Ken got his tee shot onto the three-par sixteenth and got down in two putts. He had broken the string of bogeys. Perhaps he could now get the winning birdie at No. 17 or No. 18.

The flagstick at No. 17 had been placed near the back edge of this dangerous, crowned, plateau-type green. Venturi hit a good drive and went boldly for the pin, hoping to crowd the ball so close to the hole he could not miss the birdie.

The iron shot to the green was too strong, and Ken, in horror, saw it roll down the back slope of the green. He now had a difficult, if not impossible, pitch to the pin just to save his par. He made a great effort, now under tremendous strain, for here was the loss of the tournament right before his eyes. His chip came to rest ten feet away from the cup. Those ten feet seemed to be a hundred. Ken did not get the putt down and went to the eighteenth tee one stroke behind Jack Burke. There was only an outside chance now that he could birdie the eighteenth hole, pull himself back into a tie, and then force a play-off the next day.

Ken played the eighteenth hole courageously. His drive was long and straight, and his second shot skidded to a stop only eighteen feet from the cup. The gallery held its breath, still hoping that Ken Venturi, the amateur who had played so well in this Masters, outfighting the professionals time after time, hole after hole, could sink this last putt and by tying Jack Burke might eventually become the first amateur ever to win the Masters.

The eighteen-foot putt barely missed the cup. Venturi had lost—this time. However, Ken turned professional the same year and went on to win ten championships in his first four seasons as a pro. As we shall see, he again came close to winning the Masters from Arnold Palmer in 1960, had the tournament won, in fact, until Arnie put together two incredible birdies on the last two holes to edge Venturi out of the championship.

Ken Venturi did go on to win a major championship, the 1964 U.S. Open at Congressional Country Club outside Washington, D.C., in a drama-packed finish that saw Venturi conquer his own game in the awful summer heat, haunted by the ghost of that bad finish at the 1956 Masters.

27
THE MASTERS OF 1957

Doug Ford	72	73	72	66	283
Sam Snead	72	68	74	72	286
Jimmy Demaret	72	70	75	70	287
Harvie Ward	73	71	71	73	288
Peter Thomson	72	73	73	71	289
Ed Furgol	73	71	72	74	290
Jack Burke, Jr.	71	72	74	74	291
Dow Finsterwald	74	74	73	70	291
Arnold Palmer	73	73	69	76	291
Jay Hebert	74	72	76	70	292

This was the year of one of the most sensational finishes ever seen at the Masters—Doug Ford's hole-out from the front bunker of the eighteenth hole for one of the lowest closing rounds ever played at Augusta National, a remarkable 66.

Jack Burke, Jr., defending champion, started off strongly in defense of his title with a 71, one under par, strangely the only subpar round in a huge field of 102 players. The cups were, as usual, in difficult positions, the winds unsteady and upsetting to all the golfers. Doug Ford was practically unnoticed at 72 and 73 for 145 at the halfway mark.

Doug Ford's hole-out from the front bunker at eighteen was a dramatic finish to his remarkable round of 66.

94

Sam Snead's early lead takes a turn for the worse in the third round.

Sam Snead was once more making threatening gestures and had taken the thirty-six-hole lead with a 72 followed by 68 for 140. Burke was still in contention on 71-72, 143 but would revert to his old habit of ordinary golf, two 74s for a finish at 291 and a tie for seventh place.

It was Snead who fell off in his third round with a 74, including four typically three-putted Snead greens.

After a consistent third-round 72 had left him at 217, three strokes away from Snead's leading score, Doug Ford came roaring out of the pack on the last round with birdies on Nos. 12 and 14 and a particularly brave 245-yard wood over the pond at No. 15 to catch Snead. When Snead had trouble on the back nine, Doug moved ahead of Snead by one stroke as he came to the eighteenth hole.

Doug needed a par there, and if Snead did not birdie, Ford would have a likely chance to win by one stroke over Snead.

Ford's drive at the eighteenth hole was a good one, straight and far (the bunker now in the center of the eighteenth fairway had not yet been constructed) and right down the middle. The cup was cut quite close to the front part of the green, and in trying too hard to get as near to the hole as possible Ford hooked his second shot at No. 18 into the left front bunker. He had practically buried the ball in the front upslope. Now he was faced with a most difficult shot and the strong possibility of taking a bogey because it would be a miracle if he could stop his shot out of the bunker anywhere near the hole.

Doug smashed into the sand behind the buried ball. The ball rose satisfactorily from the bunker, plopped down ten feet or so from the hole, and then proceeded to run straight into it. Doug had saved his round. In fact, he had turned it into a great 66. Snead did not come close to catching Doug Ford. He finished with a respectable 72, which was six strokes worse than Ford's 66. Ford's winning margin was three strokes, 283 to Snead's 286.

The great Arnold Palmer, four-time Masters champion, turns pro in 1954 and goes on to win his first Masters in 1958.

28
THE MASTERS OF 1958

Arnold Palmer	70	73	68	73	284
Doug Ford	74	71	70	70	285
Fred Hawkins	71	75	68	71	285
Stan Leonard	72	70	73	71	286
Ken Venturi	68	72	74	72	286
Cary Middlecoff	70	73	69	75	287
Art Wall, Jr.	71	72	70	74	287
Billy Joe Patton	72	69	73	74	288
Claude Harmon	71	76	72	70	289
Jay Hebert	72	73	73	71	289
Billy Maxwell	71	70	72	76	289
Al Mengert	73	71	69	76	289

The year 1958 saw the beginning of the era of Arnold Palmer at the Masters. Not since the days of the flamboyant Walter Hagen had such a charming personality exploded on the golf scene with as much attention and commotion as did Arnold Palmer once he turned professional in 1954, after the U.S. amateur championship of that year.

Blessed with a burly physique and the arms of a blacksmith, Arnold rifled his straight long drives and equally long accurate irons right at the hole with a daring and audacity that caused the galleries to take him immediately to their hearts. Not ashamed of showing emotion, Arnold would wince in pain as a putt failed to drop, smile broadly when an especially dangerous shot came off successfully, hitch his trousers up and stride forward with a determined face that said to the world, "No one can stop Arnold Palmer when he's playing golf like this!" And very frequently during the Palmer era no one *could* stop him.

Arnold's first important win occurred in 1955, six months after he started out on the professional trail, when he captured the prestigious Canadian Open of 1955 from a strong field. He had not won a major championship since then, although he had gathered a total of seven tournament wins of lesser importance. In the 1956 U.S. Open championship he had made his best showing to date, finishing seventh, six strokes behind Cary Middlecoff at Oak Hill Country Club in Rochester.

Arnold Palmer was overdue to win a big one, and this Masters was the tournament

Arnold Palmer, with Ken Venturi on his left, argues a rules point in 1958 with Masters officials Bobby Jones and Cliff Roberts.

that really started him on his magnificent career in golf.

The Augusta National golf course played fast on opening day of 1958. The weather was great, the winds normal, the greens, as usual, in perfect condition. There were seventeen scores under the par of 72, which shows how good to the players the Augusta course can be when it wants to be.

Ken Venturi was the lowest scorer with a fine 68. He had now turned professional and was hoping to win the Masters title he had not won as an amateur. Arnold Palmer was at 70 after sundown of the first day. He had been able to score four-three-four against par of five-four-five on Nos. 13, 14, and 15.

His long game was especially good. Arnold was making the five-pars in two strokes with long irons. He was putting for eagles and getting the birdies.

Cary Middlecoff, always a threat, was in at 70 strokes alongside Palmer. Others in the running after the first day were Fred Hawkins, Art Wall, Jr., Claude Harmon, and Billy Maxwell—all at 71. Of these four, only Hawkins would eventually threaten to win.

Venturi's second round was a typical Venturi display of good but erratic scoring. After a bad four-over-par 40 on the first nine, including a hurtful double bogey at the eighth hole, Ken had flashed back in a

32, birdieing the last three holes. He had saved a 72 and was still in the lead at 140.

Arnold Palmer was in with a respectable 73 to lie three strokes behind Ken. Middlecoff had done a 73 as well and remained tied with Palmer. Art Wall was still hanging on with a 72 for another 143 total. Maxwell, on a 70, had crept up to 141 but would come back later with 72-76 to put himself out of the running. Doug Ford had had a 74-71 start and was rather unnoticed for the moment at 145. He would make a strong move during the next two days.

Venturi fell off to a 74 on his third round and lost his leadership, never to regain it. Sam Snead had sneaked up with a great 68 for a 211 total. But tomorrow Snead would balloon to a terrible 79 and put himself right out of the tournament. Arnold Palmer was making his move. He had cracked out a 68, too, and now was in the lead going into the last day.

A drenching rain fell during the night. The course was soaked by morning, but it was playable. The skies were cloudy. The tournament officials decided to permit the players to lift, clean, and drop any ball that became embedded in its own divot mark through the green—which means all the areas of the golf course except in the hazards. This became a very important decision as far as Arnold Palmer was concerned, as we shall see.

Venturi and Palmer were paired together on the final day. Since they had heard that Snead had double-bogeyed the first hole with a six and was struggling thereafter to his eventual 79, it was clear to the two players involved—and the galleries as well—that the possible winner might be found in the Venturi-Palmer twosome.

Venturi gained one stroke on Arnold through the ninth hole with a 35 to Palmer's 36, and when Arnold went over par again at No. 10 with a five, Venturi was only one stroke behind. At the twelfth hole, Palmer's ball embedded itself in a bank above the left-hand bunker. Arnold hacked the ball out with difficulty and eventually scored what appeared to be a five on the hole. In the meantime, Venturi had made a conven-

tional three. To all appearances Ken had taken the lead away from Palmer. Then Palmer remembered the possibility of relief from his bad lie under the embedded-ball rule in effect for the day. He decided to confer with a rules committeeman (rules interpreters are readily available all the time at the Masters and other similar tournaments operating under U.S.G.A. rules). Arnold got permission from the committeeman to get relief, so subsequently he played a provisional ball, which he dropped—in accordance with the rules—away from the embedded spot. Arnold made a three with the provisional ball and had to wait for a final ruling from the rules committee as to which score was his official one for the hole, the five or the three.

Even with this cloud on his mind, Arnold was able to concentrate on the task at hand: to make up those strokes, if they were lost irrevocably. He played a typical Arnold Palmer three wood to the thirteenth green on his second shot. The ball came to rest only eighteen feet from the hole. Venturi had decided to play the hole safe, short of the green, and chip for his birdie.

Palmer then sank his putt for an eagle three to the screams of his tremendous gallery, now sensing a Palmer win. Venturi got his birdie, too, with a courageous pitch and one putt. Then came unofficial word that Palmer's three on the twelfth hole was to be counted. More pandemonium. Was Arnold truly in front now? Whether he was or not, he was charging!

A three-putt at No. 14 and Venturi had lost another stroke. He was showing signs of being rattled by the uncertainty of Palmer's score. Venturi three-putted again at No. 15 as the word at last came: Palmer had officially been given the three.

Venturi three-putted the sixteenth green and lost his last opportunity to overhaul Arnold Palmer. The psychological warfare was trying on both players as Arnold, too, stumbled in with a bogey on Nos. 16 and 18. At least Arnold was in the clubhouse with a final 73 and a 284 total.

Now there appeared a threat from two late players getting hot in their last round,

Doug Ford and Fred Hawkins. If either one of them could birdie the last hole, there would be a tie for first place and a play-off the next day.

Each man played the eighteenth hole very well. Ford got his second shot within twelve feet of his birdie, Hawkins within sixteen feet. Palmer watched most anxiously as each man made his last effort to force a tie.

It was not to be. Neither putt dropped. Doug Ford would not be a double winner, nor would Fred Hawkins ever again be so close to a win at the Masters.

America had a brilliant new Masters champion in Arnold Palmer. The era of Arnold Palmer was just beginning with this, his first major championship.

29
THE MASTERS OF 1959

Art Wall, Jr.	73	74	71	66	284
Cary Middlecoff	74	71	68	72	285
Arnold Palmer	71	70	71	74	286
Dick Mayer	73	75	71	68	287
Stan Leonard	69	74	69	75	287
Charles R. Coe	74	74	67	73	288
Fred Hawkins	77	71	68	73	289
Julius Boros	75	69	74	72	290
Jay Hebert	72	73	72	73	290
Gene Littler	72	75	72	71	290
Billy Maxwell	73	71	72	74	290
Billy Joe Patton	75	70	71	74	290
Gary Player	73	75	71	71	290

From 1934 through 1959 there appeared to be a jinx on all former Masters champions. No champion in all those years had ever been able to come back to Augusta and win the title two years in a row. Not until 1966, when Jack Nicklaus at last put an end to this hoodoo, would the same player have two Masters Tournament victories in a row.

Arnold Palmer took complete charge of the field in the 1959 Masters in the early play of the tournament, although relatively unknown Stan Leonard had opened with an excellent 69 and was only two strokes ahead of Palmer, who was alone at 71. Scores on opening day were unusually high, with only Gene Littler and Jay Hebert registering par 72s to go on the scoreboard behind Leonard and Palmer. Art Wall, Jr., was rather unnoticed at 73 and was tied with Gary Player at that figure. If any fireworks were coming, Player might be expected to supply them, it was thought. Gary never did, however.

Arnold Palmer returned a well-played 70 on the second day and took over the lead at that point. Leonard had slipped rather badly to a 74 but was able to get fired up again and score a great 69 on his third round and by the fifth hole was tied with Palmer. Art Wall, in the meantime, was playing along most steadily, putting extremely well on the fast greens. He was in with a fine 71 but at 218 strokes was believed to be much too far off the pace Palmer and Leonard were setting with their 212s. If indeed anyone were able to pick up six strokes on Masters champion Arnold Palmer in one round, surely it would not be slight, colorless, methodical Art Wall.

Art Wall, Jr. birdied five of the last six holes to take the victory from favored Arnold Palmer.

Doubtless, Arnold would break the two-win jinx and charge in with the victory.

But in that final round, Arnold Palmer suddenly found himself in serious trouble. Wall was playing in a group five holes behind the Palmer twosome when the news came that Arnold had taken a six on the short twelfth water hole. Three strokes of the lead were gone in a flash. Wall had some hope yet. Palmer had put a ball into the water, taken a penalty shot, and then gone over the green on his third shot. He had an unbelievable six strokes on a par-three hole.

The galleries were shocked. Palmer had been even par through the eleventh and was showing no signs of weakening now that he was three over par. He fought back to one over par with great birdie fours on Nos. 13 and 15. He was able to par Nos. 14 and 16. Perhaps he could win yet—get another birdie and put the championship on ice. But at No. 17, faced with a two-footer for his par, Arnold missed. Now he was two over par for the round heading for No. 18. Even a par there would earn Palmer a 74, a total of 286,

and force Art Wall to shoot a most difficult four-under-par 68 merely to tie Arnold. Wall had never broken 70 in a Masters before, and with all the pressure of the last holes on him he could scarcely be expected to do so now.

When Arnold bogeyed the seventeenth hole, Art Wall was not too far away to hear the groans of disappointment from the gallery there and get the news quickly via the huge scoreboards when the green two (two over par) went up after Palmer's name.

Wall knew what he must do: get some birdies and get them fast, because time and holes were running out on him.

He went after the birdie at No. 13 with a vengeance. His wood second got over Rae's Creek safely, but his ball stopped a long seventy-five feet away from the hole. Art chipped weakly to about fifteen feet from the cup. He couldn't afford to lose this cinch birdie hole to par. Gently, firmly, Art Wall stroked that fifteen-foot putt in for the birdie four. At the next hole, Art Wall, now gaining more and more confidence, canned a twenty-foot birdie putt. On No. 15, Wall played boldly, going for the green in two. His shot carried to the putting surface successfully and now he had a chance for an eagle from twenty-five feet. He did not get the putt down, but he cashed his third birdie in a row. He now needed at least one more birdie to beat Palmer's score. Pars in from Nos. 16 through 18 would tie him with Arnold.

The sixteenth fell to him in par. On the four-par seventeenth, Art Wall was able to get his second shot within fifteen feet of the hole. Down went the putt for his fourth birdie in twelve holes. Now, if he could just par at No. 18, he would beat Palmer by a stroke.

Wall hit a marvelous tee shot, a drive he said later was the best one he had hit during the entire tournament. The flagstick was tucked, as it is customarily on the last day, away down in the front of the green, daring the player to get close to the hole.

Wall's nine-iron shot was a sweet one and left him twelve feet below the hole. He would be putting uphill at the hole, a desirable situation on the icy Augusta greens.

With the galleries massed around the eighteenth hole in hushed silence, Art Wall sank that last putt for his fifth birdie in six holes. He had outscored Arnold Palmer 284 to 286. Art Wall's 66 to Arnold Palmer's 74 had gained eight strokes in one round on last year's champion. The jinx apparently was still in effect. Jack Nicklaus was coming along soon, and he would see what he could do about it.

30
THE MASTERS OF 1960

Arnold Palmer	67	73	72	70	282
Ken Venturi	73	69	71	70	283
Dow Finsterwald	71	70	72	71	284
Billy Casper, Jr.	71	71	71	74	287
Julius Boros	72	71	70	75	288
Gary Player	72	71	72	74	289
Wally Burkemo	72	69	75	73	289
Ben Hogan	73	68	72	76	289
Lionel Hebert	74	70	73	73	290
Stan Leonard	72	72	72	74	290

Arnold Palmer came to the 1960 Masters riding on a hot streak. He had previously won the Desert Classic in Palm Springs, the Texas Open, the Baton Rouge Open, and the Pensacola Open. He had not forgotten his weak finish in the 1959 Masters and most purposefully had decided to make up for that lapse with even better play this year. He came to Augusta early in order to get in as much practice as possible. The weather turned sour, however, and cold rain closed the golf course for some of the practice days. Besides, Arnold caught an influenza bug and was feeling miserable. All in all, things

were not very auspicious for Arnold as he began his quest for his second Masters title.

The defending champion, Art Wall, Jr., was forced to withdraw from the event because of illness, so for the first time in Masters history there was no defending champion on the course.

Seventeen amateurs were playing this year, an unusually large contingent. Among them were Jack Nicklaus, the U.S. amateur champion, and Deane Beman, the American-born British amateur champion. Ben Hogan was there seeking his third championship, but he finished seven strokes away from first place.

With the course heavy from the intermittent rains, the long hitters of golf had a distinct advantage over the less powerful players. In his opening round, Arnold Palmer, customarily a long and straight driver, showed how he could capitalize on his length when he scored three birdies and an eagle on the four par-five holes. His round was a most satisfactory 67.

Ken Venturi, again trying to quiet the

ghosts of his bad rounds at Augusta, was away with a great 31 on the first nine but then fell off on the last nine with a sorry 42 for a finishing 73 and much personal disappointment on his part. He would keep on plugging gamefully, however, and before he finished the tournament, Arnold Palmer would be aware of his considerable threat.

While Arnold Palmer had sprung out in front with his 67, there were four good players right behind him at 71—Dow Finsterwald, Fred Hawkins, Jay Hebert, and Claude Harmon. Only Dow Finsterwald would maintain his threat until the last hole.

On the second day of play, Arnold Palmer started struggling. He bogeyed three of the first eight holes and then recovered somewhat the rest of the way, getting two birdies to come in with a shaky 73 and a 140 total at the halfway mark.

Dow Finsterwald came back with a 70 after the 71 on his first round and was just one stroke off the lead. Dow had had the misfortune of a mental lapse while playing the day before. He had put down a ball on the fifth hole to try another putt, as one might do in a practice round once in a while. As he was strictly forbidden to do this by the rules, Dow had to take a two-stroke penalty on the hole. He would have had 69 on the round but for this unfortunate error in judgment. Sportsman that Dow is, though, he had called the attention of the rules committee to the fact of the practice stroke. This stroke differential eventually was the margin between a winning total score of 282 and Dow's final 284, so in retrospect it might be said that this was the Masters Dow Finsterwald lost. On the other hand, it is hard to re-create emotions and physical conditions, and who can say that Dow would have been able to finish his last two rounds of the Masters with 72 and 71, knowing that Arnold Palmer was breathing down his back?

On the third day, Palmer three-putted once and another time failed to hole a four-footer after a fine approach had left him stony. His long game was superlative, however, and Arnold checked in with an even-par 72 to remain the leader at the fifty-four-hole mark with 212 strokes. Now there were five men only a stroke away going into the customarily dramatic final eighteen holes. Venturi was still in there after a good third-round 71. Finsterwald was too, on a solid 72. The others were Billy Casper, Julius Boros, and Ben Hogan, who would put themselves out of the running on the last day with undistinguished scores of 74, 75, and 76, respectively.

On the last day, although Palmer birdied the first hole as if he were going to catch on fire, he cooled off at the short uphill third hole by three-putting. Then he bogeyed the next hole to the dismay of his army of followers. In the meantime, Venturi and Finsterwald were playing a good hour ahead of Arnold so their scores were going up on the ubiquitous scoreboards well ahead of Arnold's. They were doing very well, too. Each man had nothing but pars or birdies on the first nine, and that sight is impressive to see on the monstrous lines behind the players' names on the boards. Venturi had managed to birdie three of the first six holes, and Dow had birdied Nos. 8 and 9—Venturi out in 33, Finsterwald, 34. So when Palmer bogeyed the fourth hole he relinquished the lead to Venturi.

Venturi and Finsterwald had a nip-and-tuck battle of their own going down the last nine. Venturi picked up a bogey five on the eleventh hole, and the two men were tied at that point. Dow lost a stroke at No. 12; Venturi did not. Dow birdied No. 14; Venturi did not. So the battle between these two fine players came down to the eighteenth hole. At the eighteenth, Dow Finsterwald's second shot to the green caught the right bunker. Dow did not get up and down out of the sand, although he made a gallant try with a shot that stopped only eight feet from the hole. He had finished at 71 for a 284 total.

Venturi had carried to the green on his second shot on No. 18. By successfully two-putting under pressure-packed conditions, Ken was in with a par four for his 70 and a total of 283. He could only hope that this score would hold up before the onslaught of Arnold Palmer, now beginning his last nine.

Remember that Palmer had started out this last day at 212 or four strokes under par for the tournament. Now, as Arnold could see on the scoreboard, Venturi was in with a 70, five under par for the 72 holes. Palmer knew that he must get at least one birdie and the rest pars to tie Venturi or two birdies and the rest pars to win.

Palmer headed down into the lower corner and parred the tenth and eleventh holes. Then he got by the troublesome twelfth hole with another par. No birdies yet, but the possible birdie hole, the thirteenth, was coming up next. Surely with his long-ball driving ability this would be a drive, an iron, and a two-putt for Arnie. But it was not. The drive was not quite as long as usual, and the second was a little wild, so a chip and two putts later Arnold was glad to settle for his par five. Time was starting to run out. The fourteenth hole is not an easy hole for anyone, even Arnold Palmer, to birdie. It lived up to its reputation. Palmer's second shot was a long distance from the hole. Arnold breathed a sigh of relief when he sank his second putt for the par four.

Now, with four holes to play, it appeared that Palmer might be fighting not merely to win but even to pull into a tie with Venturi. The big red "5 under par" on the scoreboard near the fifteenth tee told Arnold more than he wanted to know. He must birdie the fifteenth.

Arnold's drive was erratic. The pressure was certainly showing now. Trying to crank up a little more distance, Palmer had hooked into the left rough. Here he had trees on the left to dodge and the pond to be carried in front of the green. He would go for the green as boldly as ever. The shot went to the right and landed in the gallery, safely over the water but still a long way from a birdie opportunity.

He chipped weakly, missed a fifteen-foot putt, and marked down another par. Three holes to go.

On No. 16, Arnold had good luck when his chip shot to the hole struck the flagstick and bounced away a short distance. With a little more luck he might perhaps have holed the shot. He got his par three but it now appeared that even fortune was against him on this fateful day.

Desperately needing a birdie on either of the last two holes, Palmer was overly cautious on his second shot to the plateaued seventeenth green. He left himself a thirty-five-foot putt. I'm sure that even Arnold Palmer sensed that he would have to get his tying birdie at No. 18. He could not hope to hole this slippery thirty-five-footer.

At last, Billy Casper, his playing partner, had putted out. It was Palmer's turn to putt—do or die. The familiar tensed pigeon-toed stance, the left forefinger down the outside of the putter grip, the steady head, the smooth unhurried backswing. The ball was on its way toward the hole, curving a foot or so from left to right. On and on it came, dead on line. Could it go in? Would it go in? Would it burn the hole and spin away? In! Right in the center of the cup, out of sight! A leap for joy out of Palmer as his white visor came off. Still alive. "Now get that birdie at the eighteenth and you can win! At least you know Venturi is tied right now, and, even if it ends in a tie, you can beat him tomorrow in a play-off!"

Arnold Palmer crushed his drive on the eighteenth hole 300 yards right down the center of the fairway. Ken Venturi was in the tournament headquarters watching the scene on television. Would this Masters be taken away from him in the same way the others were? A birdie on No. 18 is difficult for anyone. A bogey is possible. The monstrous gallery lining both sides of the eighteenth fairway and forty deep around the green itself could almost sense that Arnold would do the impossible: birdie this last hole and win the title outright from Venturi and the field.

Arnie's second shot was a magnificent six iron to within six feet of the hole. The putt was a little side-hiller, right to left about three or four inches but decidedly makable.

It was also missable, even by Arnold Palmer (or Ben Hogan, recalling 1946).

Once more the familiar crouch over the ball, the knees locked, the smooth stroke—and in went the ball for the birdie three and victory. Venturi was shut out once more in what must have been a most bitter disappointment. However, Ken's day of triumph was to come; he would win the U.S. Open at the Congressional Country Club in 1964.

31
THE MASTERS OF 1961

Gary Player	69	68	69	74	280
Charles R. Coe	72	71	69	69	281
Arnold Palmer	68	69	73	71	281
Tommy Bolt	72	71	74	68	285
Don January	74	68	72	71	285
Paul Harney	71	73	68	74	286
Jack Burke, Jr.	76	70	68	73	287
Billy Casper, Jr.	72	77	69	69	287
Bill Collins	74	72	67	74	287
Jack Nicklaus	70	75	70	72	287

Arnold Palmer was the favorite as he entered this Masters Tournament, but Gary Player of South Africa was the dark horse, coming into the tournament with an average of 69.2 strokes in his last forty-nine official rounds.

There was a field of eighty-eight players in this Masters. Intermittent rain plagued the players and the gallery of 15,000 spectators all through the day. Player was delighted that he had lengthened his wood shots and was able to reach the par-fives in two strokes. He scored an excellent 69 on the opening day. Palmer and Nicklaus played in a driving rain, with Palmer scoring a 68,

Gary Player finished the tournament with an anticlimactic 74, thinking he had "given the championship away."

Nicklaus a 70. Bob Rosburg holed a pitch shot at the fifth hole and a 100-foot putt at the fourteenth on the way to a 68, to become a first-day coleader with Arnold Palmer. Incidentally, Jack Nicklaus was playing in this tournament as an invited amateur for the second time. He had first qualified in 1960 as a result of having won the National Amateur Championship at Broadmoor Golf Club in Colorado Springs in the summer of 1959.

On the second day, Player played brilliantly, as did Arnold Palmer, and they shared the lead with almost identical scores of 69-68 and 68-69. Rosburg fell off to a 73, four strokes away in third place. Jack Nicklaus was far off the pace with a 75 for 145, eight strokes behind the leaders.

Gary Player apparently broke the tournament open with his magnificent 69 for a third-round aggregate of 206, only one stroke over the record score for a fifty-four-hole total. The weather was clear and cool as the crowd swelled to 35,000 people. Palmer started his round a half hour ahead of Gary and promptly birdied the first two holes. But Gary was able to do the same thing a few minutes later. Palmer lost a stroke to Rae's Creek at the thirteenth hole, three-putted another green, and was bunkered at two others. Jack Nicklaus came back somewhat with a 70 for a 215 total, nine strokes behind the leader Gary Player.

The final round of this tournament became an anticlimax when heavy rains washed out the day's play after Arnold Palmer and Gary Player had completed nine holes and eleven holes respectively. Player at that point had lost two strokes of his four-stroke lead. The eleventh, fifteenth, and sixteenth greens were virtually flooded by the rains, and there was a threat of a tornado, which fortunately did not materialize.

Gary Player thought he had given the championship away to Arnold Palmer when he staggered in with an unsteady 40 strokes on the second nine to finish the tournament with a 280 total. Arnold Palmer was still out on the course and apparently making one of his famous come-from-behind runs at the leader. Gary had had a ball in Rae's Creek for a double-bogey seven there and missed a short, nasty little putt at the fifteenth to bogey that hole.

Player was in the clubhouse as Palmer came to the eighteenth needing only a par to win, a bogey to tie. He had picked up five strokes on Gary and put himself into the lead. But the impossible happened. Arnold sent his second shot at the eighteenth into the right-hand bunker.* He had an uncomfortable downhill partly-buried lie and, now needing only to splash the ball out for a win or tie, skimmed the ball right over the green and down the steep bank on the left-hand side of the green. The gallery gasped in amazement. Arnold could still save a tie with a delicate run-up and a putt. But, electing to putt the ball up the slope, he ran the ball fifteen to twenty feet past the hole. He missed the attempt to tie, and Gary Player had won his first Masters in five tries.

---

*Later on, in an interview, Arnold was quoted as saying, concerning his bad shot to the eighteenth green, "Before I hit that shot I remember standing there thinking that all I needed to win was a four, just get it up there on the green and then down in two putts. That's where I made my mistake, thinking about something besides the ball. If I'd just kept my mind on swinging the club properly, there wouldn't have been any problem."—*Sports Illustrated*, April 2, 1962.

32
THE MASTERS OF 1962

Arnold Palmer	70	66	69	75	280
Play-off					68
Gary Player	67	71	71	71	280
Play-off					71
Dow Finsterwald	74	68	65	73	280
Play-off					77
Gene Littler	71	68	71	72	282
Mike Souchak	70	72	74	71	287
Jimmy Demaret	73	73	71	70	287
Jerry Barber	72	72	69	74	287
Billy Maxwell	71	73	72	71	287
Ken Venturi	75	70	71	72	288
Charles R. Coe	72	74	71	71	288

Arnold Palmer won his third Masters championship in five years and thus continued his amazing record of winning the tournament every other year. By beating Gary Player in an eighteen-hole play-off after Palmer had tied at 280 strokes with Gary and Dow Finsterwald at that figure, Arnold also gained some satisfaction for backing out of the 1961 Masters and allowing Gary to win that tournament when Arnold took his infamous six on the eighteenth hole.

Arnold Palmer narrowly misses a putt on his way to clinching his second Masters victory.

Champion Arnold Palmer shows Old Master Bobby Jones his winning ball from the three-way play-off for the 1962 title while Cliff Roberts of Augusta National looks on.

Palmer started out shakily on the first day. He was two over par through eleven holes, then birdied four of the last seven for a 70. His galleries thought that with this birdie streak he would walk away with this Masters. After a 70–66 beginning he was at 136 strokes and possessed a two-stroke lead over Gary Player, who had started strongly with a 67 but returned with a 71 on his second round. Dow Finsterwald was six strokes back when he recovered from a 74 start with a great 68 second round. At the end of the third day of play, Arnold remained in the lead by two strokes after a steady 69, which gave him a 205 three-day total. Player had scored a respectable 71 and yet lost two strokes to Arnold and was then four strokes behind the leader going into the last day of play. In the meantime, Dow Finsterwald with a great 65 had scored the best eighteen-hole total the Augusta National had seen in seven years and had moved up to second place with 207, only

two strokes away from Arnold. Dow had only 24 putts in his round; he used an old putter with a new hickory shaft.

The final day's pairing of Arnold Palmer and Gary Player added greatly to the excitement of the finish. Palmer started right out by failing to hole makable putts on the first and second holes (a twenty-incher on the latter), and at the short fourth hole he completely missed his one iron, moving the ball only 125 yards off the tee. He missed a six-foot putt at No. 7, and his lead had evaporated. Finsterwald was playing well ahead of Palmer and Player, and early in their play on the back nine, they both knew they had a total of 280 strokes to tie or beat when Finsterwald's score of 73 was posted.

Arnold double-bogeyed the tenth hole and fell two strokes behind Player (as well as behind Finsterwald's 280 complete score).

Palmer was able to recover his composure and stayed at par on the back nine as Gary matched him stroke for stroke until the sixteenth, where a dramatic forty-five-foot hooded wedge chip shot from the right edge of the green found the flagstick and disappeared into the cup for a much-needed deuce for Arnold. Player made his par at No. 16 and was then only one stroke ahead of Palmer at this time and needed pars in to tie Finsterwald.

On No. 17 Arnold hit a magnificent eight iron to within twelve feet of the flag. Then he calmly sank the putt for his birdie to set up the eventual three-way tie among himself, Player, and Finsterwald. Both Palmer and Player had putts for the outright win at the eighteenth green, but neither could find the cup.

In the play-off, Palmer very nearly duplicated the script of his previous round. He played badly for the first nine holes and fell three strokes behind Player. Finsterwald, meanwhile, was never in contention and took a 77 for the round.

Then Palmer struck back again with the lightning his army of followers had come to expect. Arnold birdied Nos. 10 and 12, two-putted No. 13 for a birdie, and followed with a sixteen-foot birdie putt on No. 14. In those five holes, Player's game fell off and Arnie had gone from three strokes down to four strokes ahead.

It was Palmer 68, Player 71, Finsterwald 77. For Palmer, it was his third Masters, and the win gave him great personal satisfaction with his comeback from near disaster.

33
THE MASTERS OF 1963

Jack Nicklaus	74	66	74	72	286
Tony Lema	74	69	74	70	287
Julius Boros	76	69	71	72	288
Sam Snead	70	73	74	71	288
Dow Finsterwald	74	73	73	69	289
Ed Furgol	70	71	74	74	289
Gary Player	71	74	74	70	289
Bo Wininger	69	72	77	72	290
Don January	73	75	72	71	291
Arnold Palmer	74	73	73	71	291

Arnold Palmer, again the favorite, found himself in a tie for fourteenth place with an opening score of 74. The wind blew in gusts up to thirty-five miles an hour, and the greens baked out in a hot sun as scores soared. There were seventeen scores in the 80s, and four players reported no cards.

Jack Nicklaus, the U.S. Open champion (victor over Arnold Palmer at Oakmont in 1962), was paired with long-hitting George Bayer. Jack three-putted twice on the way to a 74, five strokes off the pace set by Bo Wininger and Mike Souchak, who had 69s.

On the second day, Mike Souchak retained his lead on a fine 70 for a thirty-six-hole total of 139, but the threat of Jack Nicklaus began to become apparent. Playing in his fourth Masters tourney, Jack did not make a serious error in a six-under-par 66 and went into second place with 140. The wind had died away, and playing conditions were excellent.

Jack Nicklaus became the youngest Masters champion in history when he won this tournament with a closing 72 for 286 and the $20,000 prize. Tony Lema had already finished ahead of Jack and, by sinking a twenty-five-foot curling putt at the home hole, put the pressure on Jack, who was playing behind him. Julius Boros and Sam Snead were at 288, and Gary Player, Dow Finsterwald, and Ed Furgol were at 289—close to catching Jack Nicklaus.

Jack appeared to be in trouble at the eighteenth hole. Needing a par there to win by one stroke, he hooked his drive into a muddy area much trampled by the crowd. He was fortunate to obtain an official ruling that he was in casual water and thus entitled to drop away from the spot into a drier place. He did so and lofted a high pitch to the green safely. He left himself a testy three-footer but calmly put the ball in the hole to win his first Masters championship.

34
THE MASTERS OF 1964

Arnold Palmer	69	68	69	70	276
Dave Marr	70	73	69	70	282
Jack Nicklaus	71	73	71	67	282
Bruce Devlin	72	72	67	73	284
Billy Casper, Jr.	76	72	69	69	286
Jim Ferrier	71	73	69	73	286
Paul Harney	73	72	71	70	286
Gary Player	69	72	72	73	286
Dow Finsterwald	71	72	75	69	287
Ben Hogan	73	75	67	72	287
Tony Lema	75	68	74	70	287
Mike Souchak	73	74	70	70	287

Tony Lema and Arnold Palmer were among the favorites in the 1964 Masters.

Gary Player, facing a tonsillectomy, was not up to his usual fine state of physical fitness. Rains had slowed the course, so the word was out to watch out for the long hitters, Nicklaus and Palmer.

At the end of the first day, Palmer was clustered with a group of four others—Goalby, Love, Nagle, and Player—at 69. Only Player would end up in the top ten, and he would be ten strokes away from the eventual winner.

When the dust had settled on the second round's shooting, Arnold Palmer had brought in another subpar round, this time a 68, and although Tony Lema also scored a 68, Arnold was already four strokes ahead of the field. Gary Player was riding in second on a 69-72, 141 halfway count.

Arnold Palmer birdied four of the last six holes in getting his 68 and had hit a one iron to the thirteenth green on his second shot, which left him five feet from the hole. The eagle became a birdie when he rimmed the putt. Tony Lema did make his eagle at No. 13, however, on a three iron to fifteen feet from the cup.

On the third day, the script remained the same, as Palmer took a five-stroke lead on another great 69 for a 206 total at fifty-four holes. Before the largest crowd in Masters history, estimated to have been 40,000 people, Palmer birdied Nos. 14, 15, and 16. Bruce Devlin, Australian amateur champion in 1960 and winner of the Australian Open while still an amateur, made a strong move toward catching Palmer when he registered an excellent 67 and moved to second position at 211, five shots behind the leader.

114

On the last day, Palmer won with ease by six strokes when he scored a 70 for a 276 total, only two strokes away from Ben Hogan's low record total of 274 in the 1953 Masters. Palmer was in trouble twice on his last round, once at No. 11 where he hooked a three iron into the water and scored a bogey five and once at No. 13 where he again hooked, this time into the trees on the left.

He saved this hole by getting out of the woods with a wedge and then screamed a four iron to the green for a saving par.

Arnold Palmer thus became the first four-time winner of the Masters, surpassing Jimmy Demaret's record of three victories in 1940, 1947, and 1950 and Sam Snead's record of three victories in 1949, 1952, and 1954.

Six-time Masters champion, Jack Nicklaus.

35
THE MASTERS OF 1965

Jack Nicklaus	67	71	64	69	271
Arnold Palmer	70	68	72	70	280
Gary Player	65	73	69	73	280
Mason Rudolph	70	75	66	72	283
Dan Sikes	67	72	71	75	285
Gene Littler	71	74	67	74	286
Ramon Sota	71	73	70	72	286
Frank Beard	68	77	72	70	287
Tommy Bolt	69	78	69	71	287
George Knudson	72	73	69	74	288

The year 1965 was the one in which Jack Nicklaus took the Augusta National golf course apart. Jack blasted the Masters field with a third-round 64, tying Lloyd Mangrum's course record set in 1940 and setting a new fifty-four-hole record of 202, three shots better than Ben Hogan's previous record of 205 set in 1953. The longest club Jack used on a par four was a six iron. At the eighth hole, the 530 yard five-par, he was home with a three iron. The third round had started with a three-way tie among Nicklaus, Palmer, and Player at 138.

On the last day, Nicklaus scored the most one-sided victory ever accomplished in the Masters with a 69 finish for a record-shattering total of 271. Jack finished nine strokes ahead of his competitors. His 64 had put him five strokes ahead of Player and eight strokes ahead of Palmer. Player and Palmer ended in a deadlock for second place with 280; Player had a final 73 and Palmer a 70.

The winning margin of nine strokes beat Cary Middlecoff's record seven-stroke margin in 1955. The weather was clear and the greens fast. Nicklaus's putting was keen and consistently accurate. His putting total for the four days was 123 on individual putting rounds of 32, 31, 30, and 30. He had nineteen birdies and went over par five times in the four days. Nicklaus received $20,000 as first-prize money. The overall purse was $140,075, or $10,275 more than the year before.

Billy Casper took a six at the eleventh by getting into the creek and then took eight on the twelfth. He went into the pond twice and then overshot the green into a bunker. Casper ended with 80 after a 72-72-71 start and finished far down the list with 295.

Mason Rudolph was fourth at 283, Dan Sikes fifth at 285, and Spanish entrant Ramon Sota tied with Gene Littler for sixth at 286.

Jack Nicklaus's Record 64 in 1965

This is the story of Jack Nicklaus's record-tying 64 in his third round of the 1965 Masters. It is taken from an interview with Jack on September 29, 1971, and is quoted with his permission:

I remember that my tee shot on No. 1 was downwind, although there was very little wind that day. I hit it so far I used a wedge to the green. The pin was on the front left-hand side, and I couldn't hold the ball near it. I ended up on the back edge of the green about forty feet away. I trolled my putt to within one inch of the cup and made four.

On No. 2, I hit a bad drive, pretty far, but way into the trees on the right, about sixty feet from the fairway. I think I hit a three iron through the opening to about fifty yards short of the green. My putt was twenty feet or so downhill, and the green was extremely fast. I just touched the putt, and it rolled and rolled and finally just toppled into the hole for the birdie four.

On No. 3, I hit a three wood off the tee short of the bunker in the middle of the fairway and wedged to eight feet away. Did not make the putt, par four.

We were playing the short tee on No. 4 that day; that would be about between the present back tee and the lower front tee. I hit my four iron fat and was disgusted with the shot. A photographer took my picture when I made a terrible face. But the shot made the green and rolled to about ten feet away from the hole. The cup was in the front left center. I made the two for another birdie. The putt had a left-to-right bend.

On No. 5, a drive and six iron and two putts from twenty feet. Nothing unusual.

On No. 6, I hit a six iron to twenty feet above the cup, which was on the front left side of the green. Again it was a very slick situation, but I made the two.

On the seventh hole, I hit a wedge two feet from the hole and made an easy three.

I hit a very long drive on No. 8 and then a three iron, which ended up on the green but seventy-five feet

from the hole. I two-putted for a birdie four.

At No. 9, I hit a long drive and wedge to about twenty feet from the hole, took two putts for the par four and 31 on the nine.

On No. 10, I hit a drive to the right-hand side of the fairway. You know that's where you shouldn't hit it, because it makes the hole a lot longer. But I still had only an eight iron to the green. I made the green twenty feet from the hole and two-putted for the par four.

Again, on No. 11, I hit my drive pretty long but on the right side. The pin was on the left-hand side of the green. I got on the green but about fifty feet from the hole. I two-putted for the par four.

At No. 12, the pin was on the front left side of the green. I hit an eight iron to four feet away and missed the birdie.

On No. 13, I hooked my drive around the corner and hit a five iron just barely on the green, took two putts from forty-five feet for the birdie four. [The film of the Masters of 1965 shows that Jack nearly three-putted this green. His first putt left him about eight feet short and with a slippery downhill putt to make. His putt just barely toppled into the cup to save his birdie there.]

On No. 14, I drove into the rough again, this time on the right side of the fairway. I hit a seven iron to twenty-five feet and took two putts for the par four.

I hit a very long drive on No. 15, about 325 yards but into the left rough so that I was blocked by trees on my second shot. I couldn't hit straight for the pin, which was on the left side of the green. I hit a five iron to the back right fringe, chipped a six iron to eighteen inches, and made the putt. I remember that the chip was really a great one, that it kept rolling and rolling closer and closer to the pin.

At No. 16, I hit a six iron to fourteen feet from the hole. I remember the pin was in exactly the same position and the putt was from exactly the same place as it was when I made a birdie two in 1963 and went on to win the Masters. It broke about six inches, right to left. I made the putt again for a birdie two.

No. 17 was rather routine. I drove very far and hit an eight iron to the front fringe. I putted from the fringe, put it close, and holed for the par four.

I hit a very long drive way up the fairway. Remember, this was before the trap was put in the center of the fairway where it can catch your drive. The pin was down in the lower front right, and my second shot, with my wedge, went about twenty-five feet beyond the hole. I two-putted for the par four, had a 33 on the last nine, and a total of 64. There were eight birdies and ten pars, not one five on the scorecard.

36
THE MASTERS OF 1966

Jack Nicklaus	68	76	72	72	288
Play-off					70
Tommy Jacobs	75	71	70	72	288
Play-off					72
Gay Brewer, Jr.	74	72	72	70	288
Play-off					78
Arnold Palmer	74	70	74	72	290
Doug Sanders	74	70	75	71	290
Don January	71	73	73	75	292
George Knudson	73	76	72	71	292
Raymond Floyd	72	73	74	74	293
Paul Harney	75	68	76	74	293
Billy Casper, Jr.	71	75	76	72	294
Jay Hebert	72	74	73	75	294
Bob Rosburg	73	71	76	74	294

Gay Brewer, Tommy Jacobs, and Jack Nicklaus finished in a three-way tie at the end of the regulation seventy-two holes of the Masters of 1966. Brewer missed a seven-foot putt for a par four on the eighteenth hole. He had a side-hill forty-footer from the back of the green and tried to lag it close enough to get down in two, but the ball slipped seven feet beyond the cup. Although he hit his second putt firmly, the ball broke more than he expected.

Nicklaus and Jacobs shared the lead at the end of the third round, and each shot a 72 in the final round, while Brewer came in with a 70. The three tied at 288, a seventy-two-hole aggregate only one stroke less than the record high when Jack Burke won with a 289. Hogan and Snead also tied at that figure in 1954 before Snead won in the play-off.

Jack Nicklaus missed a three-and-a-half-foot putt for a birdie at No. 17 as Jacobs and Brewer, who had already completed their rounds, awaited Jack's finish. On the eighteenth Jack had a downhill, side-hill forty-footer that just missed the cup, or Jack would have won the tournament outright.

In the play-off, Nicklaus and Jacobs each went out in 35, while Brewer stumbled to a 38. Jacobs started out the play-off round strongly with a birdie three to take an early lead, but Jack Nicklaus caught him with a birdie at the second hole, where Jack's three-wood second shot struck the pin on the fly and bounced thirty feet away. Jacobs went ahead again at the fourth, where Nicklaus was bunkered and took four, but Jack made a downhill eighteen-foot putt on No. 6 for a deuce to draw even again. Both played the ninth badly for bogeys. Jack picked up two strokes on Jacobs on Nos. 10 and 11 with 4-3 against Jacobs's 5-4. Jack holed a twenty-five-foot putt for his birdie at No. 11. They matched each other's cards all the rest of the way for 37s and 70-72 totals while Brewer was never in contention. He took 40 strokes on the second nine, including a double-bogey six at the seventeenth hole.

Jack Nicklaus became the first Masters champion to succeed himself.

37
THE MASTERS OF 1967

Gay Brewer, Jr.	73	68	72	67	280
Bobby Nichols	72	69	70	70	281
Bert Yancey	67	73	71	73	284
Arnold Palmer	73	73	70	69	285
Julius Boros	71	70	70	75	286
Paul Harney	73	71	74	69	287
Gary Player	75	69	72	71	287
Tommy Aaron	75	68	74	71	288
Lionel Hebert	77	71	67	73	288
Roberto de Vicenzo	73	72	74	71	290
Bruce Devlin	74	70	75	71	290
Ben Hogan	74	73	66	77	290
Mason Rudolph	72	76	72	70	290
Sam Snead	72	76	71	71	290

This was the year that Gay Brewer redeemed himself for failing to win the Masters of 1966. He scored a magnificent 67 in a final round played with his closest pursuer and good friend, Bobby Nichols, who scored a 70 to finish one stroke behind Gay, 280 to 281. Brewer had three straight birdies on the last nine holes in his final round, at Nos. 13, 14, and 15. A crucial exchange occurred at the uphill fourteenth, where Nichols had a makable putt for a birdie that would have put him into a tie with Gay should Gay miss his twenty-foot birdie attempt. Gay holed his putt, and then Bobby holed his as well to remain one stroke behind.

Bert Yancey, twenty-eight years old and playing in his first Masters, made an impressive start and was considered to be the possible winner after the first two days' play. Bert started out with 67 in the first round and took a three-stroke lead over Billy Casper and amateur Downing Gray, who had scores of 70. Jack Nicklaus opened with a par 72 and, when he followed with a poor 79, found himself in the unenviable position of being the only former champion who did not qualify for the last two rounds of play.

Yancey kept the lead on the second day with a 73 for a 140 total as Gay Brewer started his move toward the eventual championship. Gay scored a 68 after his first-round 73. Julius Boros, Tony Jacklin, and Bobby Nichols were also in very close pursuit at 141. Incidentally, this was Tony Jacklin's first appearance at the Augusta National course. He had gained his invitation when Neil Coles, ahead of Tony on the English "select list," decided to forgo the tournament.

The third round was highlighted by the electricity of Ben Hogan's remarkable 66, a score he personally had equaled only once at Augusta, in 1953, when he captured the British Open and the United States Open championships in the same year.

At the end of the third day, Boros, Nichols, and Yancey shared a three-way tie for the lead at 211 strokes, while Gay Brewer was only two strokes back of the leaders. Hogan had begun his third round eight strokes behind Nichols and had pulled up to a tie with Brewer, two strokes away from the top. Hogan's day was over, however, as he finished with a tired 77 for a tie at tenth place.

Gay Brewer carded a final round of 67 for a 280 total to win by one stroke over Bobby Nichols, who had a 70 for 281 and second place all alone. Brewer and Nichols were paired together on the final day to the pleasure of the galleries. Brewer won the tournament by shooting those three straight birdies on the back nine.

After he had won, Brewer said, "I think I redeemed myself," meaning that he felt that he had atoned for his failure to win the year before.

One of the most heart-warming scenes in the history of golf happened in mid-afternoon of the third day of the 1967 Masters. The "wee ice mon," Ben Hogan, as the Scots had called him at Carnoustie when he won their prized Open Championship so coolly in 1953, came back to life again for four hours at the Augusta National golf course. After missing several Masters, as a result of illness, and putting in token appearances in several more, Ben Hogan returned to his old form this particular day. Out in a respectable 36 strokes on the first nine, he gave no sign of the fireworks he intended to show on the second nine.

At the tenth hole he placed a seven iron seven feet from the cup and sank his putt for a birdie three. A roar went up at the main

Gay Brewer, Jr. comes back from his loss in the play-offs of 1966 to win the 1967 title.

scoreboard near the eighteenth green as Ben's three was recorded and some of the spectators left to head down into the Amen Corner. Perhaps Ben could still play golf in his old style and would be interesting to watch.

At the eleventh a six iron stopped twelve inches from the hole, and Ben had birdied two on the second nine. Again, a roar went up when his score was posted on the huge scoreboard. His crowd again increased.

But Ben did not stop there. He put a six iron within fifteen feet of the twelfth flagstick and down went the putt for a two. Three birdies in a row! And the five-par thirteenth, eminently birdieable, was coming up next. A drive, a comfortable four wood to twenty feet from the hole, and Ben had made a normal birdie four for his fourth birdie in a row. The roars of the crowds at the scoreboards in every corner of the golf course became louder and louder as

OFFICIAL SCORE CARD

APR 8 1967

Hole	1	2	3	4	5	6	7	8	9	Out	10	11	12	13	14	15	16	17	18	In	Totals
Yardage	400	555	355	220	450	190	365	530	420	3485	470	445	155	475	420	520	190	400	420	3495	6980
Par	4	5	4	3	4	3	4	5	4	36	4	4	3	5	4	5	3	4	4	36	72
Player	4	5	5	3	4	3	3	5	4	36	3	3	2	4	4	4	3	4	3	30	66

I HAVE CHECKED MY SCORE, HOLE BY HOLE.

PLAYER SIGNATURE _Ben Hogan_
BEN HOGAN

ATTEST _____

Ben Hogan sets a course record 30 on the back nine in 1967.

the red numbers went up after Ben's name on hole after hole. Could Ben keep up that torrid pace? He did. A par at No. 14 brought him to another possible birdie hole.

Again, a typical long, straight Hogan drive left him a four wood away from another birdie opportunity. The tremendous crowd now following him held its collective breath as he dared to carry the water in front of the fifteenth green. Over the water and twenty feet from the hole, the ball came to rest. There followed two putts, and Ben Hogan had his fifth birdie of the nine. Could he keep on going? Would his tired legs give out on him? The sixteenth and seventeenth fell to Ben in normal pars—on the green in regulation strokes and two putts for the pars.

To the eighteenth, the tough uphill finishing hole, with the blind pin position. Now there were between 10,000 and 12,000 people lining both sides of the eighteenth fairway, hoping for Ben, praying that he could solve the last hole in par. A birdie would be miraculous, of course. Ben's tee shot was straight and just short of the dangerous mid-fairway bunker. Without any hesitation, he cracked a sweet five iron up the hill to the plateau green now completely surrounded by the massed gallery.

The ball carried the bunker in front of the green and came to a skidding stop twenty-five feet from the hole, too far away, everyone thought, to hope for a birdie. Then poor tired Ben Hogan began to climb that last 160 yards uphill to the last green. The galleries came to life. They realized that they were seeing a living legend, one of the greatest golfers of all time, proving his courage and his skill in one last magnificent effort of concentration and perfect execution of the golf swing.

The roars of the crowd started as he passed the center fairway bunker. They increased in intensity as Ben laboriously placed one foot down after the other in his climb up the hill. It takes four minutes for a man in good health to climb that hill. I think it took Ben Hogan five minutes, for I was there to see the scene and to feel the drama unfolding. He tipped his little white-visored cap several times as he neared the green. Whether there were tears in his eyes, we will never know, but I suspect that the great golfer's heart melted at this thundering, unending display of admiration.

Of course, he rolled that twenty-five-foot putt right into the hole for his sixth birdie and a course record score of 30 strokes. Do you think his guardian angel would have allowed him to miss that putt? I don't.

38
THE MASTERS OF 1968

Bob Goalby	70	70	71	66	277
Roberto de Vicenzo	69	73	70	66	278
Bert Yancey	71	71	72	65	279
Bruce Devlin	69	73	69	69	280
Frank Beard	75	65	71	70	281
Jack Nicklaus	69	71	74	67	281
Gary Player	72	67	71	72	282
Raymond Floyd	71	71	69	71	282
Tommy Aaron	69	72	72	69	282
Jerry Pittman	70	73	70	69	282
Lionel Hebert	72	71	71	68	282

The year 1968 was the one of the wrong scorecard incident at the Masters, an unfortunate occurrence that cost Roberto de Vicenzo a tie for the championship of that year and allowed Bob Goalby to don the green winner's coat as undisputed champion.

The golf course at Augusta National was once again rain-drenched and slow as the play began with the smallest field in years, only seventy-four players. Billy Casper had won in Greensboro and was on his game. It was apparent, too, for on the first day Casper used only 29 putts in a fine 68 to take the early lead in the tournament. Tommy

Going into the final round eight golfers were within two strokes of each other for the lead. Bob Goalby emerged victorious.

Aaron, Roberto de Vicenzo, Jack Nicklaus, and Bruce Devlin were at 69. Bob Goalby, in the first pairing of the day after 86-year-old Fred McLeod and 83-year-old Jock Hutchinson had started the field in traditional fashion, was unnoticed behind the clustered leaders with a sound 70.

On the second day, there were nine players in a bunch from Don January and Gary Player at 139 to de Vicenzo, Devlin, and Floyd at 142. Goalby, still not in the spotlight, had put together two 70s now to be only one stroke off the leaders' pace. Arnold Palmer missed the thirty-six-hole cutoff after a 79, which included a horrendous eight at the fifteenth hole. Bruce Devlin at one time was leading the field by three strokes until he, too, took an eight on the eleventh hole.

It was apparent that the tournament was a wide-open one, with no one so far ready to establish a firm grip on the leadership.

Going into the last round, the field remained in a tight cluster. The scoreboard showed:

Player	72	67	71	210
Beard	75	65	71	211
Devlin	69	73	69	211
Floyd	71	71	69	211
Goalby	70	70	71	211
January	71	68	72	211
de Vicenzo	69	73	70	212
Trevino	71	72	69	212

Bob Goalby emerged from this jam of great golfers with a magnificent 66. Bob was playing behind the pairing of de Vicenzo and Tommy Aaron and was able to birdie the thirteenth hole with an eight-foot putt and the fourteenth hole on a fifteen-foot putt, and eagle the fifteenth when he stroked a three iron within eight feet of the cup and sank the putt to go twelve under par for the tournament.

Roberto de Vicenzo had started out brilliantly ahead of Bob Goalby. At the first hole, Roberto sank his second shot for an opening eagle two. Later on he birdied No. 12 for a two, No. 13 for a four, No. 15 for another four. He had 31 strokes on the outward nine and finished with what ap-

peared to be a 65, bogeying No. 18 on a shot into the crowd surrounding the green.

The scoreboards were then showing de Vicenzo apparently eleven under par, so when Goalby, playing behind de Vicenzo, three-putted the seventeenth hole, it was evident that he needed to par the eighteenth hole for an apparent tie with Roberto de Vicenzo. A national television audience had watched de Vicenzo sink a five-foot putt on the seventeenth hole for what they thought was the birdie three to put de Vicenzo into the eleven-under-par situation and on the way to a tie with Goalby, provided that Goalby could par the eighteenth hole.

Goalby managed to sink a tricky five-foot putt for his par four and a great round of 66 for a total score of 277. The scorecards were signed by the scorers of the twosomes, Tommy Aaron for de Vicenzo and de Vicenzo for Aaron, as is customary in golf tournaments run under the rules of the United States Golf Association, the Masters Tournament being one of them.

Suddenly, before the national television audience, it was clear that something had gone wrong. The usual speeches and presentations were being delayed.

Then, it was announced that the de Vicenzo scorecard attested by Tommy Aaron and countersigned as correct had reported a four as de Vicenzo's score on the seventeenth hole, not the three the millions of television viewers had seen him make.

Furthermore, under the rules of golf, unfortunate as the circumstances were, Homer E. Shields, the tournament director, declared that de Vicenzo's score was a 66, not the 65 everyone thought he had scored, and that his total score was therefore 278, which left him one stroke behind Goalby, the runner-up, rather than tied with Goalby for the championship.

The official U.S.G.A. rule 38, paragraph 3, specifies: "No alteration may be made on a card after the competitor has returned it to the Committee. If the competitor returns a score for any hole lower than actually played, he shall be disqualified. A score higher than actually played must stand as returned."

Roberto de Vicenzo was quoted in the newspapers as having said en route to the television area, "I just signed a wrong card. The other fellow [Tommy Aaron] put down a four. It's my fault." Roberto de Vicenzo made millions of friends in the golf world by graciously accepting this regrettable occurrence that cost him the chance of a lifetime to be a Masters champion. Bob Goalby, under the circumstances totally beyond his own control, became sole and undisputed Masters champion of 1968.

39
THE MASTERS OF 1969

George Archer	67	73	69	72	281
Billy Casper, Jr.	66	71	71	74	282
George Knudson	70	73	69	70	282
Tom Weiskopf	71	71	69	71	282
Charles Coody	74	68	69	72	283
Don January	74	73	70	66	283
Miller Barber	71	71	68	74	284
Tommy Aaron	71	71	73	70	285
Lionel Hebert	69	73	70	73	285
Gene Littler	69	75	70	71	285

Billy Casper, Jr., started the 1969 Masters with a sparkling 66 and at the end of the first day it appeared that this Masters might have one of the lowest scoring fields in its history. Sundown of the first day found George Archer at 67 and no fewer than six players—Gene Littler, Lionel Hebert, Mason Rudolph, Dan Sikes, Bert Yancey, and Bruce Crampton—at 69.

And who was this George Archer in second place? A tall—six-foot, six-inch—former California amateur champion who had recently turned professional and had won the Pensacola and New Orleans Open championships in 1968. George was consid-

George Archer, thought of as a long shot to win the 1969 Masters, comes out on top.

The infamous Rae's Creek finds George Archer and his second shot on the thirteenth.

ered a long shot to win this Masters, especially when Billy Casper was apparently taking complete charge of the situation this April. For Bill had followed up his great 66 beginning with a 71 to be coleader at the halfway mark and on another 71 was leading the field all alone as he began his last round.

Both George Archer and Charles Coody, however, climbed into contention on third-round 69s and were riding at 209 and 211, respectively one and three strokes behind Casper.

Casper had a most unfortunate first nine, actually ten, holes on the last day. He had scored only two bogeys in all three of his previous rounds, but incredibly, in a sudden reversal of form, racked up five bogeys in ten holes to be five over par for the round.

In the meantime, both Coody and Archer were playing steady, if not spectacular, golf. When Coody laced a two iron to within twenty-five feet of the thirteenth hole and downed the putt for an eagle three, he went eight under par for the whole tournament and was one stroke ahead of George Archer, who was playing just behind him.

Casper was making a comeback, too; he got a birdie at No. 11 and two brave fours at the five-par thirteenth and fifteenth in an attempt to salvage what had appeared to be the best chance he had ever had to win his first Masters Tournament.

Archer also birdied the thirteenth hole to pull even with Coody. Coody bogeyed No. 14 and then promptly recovered from that mistake with a good birdie at No. 15. Actually, Coody took the sole lead at this point when Archer also bogeyed No. 14.

Then Coody's game went to pieces, and he stumbled in with three straight bogeys on the last three holes.

Archer, now coming on strong, could sense his chance to win. A crucial situation occurred when Archer's second shot at the watery fifteenth found the pond. Archer calmly pitched over the water and sank a ten-foot putt to save his par there. He came in with three straight pars, including a very comfortable one at the eighteenth hole, where his second shot landed only twelve feet from the cup. He putted to a few inches away from the cup, sank the next putt, and was the new Masters champion. He had scored a 281, seven strokes under Augusta National's par. It took a size forty-two extra-long green coat to fit George Archer, the tallest champion in Masters history.

There was a three-way tie for second place among George Knudson of Canada, who finished his last two rounds with 69-70; Tom Weiskopf, who had 69-71; and Billy Casper, Jr., who almost salvaged his bad start with a 34 back nine and a round of 74 strokes. Billy had an unsuccessful thirty-yard chip for a birdie at No. 18, which meant he didn't tie George Archer after all. It was just not Billy Casper's year to win the Masters. But wait until next year, he would show them!

40
THE MASTERS OF 1970

Billy Casper, Jr.	72	68	68	71	279
Play-off					69
Gene Littler	69	70	70	70	279
Play-off					74
Gary Player	74	68	68	70	280
Bert Yancey	69	70	72	70	281
Tommy Aaron	68	74	69	72	283
Dave Hill	73	70	70	70	283
Dave Stockton	72	72	69	70	283
Jack Nicklaus	71	75	69	69	284
Frank Beard	71	76	68	70	285
Bob Lunn	70	70	75	72	287
Juan Rodriguez	70	76	73	68	287

Billy Casper's skilled putting in the play-off against Gene Littler earns him the 1970 title.

The 1970 Masters was one of the most suspenseful tournaments in recent years. During the play on the last day, at one moment in time seven players were within one or two strokes of the lead and of each other: Billy Casper, Jr., Gene Littler, Gary Player, Bert Yancey, Dave Hill, Dave Stockton, and Tommy Aaron. Each one of them had an excellent chance, but when it came down to the final putts on the eighteenth hole, Billy Casper and Gene Littler found themselves in a tie at 279 strokes and thus entered the sixth play-off in Masters history.

Billy Casper blasts from the bunker at No. 4.

On the first day, Tommy Aaron was off to a one-stroke lead over the field on a great 68. Close behind were Littler and Yancey at 69. Casper had a sound 72 and followed with a strong 68. Littler was back the second day with a 70. So, at the halfway mark, there were Littler at 139, Yancey at 139 (having matched Gene's 69-70), Casper at 140, Aaron and Player at 142.

Casper, putting phenomenally all the way, kept saving pars on one-putts when he wasn't making them conventionally. Littler remained steady and came in with a third-round 70. Casper's 68 gave him a one-stroke lead at 208 to Gene's 209. Player had moved up on a 68 to 210 to set the stage for the dramatic finale on Sunday. With only nine holes to play, Casper, Littler, and Yancey were tied for the lead, and Player was one stroke behind.

Casper had shown signs of weakening and no doubt had memories of his sagging finish in 1969 to lose that tournament to George Archer. Billy had hit his drive into the right-hand bunker at No. 8 and had taken a double bogey there. However, he managed to run down a long birdie putt at No. 9 and get some of his confidence back.

Casper and Littler both birdied No. 13 and showed the strength coming down the stretch. Casper made a necessary and typical save for his four at No. 15 to match Littler's birdie there a few minutes ahead of him. Both Casper and Littler had possible winning birdie putts at both No. 17 and No. 18, but neither man was able to hole the ball and win the title outright. Their scores of 71 and 70 gave them each a 279 total for the four rounds.

Player stumbled to a bogey five at No. 18 after hooking his second shot into the bunker and was out of the race when he missed his putt for the par. He took third place at 280. In the meantime, Yancey had failed to get his birdie at No. 15 when the others did, and when he, too, bogeyed No. 18 he fell behind Gary Player and finished at 281 in fourth place.

The play-off between Casper and Littler was anticlimactic. Both men played erratically and sometimes badly, but Casper, as usual, saved himself with his magic putting stroke. He registered six one-putt greens in the first seven holes and was then three under par and in the lead over Gene by five strokes. The second hole was a turning point in the match when Littler dubbed his third, a little wedge shot, only ten feet into a bunker.

Casper saved his par there after being in trouble at the start of the hole and was never headed during the rest of the match. Casper shot 69 to Littler's 74 in the play-off. Billy Casper, Jr., National Open champion of 1959, had finally won the Masters.

41
THE MASTERS OF 1971

Charles Coody	66	73	70	70	279
John Miller	72	73	68	68	281
Jack Nicklaus	70	71	68	72	281
Don January	69	69	73	72	283
Gene Littler	72	69	73	69	283
Gary Player	72	72	71	69	284
Ken Still	72	71	72	69	284
Tom Weiskopf	71	69	72	72	284
Frank Beard	74	73	69	70	286
Roberto de Vicenzo	76	69	72	69	286
Dave Stockton	72	73	69	72	286

Charles Coody became the thirty-fourth Masters champion, winning by two strokes over young John Miller and formidable Jack Nicklaus, with scores of 279 to 281.

Jack Nicklaus had already won the P.G.A. Championship (played earlier this year in an experiment by the Professional Golfers Association to increase public interest in the event) and was attempting to take the second part of his much desired grand slam. The year before, after being in the lead with only three holes to play, Charles Coody had finished with three consecutive bogeys to lose the coveted championship and fall into

Charles Coody, winner of the 1971 Masters.

Top contender Johnny Miller explodes from the bunker at nine.

a tie for fifth place. This year he wanted badly to prove that he could win the championship. On the first day, Coody shot a subpar-34 first nine and then fashioned a beautiful 32 on the second nine for a sparkling 66, which brought him a three-shot lead over the field. He birdied Nos. 10, 13, 14, and 15 on the way to this great start. In the meantime, Nicklaus and Miller were off with 70 and 72 respectively. There was a five-way tie at 69 among Don January, Ray Floyd, Bob Lunn, Bob Murphy, and Hale Irwin. Only January fulfilled this promising beginning, as he finished in 69-73-72 for 283 and a tie for fourth place with Gene Littler, who had 72-69-73-69 for his 283.

Coody slumped a bit on his second round, shooting a 73. Out in a shaky 39 strokes, he lost another stroke to par at the short twelfth but again accomplished a birdie spree at Nos. 13, 15, and 16 to save the round with a 33 back nine. Nicklaus had a 71 and picked up two valuable strokes on Coody.

Coody came back with a 70 on the third

day while Jack closed up the stroke margin with a 68. They went into the third round tied at 209. In the meantime, John Miller, by scoring a fine 68 on his third round, came within two strokes of the leaders at the start of the final round, 211 to 213.

Miller started the last day and proceeded to burn up the course. He scored three birdies on the first nine and then three more on the second nine at the eleventh, twelfth, and fourteenth holes to put himself nine under par and to lead the field at that time by two strokes over Coody and Nicklaus with only four holes to play. But John bunkered his second shot at a birdie hole, No. 15, and scored no better than par. Then he stumbled to two more bogeys at Nos. 16 and 18, and his chances were gone.

Meanwhile, Coody had followed Miller and, with a birdie at No. 15, cut Miller's margin to one stroke. When Coody stroked a sweet iron to fifteen feet from the sixteenth flagstick and then holed the putt, the lead had changed hands. Nicklaus, like Miller, failed to birdie No. 15. His four iron went over the green, and his chip left him too far away for the birdie.

Now leading both Nicklaus and Miller by two strokes, Coody scrambled to a chip and seven-foot putt to save his par at No. 17. With a two-stroke lead at No. 18, Coody was able to make his par at the final hole, and a few minutes later Billy Casper, 1970 Masters champion, raised Charles Coody's arm in triumph after he had helped him don his green Masters coat. The 1970 Masters had truly been avenged by Charles Coody.

42
THE MASTERS OF 1972

Jack Nicklaus	68	71	73	74	286
Bruce Crampton	72	75	69	73	289
Tom Weiskopf	74	71	70	74	289
Bobby Mitchell	73	72	71	73	289
Jim Jamieson	72	70	71	77	290
Homero Blancas	76	71	69	74	290
Jerry Heard	73	71	72	74	290
Bruce Devlin	74	75	70	71	290
Jerry McGee	73	74	71	72	290
Gary Player	73	75	72	71	291
Dave Stockton	76	70	74	71	291

Jack Nicklaus tied Arnold Palmer's record of winning four Masters championships when he added the 1972 Masters title to his impressive record of eleven major golf championships and achieved the first leg of the grand slam of golf—the United States and British Open championships, the Professional Golfers Association Championship, and the Masters.

Jack started out slowly in his first round. He was in and out of trouble on the first nine for a one-over-par 37. When he bogeyed the tenth hole, he appeared to be in even more difficulty. In the meantime, defending

A winning Nicklaus bunker shot.

137

Power hitter Tom Weiskopf tees off at No. 1.

champion Charles Coody had started off well. To the delight of his followers, he had scored a hole-in-one on the hard three-par sixth hole to put himself four under par and become the leader of the field at that time. But Coody had trouble extricating himself from the sand of the front bunker at the seventh hole and took a horrendous seven there, three over par. He was never in contention again.

Nicklaus started his move toward the lead with a remarkable stretch of fine golf, beginning with the eleventh hole, which he birdied. At the twelfth hole he sank a twenty-five footer for a birdie two. At thirteen, he hit a three wood from the tee and a six iron to the left bunker, recovered nicely to three feet, and had another birdie. He parred No. 14 normally. No. 15 fell to him in three strokes, an eagle, when he hit a long drive and a 235-yard one iron to within thirty feet of the cup. Jack holed his birdie

Former Masters champion George Archer at the fourth tee.

two from the fringe of No. 16 as the galleries became hysterical with delight. He had played the last six holes in six under par.

At this point, Jack Nicklaus moved past aging Sam Snead, who had played magnificently, only to falter a bit with his putter and end at 69 to Jack's leading score of 68.

Jack was never seriously threatened from then on. Several players made moves as if they were going to catch him. Jim Jamieson, a young newcomer in his first Masters, played extremely well through three rounds of 72-70-71, but could manage only 77 on the last day. Bruce Crampton, Bobby Mitchell, and Tom Weiskopf closed with 73, 73, 74, respectively, to share a tie for second place at 289, three strokes behind Jack Nicklaus's conservative 74. If Jack had not had trouble with the fifteenth hole, where he scored double bogeys on his third and fourth rounds, he might have broken open the tournament as decisively as he did when he won in 1965 by nine strokes.

The low amateur was twenty-year-old Ben Crenshaw, who scored a very creditable 295 to tie for nineteenth place, ahead of such formidable Masters stars as Bob Charles, Roberto de Vicenzo, Tony Jacklin, Bobby Nichols, Arnold Palmer, and Lee Trevino. Palmer fell off to a dreadful 81 on his last round after being in moderate contention with a 70-75-74 start for a 219 total at the third-round mark. This was the worst round Arnold had ever played in eighteen Masters Tournaments. All the contestants were bothered by gusty winds and difficult pin placements on very slick, close-cut greens.

43
THE MASTERS OF 1973

Tommy Aaron	68	73	74	68	283
J. C. Snead	70	71	73	70	284
Peter Oosterhuis	73	70	68	74	285
Jim Jamieson	73	71	70	71	285
Jack Nicklaus	69	77	73	66	285
Bob Goalby	73	70	71	74	288
John Miller	75	69	71	73	288
Masahi Ozaki	69	74	73	73	289
Bruce Devlin	73	72	72	72	289
Gay Brewer	75	66	74	76	291
Juan Rodriguez	72	70	73	76	291
Gardner Dickinson	74	70	72	75	291
Don January	75	71	75	70	291

This was the year that bridesmaid Tommy Aaron finally became a bride and won his first major tournament, the Masters. Aaron, a tall, quiet, soft-spoken Georgia gentleman-golfer, had had a twelve-year-long successful career on the professional circuit but, outside of two championships, the Canadian Open in 1969 and the Atlanta Classic in 1970, had distinguished himself primarily by finishing second no fewer than fourteen times.

So, when the first day's scores were in and showed Aaron at 68, an excellent score over a cool, wind-swept Augusta National course, the murmurs of the experts were "wait until the tournament is over, and then see where Tommy Aaron will be." Jack Nicklaus, who entered the tournament a four-to-one favorite to win, had scored a sound 69 and rested only one stroke off Aaron's pace. Aaron's 68 was constructed of a brilliant first-nine 32 with four birdies, no bogeys, and a second-nine 36 played in straight par except for a bogey at the eleventh hole, which was promptly cancelled by a birdie two at the twelfth hole.

Also tied with Nicklaus in second spot behind Aaron was Masahi Ozaki, the long-driving Japanese in his second guest appearance at the Masters. Bob Dickson, former American and British amateur champion, and J. C. Snead, a nephew of the famous Sam Snead, reported excellent 70s.

On the second day of play, when Jack Nicklaus tapped in an eighteen-inch putt to birdie the first hole, the spectators began to nod to each other and say, "Jack is off to the lead, and now no one will catch him." Nick-

With a career of fourteen second-place finishes, Tom Aaron secures the blue ribbon in 1973.

laus parred the second hole, normally a natural birdie hole for him, when a bunkered drive kept him from making the green in his customary two strokes—par five for Jack at the second hole, still one under par for the round and four under par for the tournament. At the uphill, short third hole Jack placed a delicate wedge shot six feet from the hole for what his gallery felt would be a sure birdie for him. But the ball nicked the cup and spun out. The score was a par four.

The strong, young amateur Ben Crenshaw was the playing partner of Nicklaus on that second day. Before the eyes of a shocked gallery, Ben Crenshaw, playing superlative golf himself (a 32 on the front nine, which included an eagle three at the eighth hole, for example), proceeded to gain nine strokes on Jack Nicklaus in the space of ten holes. Jack's putter had failed him completely. He three-putted the fourth, the fifth, the sixth, and the eighth holes, the eighth after being on the five-par green in two. Furthermore, he had hooked wildly

into the left-hand trees at the seventh hole and was lucky that he escaped with no more than a double-bogey six. That Crenshaw faltered a bit on the back nine and Jack recovered his touch to save the round with a 35 to add to his outgoing 42 and 77 total strokes was almost beside the point. Nicklaus had probably put himself out of the tournament with the highest single round he had had since missing the cutoff total with a 79 in 1967. At the close of the day Nicklaus found himself in a tie with nine other players for nineteenth place.

That second day, in beautiful, warm, calm weather, Gay Brewer, putting the way he did when he won his Masters title in 1967, turned in a sparkling 66 to add to his first-round 75 for 141 strokes at the halfway mark. Tommy Aaron slipped a bit from his 68 pace to a 73 but remained one of four leaders of the tournament at 141. Bob Dickson was still in the running with a great 71 that followed his first round 70 and was also at 141. J. C. Snead, too, had matched Dickson's scores exactly and joined the foursome leading at 141. Comparatively unnoticed at this moment was Peter Oosterhuis, English Ryder Cup member playing in his second Masters Tournament. Peter had scored a respectable 73 on the first day and a sparkling 70 on the second day. With his total score of 143, he was only two strokes away from the cluster of players in the lead.

On Saturday the rains came early, and by tee-off time at 10:00 A.M. the course was almost unplayable. By the time a few twosomes had played two holes, all play was cancelled for the day. The torrential rains continued all day long, and the ominous forecast was that there would be more thundershowers on Sunday. Fortunately, the Sunday golf was played in clear, sunny weather as the rain threat never materialized.

The surprise score of the third round was a 68 shot by Peter Oosterhuis. Peter's game was sound and his putter hot. He holed a sixty-foot putt for an eagle on the second hole, an eighteen-footer on the eighth, and a large assortment of six- to twelve-footers along the way to a 27-putt total round.

Tommy Aaron had played badly on the front nine and had lost six strokes to par by the time he reached the treacherous twelfth hole. Aaron, then several twosomes behind Oosterhuis, played a brave second shot, a three iron, to the thirteenth hole, safely two-putted, and put himself only two strokes behind Oosterhuis.

Oosterhuis appeared to be charging into a large lead at this point when, after birdie-ing the twelfth hole with a fifteen-foot putt, he was able to reach the five-par thirteenth hole in two strokes with a beautiful drive and a long, straight three iron, and then two-putt for his birdie four.

At the sixteenth hole, Oosterhuis pushed his tee shot to the right, short of the green, and left himself a tricky thirty-yard chip. He approached badly and left himself a twelve-footer but rolled home a courageous curling putt for his par.

In the meantime, Jack Nicklaus was playing well ahead of the Oosterhuis-Aaron groups and appeared to be picking up some ground on the leaders. Suddenly, the report came that Nicklaus had gone into the water on his second shot at the fifteenth hole and, incredibly, after dropping his ball behind the water hazard, had put his fourth shot into the pond again and had eventually taken a triple-bogey eight.

Jack Nicklaus finished his round at 73, a remarkable comeback, but it was still spoiled by his disaster on the fifteenth hole (Jack's three-round total was 219). Because Oosterhuis finished his round with a marvelous 68 for a 211 total, Nicklaus found himself tied with four others in fifteenth place, eight strokes away from the leader.

J. C. Snead, with 73; Bob Goalby, with 71; and Jim Jamieson, on a steady 73-71-70 track, were all tied in second place at 214, three strokes behind Oosterhuis. Four strokes away after a sagging round of 74 was Tommy Aaron. Perhaps the gallery experts were right about Tommy. Could Aaron hope to pull himself up to his usual runner-up position?

The final day was played in beautiful weather. Jack Nicklaus started earlier than the clutch of leaders and proceeded to burn up the course with seven birdies through the seventeenth hole. By the time he reached the front edge of the eighteenth hole, he was two under par for the tournament. When Jack Nicklaus sank his thirty-foot chip shot for his eighth birdie of the round and 66 strokes for the day, he was in with a total of 285, a three-under-par score that the leaders on the course would have to match or exceed in order to tie or win.

Since Aaron had slipped out of the lead on the third day, he was playing fifteen or twenty minutes ahead of J. C. Snead and Peter Oosterhuis. At the time Aaron received word about Jack Nicklaus's closing birdie via the monstrous scoreboards and the yell of the crowd at the eighteenth hole, Tommy was three strokes under par playing the thirteenth hole. Snead was then five strokes under par and about to tee off on the devilish twelfth hole. Oosterhuis had relinquished part of his lead and was also under par at this point.

Aaron played the five-par thirteenth as a simple four-par with a long, straight drive and a four iron twenty-five feet from the hole. He two-putted easily for his birdie and simultaneously shot into the lead of the tournament as J. C. Snead's tee shot at the twelfth hole hit the bank and rolled back into the water there. Snead took a double-bogey five and never recovered from the blow. He fell to three under par, and, now desperately needing birdies, all he was able to do was match Aaron's ensuing birdie at the fifteenth hole.

Under great pressure along the way in from the thirteenth hole, Tommy Aaron holed several dangerous two-and-a-half- to three-foot putts and came to the eighteenth needing a par to force Snead to make a birdie there to tie. Oosterhuis, in the meantime, had taken a nasty six at the fifteenth, which for all practical purposes put him out of the running for first place. Needing an impossible eagle at the eighteenth hole to tie, he did accomplish a scrambling four there to save part of his honor and a share of third place with Jack Nicklaus and Jim

Jack Nicklaus and Clifford Roberts congratulate Tommy Aaron, the first native-born Georgian to win the Masters.

Jamieson, who had played steadily and well in his last round for a 71 and a 285 total, up among the leaders for the second year in a row.

Snead made valiant efforts at both the seventeenth hole, where he holed a ten-footer to save par after bunkering his second shot, and the eighteenth, where he barely missed another similar-length putt, which would have put him into a tie with Aaron.

Can you imagine how delighted Bob Jones would have been if he had lived to see the green Masters coat on Tommy Aaron, the first native-born Georgian to win the tournament in its thirty-nine-year history?

44
THE MASTERS OF 1974

Gary Player	71	71	66	70	278
Dave Stockton	71	66	70	73	280
Tom Weiskopf	71	69	70	70	280
Jim Colbert	67	72	69	73	281
Hale Irwin	68	70	72	71	281
Jack Nicklaus	69	71	72	69	281
Bobby Nichols	73	68	68	73	282
Phil Rodgers	72	69	68	73	282
Maurice Bembridge	73	74	72	64	283
Hubert Green	68	70	74	71	283
Bruce Crampton	73	72	69	70	284
Jerry Heard	70	70	73	71	284
Dave Hill	71	72	70	71	284
Arnold Palmer	76	71	70	67	284

Gary Player, proving that he was fully recovered from the kidney surgery that had kept him out of the 1973 tournament, won the 1974 Masters. This was Gary's second Masters championship and gave him a seventh leg toward his own personal goal of winning each of the major titles twice—a feat no other golfer has accomplished. Player already had to his credit the United States Open Championship of 1965, the P. G. A. Championships of 1962 and 1972, as well as the 1959 and 1968 British Open Championships, and the 1961 Masters (and would win the 1978 Masters).

The Augusta National Golf Course was in magnificent condition, the fairways cropped close and carpeted with a new strain of grass that gave players more opportunity to control their iron shots. The greens, velvety smooth and true, were lightning fast as usual. Morning showers on the third day gave some relief and allowed the golfers to charge the cup a little more. Sunday they were again like ice.

As often happens, there were fireworks the first day. Art Wall, Masters champion of 1959, set a tournament record with three consecutive twos. Wall birdied the three-par fourth hole, followed with a sensational four wood to eagle the four-par fifth hole—the first eagle ever scored on that treacherous 465-yard hole in Masters history—and concluded his string of twos with a birdie on the 190-yard, three-par sixth. Wall posted a first-round 70 and an eventual 291.

To balance the ledger, golfing tragedy struck England's Tony Jacklin, whose sec-

144

ond shot on the four-par thirteenth went over the green. Tony came out of the rear bunker too strongly and found Rae's Creek. His pitch back to the pin again found the creek. Tony marked down nine on his card, and although he recovered the next day with a sound 71, he was out of the '74 Masters.

Hale Irwin put his name into the Masters record book too, scoring five successive birdies on the twelfth through sixteenth holes en route to a great 37-31-68, one stroke behind the first-day leader, Jim Colbert, who had a 33-34 for a startling 67. While Colbert held the lead alone, eight other players broke 70, and six more were at an even 70. Jack Nicklaus was at 69, two strokes back, while Gary Player and Tom

Gary Player on his way to capturing his second Masters title.

Weiskopf were tied for sixteenth place.

On the second day, in gorgeous weather, Dave Stockton made a strong bid for the championship. His 66 was a typical Stockton scramble with Dave up and down nearly every time he found himself in trouble. For instance, he had to play a five iron from out of the eighth fairway to get to the second green but managed a birdie. The fifteenth hole fell to him with an eagle three when his five-iron second shot stopped thirty feet from the hole and the putt dropped to the accompanying screams of delight from the huge gallery. Eight players either led or shared the lead during the second round. The end of the day found nineteen players within five strokes of Stockton, whose 66 moved him into the lead at 137, one stroke ahead of Hale Irwin and Hubert Green. Colbert slipped to 72 and a 139 total. Gary Player scored his second 71 and remained in a tie for sixteenth place. Jack Nicklaus also had a 71 and lay three strokes behind Stockton. The field shrank to forty-four at the cutoff mark of 148 strokes. For the second time in Masters history, the former champion failed to make the cut. Tommy Aaron's 77-73, 150 total missed by two strokes.

On Saturday, the third day, the first twosome teed off at 11:12 A.M., and by the time it got to the second tee a rain began to fall. The skies looked gray and forbidding. Would there be a replay of the '73 tournament with a third-day washout? For a time intermittent showers splashed the galleries and slowed the players. But at about 1:00 P.M. the sun came out and the gallery burst into a spontaneous cheer. The weather remained clear for the rest of the day as well as on Sunday.

Now excitement came from the second nine. Playing well ahead of the leaders, Gary Player suddenly found his putting touch and tied the newly set Hale Irwin birdie record when he, too, scored birdies on the twelfth through the sixteenth holes. As each successive red number appeared after Gary's name on the many scoreboards, great cheers went up from the gallery. Gary moved up to a tie for second, one stroke behind Dave Stockton, who came in with a good 70 and a 207 three-round total. Stockton again putted sensationally, having only 26 putts. Dave had started out in incredible fashion. He holed a seventy-five-yard wedge for an eagle three on the second hole and then birdied the third for a three-under-par start. Colbert, too, tried to get back into the lead, with a 69 for a 208 total, to tie Player. Jack Nicklaus slipped to a 72, five strokes off. Almost unnoticed in the pack after two days of play, Bobby Nichols and Phil Rodgers had scored 68s and posted 209 totals and were only two strokes away from Stockton going into the last day. In all, eighteen golfers were within seven strokes of the lead. True to Masters tradition, the last day promised a dramatic finish. There was even speculation about the chances for a tie and a Monday play-off.

Hollywood could not have written a more dramatic scenario for Sunday's play. Player and Stockton would battle head to head in the final twosome. Nicklaus would tee off thirty minutes ahead of Gary and Dave. Strung between them were the young lions, any one of whom could explode and seize the coveted championship—Stockton, Colbert, Rodgers, Nichols, Irwin, Weiskopf, all non-winners of the Masters; and Nicklaus and Player, former champions and Masters-tested.

The excitement of the championship race overshadowed the third 64 ever shot in Masters competition, a score that tied the course record jointly held by Lloyd Mangrum (1940) and Nicklaus (1965). Maurice Bembridge, a strong and wiry Ryder Cup star from England, played this almost unbelievable round. After starting out with 73, 74, and 72, his final 64 brought him in at 283 and earned him $3,900.

Maurice had no bogeys on his card. He started out mildly enough with birdies at the fifth and sixth holes. Beginning with the tenth hole, he put together four more birdies in succession, the first two on putts of fifteen and twenty-five feet, and then sank three-footers on the twelfth and thirteenth holes. Maurice came to the last hole needing a thirty-foot downhill putt for the record.

His chances of getting it on the slippery, tricky green were remote. The crowd gave him a tremendous ovation, hoping he could get down in two putts so as not to spoil the fine round. Undaunted by the pressure of his low score, Bembridge gave the putt a good go—it disappeared, dead center in the hole, for his eighth birdie. So Maurice Bembridge's name went into the Masters record books alongside those of many golfing immortals. The international aspect of the tournament was certainly enhanced by his performance.

On the last day, Gary Player started out one stroke behind Dave Stockton. He drew even with Stockton at the sixth hole when he put his seven-iron tee shot twelve feet from the hole and sank the putt while Dave made his par three.

At the ninth hole Gary charged into the lead when his six-iron second shot missed the bunker and caught the fringe of the green, stopping quickly only six feet from the hole. Stockton's second shot was about fifteen feet above the cup. Dave was determined not to be short on his first putt. He wasn't. In fact, he was horror-stricken to see the ball continue rolling, finally stopping about three-and-a-half feet below the cup.

Gary made the most of his opportunity. He took three little, smooth practice strokes with the feet close together. The putt went in for a one-stroke lead even if Dave Stockton sank his putt. When Dave missed, Gary's lead was suddenly two big strokes. He would never relinquish the lead again, though it would be threatened at several points during the second nine.

When the Stockton-Player twosome, the last pairing on the course, completed the eleventh hole, Gary Player was leading at nine under par. His partner-opponent, Dave Stockton, was eight under par. Tom Weiskopf, ahead of them, was seven under par at the twelfth hole. Nicklaus was six under par but had a chance to birdie the thirteenth, gain a stroke, and put more pressure on Gary. The crowd roar in the distance told everyone that Nicklaus had made his birdie four at the thirteenth hole. But the scoreboard changed for Nicklaus from -6 to -8. Jack had made an eagle three on No. 13 and was now only one stroke behind Player.

Player executed his pitch shot on the eleventh, and his ball stopped six feet short of the hole. The crowd sensed that Nicklaus would go into a tie for the lead at this point should Gary miss his putt. However, Gary made his putt and held his lead over Nicklaus and over Stockton, who also parred the eleventh hole.

Now it was Tom Weiskopf's turn to add to the drama. At seven under par, if he could birdie the thirteenth hole he would go into a tie for the lead. Reaching the green in two, Tom was on the left side of the putting surface. He just barely missed his eagle, the ball sliding away by an inch. Now it was Weiskopf tied with Player, with Nicklaus a stroke behind and playing the fourteenth hole.

The flagstick on the fourteenth hole had been placed at the right rear of the green in a most difficult position. The choice was to go for the hole and chance going over the green, or play it safe. Jack's second shot was bold, a little to the left on the back fringe of the green, thirty-five feet away from the hole. Furthermore, Jack had to negotiate a wicked upslope in front of the flagstick. He elected to putt but came up short by five feet and missed the putt to slip back another precious stroke.

Player knew he had to birdie the five-par thirteenth hole to have any chance of holding his lead against Nicklaus, Weiskopf, and Stockton. He played the hole bravely and put his second shot on the left side of the green. While he did not come close to the eagle, he did get down in two with a seven-foot second putt to go nine under par. Stockton matched Gary's birdie to remain one stroke behind him.

Weiskopf played the fourteenth hole beautifully, putting his second shot about fifteen feet from the hole and just missing his birdie, his putt falling short by inches but dead on the line. Nicklaus, ahead on the five-par fifteenth, now desperately needed a birdie. Hitting a long iron, he fell short of the green and rolled back into the edge of the pond. Disappointment was written all over his face.

The situation, while bad, could have been worse. It appeared that the ball was lying in heavy grass and muck at the water's edge and might even be playable. Jack decided to try. Taking off his sock, rolling up his trouser leg, and replacing his shoe, Nicklaus stepped into the pond with his right foot under water, his left foot on the bank. There was a mighty swing, and out of the mud and heavy grass came Jack's ball, stopping only six inches from the hole for a certain and incredible birdie. He was not out of it yet by any means.

Needing birdies, Jack went for the flagstick on the three-par sixteenth hole. The hole had been cut on the far left rear of the green, daring the players to go for the pin. Jack's shot, a six iron, was a foot or so too far left and just caught the edge of the left bunker. He was faced with a delicate bunker shot, very little green to work with, and the green sloping away from him. Just barely clearing the bunker's edge, he needed to sink a twenty-foot putt to save his par and remain in the running. He missed, and took a bogey four to fall out of contention. He eventually bogeyed the eighteenth hole as well after a bad drive, and finished at 281, three strokes behind Gary Player.

In the meantime, Gary Player missed a birdie at the fourteenth hole by only an inch and came to the fifteenth needing a birdie to keep his one-stroke lead on the field. Gary's drive was long; his second shot, a long iron, went to the right and into the bunker. Renowned as a premier sand player, he proved his adeptness by executing a brilliant explosion shot from fully sixty feet to within five feet of the flagstick. Another pressure putt, and down went his birdie. Gary would not surrender his lead.

Dave Stockton was playing along steadily, trying to pick up a stroke on Gary, but was not able to sink the putts that had gone in on the previous days. Tom Weiskopf had birdied the fifteenth hole ahead of Player and had moved into a scoreboard tie with

Gary Player executes a great bunker shot and places it close to the hole.

Gary at nine under par. The sixteenth hole cost Weiskopf, however, when his tee shot found the lake just a few feet away from safety and from a close position to the pin. Tom walked up to the drop area at the edge of the pond, hit a lofted iron close to the hole and salvaged a bogey four, but, like Nick-laus, had put himself out of the tournament.

The seventeenth hole proved to be the climax of the tournament. Player's drive was excellent, right in the center of the fairway, so long that his club choice for the second shot was only a nine iron on this 420-yard, four-par hole. At this time Gary turned to his genial caddie, Eddie McCoy, and told him, "Eddie, in all the years I've played here, I've only hit this green six times. In 1961 this was the hole that won the tournament for me. I think it's going to win it for us again."

The shot was a magnificent one, so good that Gary knew he had done it and merely tossed his club aside without even looking any longer at the green. And he had done it. The ball was six inches from the birdie that would put him two strokes in front of the field with one hole to play. The crowd came to its feet and roared its cheers for the South African, dressed as usual in black, as he dropped the short putt that put him ten under par.

Stockton came over to congratulate Gary on his remarkable shot. The eighteenth hole was anticlimactic. Gary drove perfectly and placed his second shot twenty-five feet from the hole. He putted to within a foot and a half and calmly sank the putt that gave him his second Masters championship.

45
THE MASTERS OF 1975

Jack Nicklaus	68	67	73	68	276
Tom Weiskopf	69	72	66	70	277
Johnny Miller	75	71	65	66	277
Hale Irwin	73	74	71	64	282
Bobby Nichols	67	74	72	69	282
Billy Casper	70	70	73	70	283
Dave Hill	75	71	70	68	284
Tom Watson	70	70	72	73	285
Hubert Green	74	71	70	70	285
Lee Trevino	71	70	74	71	286
J. C. Snead	69	72	75	70	286
Tom Kite	72	74	71	69	286

In a showdown finish that brought, as Herbert Warren Wind, famous golf writer, said, "the most unbearable of sporting pressure and the most inconceivable of thrills," Jack Nicklaus won an unprecedented fifth Masters championship this year—his fifteenth major title—when he scored a brilliant 68 on his last round for a 276 total. Jack's score was twelve strokes under the Augusta National's par, and he edged out, by a single stroke, Tom Weiskopf and Johnny Miller in what was undoubtedly the most exciting

Jack Nicklaus receives his fifth Masters jacket from 1974 champion Gary Player.

149

and dramatic finish the Masters Tournament had ever witnessed.

The tournament started out calmly enough in excellent weather with greens softened by early-morning rains. The evening of the first day showed Bobby Nichols in the lead with an excellent 67, but the ominous Nicklaus was only one stroke behind at 68. Allen Miller, J. C. Snead, Tom Weiskopf, and, surprisingly enough, veteran Arnold Palmer were close behind the leaders at 69 strokes apiece.

On the second day, all the experts thought Jack Nicklaus had broken the back of the tournament as he opened up a monstrous five-stroke lead with a sparkling 67 for a 135 total.

The course was drenched by an overnight rain. The result was that the greens held the pitches well and the players were able to putt boldly for the cups. Nicklaus's close pursuers fell off the chase somewhat: Palmer to a 71 and a 141 total, Weiskopf also to 72 for a 141 total, while Tom Watson and

Billy Casper began to threaten with 70s each for 140 totals. The consensus was, however, that Nicklaus had started to walk away from the illustrious field of international golfers. The question seemed to be who would be second to Jack.

At the close of the third day, however, everyone woke up to the fact that Nicklaus did not have the title locked up. The fight was on. Tom Weiskopf made a strong move and by nightfall had taken over the lead by a single stroke. Playing earlier than Nicklaus, who played in a sentimental pairing with Arnold Palmer, Tom was able to take advantage of the good weather and balmy breezes as he fired a six-under-par 66 for a 207 three-day total by nightfall and found he had vaulted past Jack into first place. Jack and Arnold, with monstrous galleries following them, were never able to get it going and, playing in weather that got gustier as the day went on, stumbled in with 73 for Nicklaus and 75 for Palmer.

The eventual dogfight for the champion-

Jack Nicklaus at the fifteenth green.

ship was shaping up now. The scoreboard at the end of the third round showed:

Weiskopf	69	72	66	207
Nicklaus	68	67	73	208
Miller	75	71	65	211
Watson	70	70	72	212
Casper	70	70	73	213
Nichols	67	74	72	213

At the same time that Weiskopf was making his move to the top, Johnny Miller, who had gotten off to a disappointing 75–71, 146 start and was lying eleven strokes behind Jack Nicklaus, caught fire too. Miller scored six straight birdies starting with the second hole and checked in with a startling score of 65, only one stroke more than the course record of 64. Miller's 30 was a new Augusta National record for the first nine.

The scene was now set for the unbelievable drama of the last day. As a result of his falling from the lead, Jack Nicklaus was paired with young Tom Watson, British Open champion of 1975. They would constitute the second-to-last twosome on the course. Weiskopf and Miller, both mounting Palmer-like charges at the lead and the victory, would play in the final twosome.

The play-by-play went this way: Nicklaus, playing first, bogeyed the first hole and fell two strokes out of the lead. Nicklaus birdied the second hole to gain the stroke back. Nicklaus, one behind. Weiskopf and Miller then started and parred No. 1. Miller birdied No. 2; Weiskopf made his par. Miller closed the gap to three strokes between himself and Weiskopf.

Nicklaus and Weiskopf both birdied the third hole, while Miller slipped to a bogey and four strokes behind. Nicklaus and Weiskopf both parred the fourth hole as Miller birdied. Weiskopf was then leading Jack by one stroke, Miller by three. Jack's second shot at the four-par fifth was a sensational one, close enough for his birdie, and now Jack and Tom were tied for the lead.

Miller and Weiskopf both birdied the sixth hole as Jack got his par. All three golfers parred No. 7. Miller was the only one to birdie the eighth, and when Miller also

birdied the ninth hole he was out in 32 and only two strokes behind Nicklaus and Weiskopf.

Jack's fifteen-foot putt for a birdie at No. 9 brought him even with Tom with nine holes to go.

The back nine were equally excruciating, with Miller missing a short birdie attempt at the tenth hole and a tiny two-footer at the eleventh for a bogey. It began to appear that Miller was falling out of the three-way contest, that Weiskopf and Nicklaus would fight out the title to the end.

Then disaster struck Weiskopf as he dunked his second shot at the eleventh hole into the treacherous pond in front of the green. A sensational wedge shot of seventy-five yards helped him to salvage a bogey five. But, as it turned out, that was a costly penalty stroke for Tom.

But now Jack Nicklaus, ahead of the Miller-Weiskopf pairing, could hear the groans of the huge crowds as they sympathized with Johnny Miller and Tom Weiskopf behind him.

Neither Weiskopf nor Nicklaus was able to cash in a four at the thirteenth; Miller did and tightened the race again. Weiskopf now heard the lamentations of Nicklaus's gallery ahead on the fourteenth hole, normally a simple four for Jack. This time it appeared that Jack's nerves were completely shattered. From a spot on the front edge of the green, Jack putted completely off the back edge of the green. Bogey five for Jack and back to ten under par.

The fourteenth was a lead-saving hole for Weiskopf, who immediately followed in the wake of Jack's bogey with a great birdie three. Weiskopf was now back in the lead by one stroke, eleven under par, Jack now ten under par, but heading for the birdieable five-par fifteenth, while Miller was nine under.

All three players made birdie fours on the fifteenth. The race remained unchanged.

Now Nicklaus, on the sixteenth green, was facing a nasty forty-foot left-to-right breaking putt. Jack was aware that Weiskopf and Miller had both birdied the fifteenth, Weiskopf to remain a stroke ahead of Jack with Miller closing two strokes behind.

The cup on the sixteenth hole was cut that day on the far right top corner of the green, in a most awkward place. Jack later said that he "knew he could make the putt, that he'd had a putt some years before from the same spot and had holed it." He struck the putt firmly and knew he might make it. He started to dance to his right with his putter raised in the air as the ball made its last necessary veer for the center of the hole. Down it went for the birdie two. The customarily reticent Nicklaus leaped into the air in elation.

Jack's birdie and the resultant roars of the massed crowd must have affected Tom Weiskopf, who was waiting on the sixteenth tee. He had memories of other tee shots into the water on the left and, overly cautious, hit a weak iron to the front of the sixteenth green, never having a chance for his par as he left his first putt woefully short of the cup eighteen feet away. Miller made three on No. 16 to stay in contention, still two strokes behind.

Nicklaus was once more in the lead and, sensing the chance of nailing the victory down for certain, made valiant attempts at birdies on both the seventeenth and eighteenth holes, but his putts would not fall. As Jack played his last hole, a tremendous roar went up from the seventeenth green where Weiskopf and Miller were putting. If the roar were for Tom, it meant that he and Jack were tied. Jack sighed in relief as the score posted on the giant leader board at the eighteenth hole showed the latest birdie to be Miller's, not Weiskopf's. So each player was one stroke behind Nicklaus, each needing a three at No. 18 to tie for the championship.

Down the eighteenth fairway came Weiskopf and Miller, each with perfectly placed drives. Two high soft shots arched toward the elevated green, toward the flagstick in the hole cut fairly close to the front edge of the green. Both skidding-to-a-stop crisp iron shots brought Weiskopf and Miller within birdie range and the ultimate oppor-

Hale Irwin tied the course record of 64 in the final round, enabling him to take fourth place and $9,600,000.

tunity to tie Jack Nicklaus for the championship.

Their putts were very much alike, almost on the same line to the hole. Johnny Miller's ball was away, about twelve feet from the pin, above and to the right of the cup. His putt would break from four to six inches from right to left. Tom Weiskopf's putt was only eight feet away on practically the same line Miller would use. Tom would have the benefit of watching how Miller's putt would break.

The monstrous, hushed and expectant gallery sensed that at least one of these great golfers would sink his birdie putt and force a play-off the next day. Perhaps both players could do it.

Miller putted and, in agony, watched his ball take too much of the break and finish below the hole, not in it.

Then Weiskopf, having watched Miller's ball break more than might have been expected from right to left, stepped up to putt his ball along the same line. Surely Tom would not under-allow for the sharp break.

Nicklaus is greeted with a standing ovation as he approaches the eighteenth green.

Any putt at Augusta is missable. This one was a miss, too. Tom's ball never did take the break to the left and finished on the right side of the cup and then rolled behind it.

Almost unnoticed in the dramatic histrionics of the day, Hale Irwin, who had played a disappointing game all week, came to life with a spectacular round that included eight birdies to score a 64 and tie the course record jointly held by Mangrum, Nicklaus, and Bembridge. Irwin came within an eyelash of breaking the historic record when his bid for a birdie three on the final hole failed to drop.

So, it was Jack Nicklaus, champion for the fifth time of the Augusta National Masters Tournament.

Here are the score cards showing the final hole-by-hole duel of Nicklaus, Weiskopf, and Miller:

Par Out	4 5 4 3 4 3 4 5 4-36
Nicklaus Out	5 4 3 3 3 3 4 5 3-33
Weiskopf Out	4 5 3 3 4 2 4 5 4-34
Miller Out	4 5 4 2 4 2 4 4 3-32
Par In	4 4 3 5 4 5 3 4 4 36-72-288
Nicklaus In	4 4 3 5 5 4 2 4 4 35-68-276
Weiskopf In	4 5 3 5 3 4 4 4 4 36-70-277
Miller In	4 5 3 4 4 4 3 3 4 34-66-277

46
THE MASTERS OF 1976

Raymond Floyd	65	66	70	70	271
Ben Crenshaw	70	70	72	67	279
Jack Nicklaus	67	69	73	73	282
Larry Ziegler	67	71	72	72	282
Charles Coody	72	69	70	74	285
Hale Irwin	71	77	67	70	285
Tom Kite	73	67	72	73	285
Billy Casper, Jr.	71	76	71	69	287
Roger Maltbie	72	75	70	71	288
Graham Marsh	73	68	75	72	288
Tom Weiskopf	73	71	70	74	288

Raymond Floyd won the fortieth Masters Tournament by an eight-shot margin over runner-up Ben Crenshaw, 271 to 279. Floyd tied the 1965 Jack Nicklaus record score for the event, seventeen strokes under par, and set several other records along the road to his victory. He held the outright lead after each round. Only Craig Wood, Arnold Palmer, and Jack Nicklaus had ever performed that feat before.

Golfing weather was close to perfect with temperatures in the mid-seventies and cloudless skies.

On the opening day, Ray Floyd had an early starting time and checked in with a brilliant 32 on the first nine. He was such a dark horse in the event that his name was not entered on the leader boards as one of the players to watch. Furthermore, in a pretournament poll of professionals and sportswriters, sixteen players' names had been mentioned as possible winners. Floyd's name was not among them. Floyd had an equally strong second nine and by 2:30 of the opening day was in front with 65, never to be headed again. Floyd's 65 start was the best start by any champion.

This Masters Tournament was Floyd's twelfth, but he had not done very well in any of the previous events—a seventh finish in 1968 and a tie for eighth in 1966 as well as a number of no-shows in the top slots. After winning the P.G.A. championship in 1969, Floyd's game had deteriorated to the point that he did not make the top sixty players of the year in 1972 or 1973. His earnings had fallen to as low as $39,000 in 1973. He was, however, having a comeback of sorts and had earned more than $100,00 a year again

"Dark horse" Raymond Floyd runs away with the fortieth Masters Championship.

in both 1974 and 1975. But major titles were eluding him.

Jack Nicklaus scored a 67 on his first round, and so did Larry Ziegler. Other good opening scores were those of Lou Graham at 68, Dave Hill at 69, Bud Allin at 69. They were not heard from again, however. Pretournament favorites Tom Weiskopf and Johnny Miller were at 144 after rounds of 73-71 and 71-73 respectively. But they also fell off the pace, never to challenge in the Floyd one-man runaway.

At the close of the second day of play, Floyd had again shown his domination of the course with a remarkable six-under-par 66 that gave him a 131 total and a five-stroke lead over Jack Nicklaus, who reported a 69. Floyd's 131 two-day total was four strokes under the prior Masters Tournament two-day record score of 135 held jointly by Picard, Nelson, Venturi, and Nicklaus.

The crowd's sentiments seemed to be that Floyd might be expected to shoot a more normal round, that Nicklaus would get hot and catch him for an exciting finish remi-

niscent of the 1975 three-way duel among Nicklaus, Weiskopf, and Miller.

Ben Crenshaw, playing with Nicklaus on the second day, had a remarkable start of a birdie, eagle, birdie, and par—four straight threes—to put him four under par at that point. But Ben struggled home no better and two strokes worse for a 70 and two-round score of 140, nine strokes back of Floyd.

Truly, the event was shaping up for a one-man show. Floyd did not let down. He had missed only one green (the eighteenth) in his first round and one (the third) in his second round. On the other hand, he was simply murdering the five-par holes.

Floyd had decided to abandon his one iron and replace it with a five wood. The result was that he was getting home comfortably on many of the five-pars in two strokes. By the tournament's end, the score sheets would show that Floyd had played the five-pars in fourteen strokes under par, breaking the previous record for five-par play set by Jimmy Demaret in 1950, thirteen under par.

The scoreboard at the end of the third day of play read:

Ray Floyd	65	66	70	201
Jack Nicklaus	67	69	73	209
Larry Ziegler	67	71	72	210
Charles Coody	72	69	70	211
Ben Crenshaw	70	70	72	212
Tom Kite	73	67	72	212

On the last day of the tournament the winds came up and occasionally were gusting at twenty-five to thirty miles an hour. The only way Raymond Floyd would be caught would be a sensational subpar round by someone else coupled with a weak finish by Raymond himself. But the Augusta National course does not yield low scores in windy weather. The greens become dry and are blown out, faster than the proverbial downhill marble stairway.

Floyd played steady golf that last day, and soon it was evident that he was not going to weaken, that his closest pursuers were merely playing for second place. Floyd

At the awards presentation, Ben Crenshaw explains just how Ray Floyd happened to beat him by eight strokes.

was out on the first nine in par 36; he was in trouble only once, and that time, on the very first hole, he punched a shot around a tree and still made his par. That was a good omen for the sort of day Floyd would have.

He played the thirteenth hole bravely, going for the green with his new five wood, but missed a ten-foot putt for his birdie there. On the fifteenth, he played conservatively, short of the water in two, but still was able to cash in his birdie with a sparkling wedge shot and fifteen-foot putt.

Ben Crenshaw, admitting later that he was playing for second, moved out of the pack behind Floyd. He was helped by a sensational eagle three on the thirteenth hole as well as by a spectacular splash-out birdie at the fifteenth, accomplished by rolling up his trousers and standing with one bare leg in the pond at No. 15.

Larry Ziegler never challenged either Crenshaw or Floyd, nor did Jack Nicklaus.

They finished tied for third at 282, eleven strokes behind the victorious Floyd, on final scores of 72 and 73 respectively.

Curtis Strange was low amateur in the event on scores of 71, 76, 73, and 71 for 291, a tie for fifteenth place, a most respectable showing for the young Walker Cup player.

Here is Raymond Floyd's record-tying score:

OUT	IN
Par	4 4 3 5 4 5 3 4 4-36-72
4 5 4 3 4 3 4 5 4-36	
1st Round	4 4 4 4 3 4 2 4 4-33-65
4 4 4 3 3 3 4 4 3-32	
2nd Round	4 4 3 4 3 3 3 5 4-33-66
4 4 4 3 4 2 4 4 4-33	
3rd Round	4 6 3 4 4 4 3 4 3-35-70
4 4 4 2 5 4 4 4 4-35	
4th Round	4 4 2 5 4 4 3 4 4-34-70
4 5 4 4 3 3 4 5 4-36	
	271

47
THE MASTERS OF 1977

Tom Watson	70	69	70	67	276
Jack Nicklaus	72	70	70	66	278
Tom Kite	70	73	70	67	280
Rik Massengale	70	73	67	70	280
Hale Irwin	70	74	70	68	282
David Graham	75	67	73	69	284
Lou Graham	75	71	69	69	284
Ben Crenshaw	71	69	69	76	285
Ray Floyd	71	72	71	71	285
Hubert Green	67	74	72	72	285
Don January	69	76	69	71	285
Gene Littler	71	72	73	69	285
John Schlee	75	73	69	68	285

Tom Watson won the forty-first Masters Tournament after withstanding tremendous pressure: the sight and sound of Jack Nicklaus playing directly in front of him on the last day and birdieing six out of the first thirteen holes. Watson matched him practically stroke for stroke, birdie for birdie, and returned a 67 to Nicklaus's 66 to win by two strokes, 276 to 278, as Tom Kite and Rik Massengale tied for third with scores of 280.

The usual balmy spring weather of Augusta in April did not prevail during the first two days, as raw winds and occasionally blustery rains swept the course. When the storms had passed through at last, the temperature moderated, and by late Saturday and all day Sunday the weather was sunny and as beautiful as ever.

Hubert Green took a two-stroke lead on the first day on a card of 67 that showed six birdies and one bogey. Veteran Don January checked in with a 69, and so did young Bill Kratzert. Behind these three were Jerry Pate, Rik Massengale, Tom Kite, and Tom Watson, all at 71. Altogether there were twenty-three players at par or better, a situation that was attributed to the softness of the course after the rains and to the slowness of the greens, which permitted aggressive putting for the hole. Green followed his good start with undistinguished rounds of 74, 72, and 72 and finished well down the list in a tie for eighth place.

By the end of the second day Watson was starting to assume command of the tournament, it appeared, as he scored a three-under-par 69 that included five birdies and two bogeys. His halfway total was 139. Al-

Tom Watson, 1977 Masters Champion.

most unnoticed by the crowds, Rod Funseth had an excellent round and vaulted from nowhere in sixteenth place as the day started to a tie for the lead at the thirty-six-hole mark. Rod had only 28 putts in his round with birdie putts that ranged from four to twenty-five feet. Regrettably, he finished his last two rounds in 74 and 73, ten strokes behind the winner.

Here was the scoreboard as play began Saturday morning, the third day:

Tom Watson	70	69	139	5 under par
Rod Funseth	72	67	139	5 under par
Bill Kratzert	69	71	140	4 under par
Ben Crenshaw	71	69	140	4 under par
Gary Player	71	70	141	3 under par
Hubert Green	67	74	141	3 under par
Jack Nicklaus	72	70	142	2 under par

On the third day, Watson and Nicklaus matched cards with 70s while young Rik Massengale sprang into contention after a 70–73, 143 start, with a fine 67. Crenshaw was in with his second successive 69 and

was also a threat at 209. But Crenshaw finished diappointingly while playing with Jack Nicklaus on his last round. He found two bunkers on the second and bogeyed that hole, was lucky to sink a ten-footer on the third for a bogey after his second shot went over the green, and chipped back clear across the green into another bunker. Crenshaw was finished for the day and eventually staggered in with a 76 for a 285 total and a tie for eighth place.

Heading into the last day, the four leaders looked like this on the monstrous scoreboard:

Tom Watson	70	69	70	209	7 under par
Ben Crenshaw	71	69	69	209	7 under par
Rik Massengale	70	74	67	211	5 under par
Jack Nicklaus	72	70	70	212	4 under par

When play started on Sunday, it appeared that the finale would be a head-to-head match between Watson and Massengale, who were scheduled to play together in the last twosome of the day. As it turned out, Massengale was Watson's closest pursuer for the first eleven holes, but he fell off the pace with successive bogeys at the tenth and eleventh holes. He dropped back and out of contention just as Jack Nicklaus was making his serious move toward catching Tom Watson.

Watson and Massengale had a marvelous duel against each other and against par on the first nine. Watson began his round at seven under par and held that red figure as he parred the first four holes. The crowd roared with mounting excitement as Rik Massengale birdied the second hole to draw within a stroke of Watson. The real excitement began at the fifth hole and left the onlookers gasping in astonishment as the two players rammed in seven out of eight possible birdies in the next four holes, the fifth through eighth. Watson had gained four strokes on par by then and stood at eleven under par after eight holes. Massengale was then ten under par.

Both Watson and Massengale parred the ninth hole, but each player lost a stroke at the treacherous tenth hole. At the eleventh,

The victorious Tom Watson prevails in a dramatic head-to-head duel with Jack Nicklaus in the final round.

they both missed the green with their second shots, playing safe to the right side, and only Watson salvaged his par. Massengale needed three strokes to get down. That put Watson two ahead of Massengale, Watson at ten under par.

In the meantime, Jack Nicklaus was playing in the twosome ahead of Watson and

Watson sinks an "impossible" birdie putt on the seventeenth, giving him the lead he held to win the 1977 Masters.

Massengale. Jack, always dangerous, had been making threatening gestures most of the day. Jack started at four under par and promptly birdied the first two holes to go six under par. Watson was only seven under when Jack reached six under par, within a stroke then of tying Watson for the running lead.

Then Jack seemed to fall off his hot pace and was able to do no better than par on the third through seventh holes. Par was good, but not good enough it seems, because while Jack was making his steady pars, Watson, right behind him and watching every shot Jack made, was on his hot birdie streak and moving to eleven under par.

Jack got home in two on the uphill eighth

and finally cashed a birdie there. The hole is really no more than a long par four for him, and he should make a birdie there every time. That put Nicklaus at seven under par and four strokes behind Watson.

The race narrowed minutes later when Nicklaus was able to birdie No. 10 ahead of Watson's bogey five there—Nicklaus eight under, Watson slipping back to ten under, only two shots ahead.

Nicklaus frightened the crowd and himself at the eleventh when he overran the green and found his ball in a shallow green-side bunker. Knowing that the tournament might well turn on the next shot, Jack skimmed his ball out with a well-played shot to about twelve feet from the hole. With his usual calmness and steady stroke on the six- to ten-footers, Jack downed the putt and saved his par. He could not afford to lose any more strokes to Watson and hope to win.

Jack's confidence was high as he played the nasty little three-par water hole, the twelfth. He clicked a sweet seven iron straight at the flag. His ball ended in a nice flat place on the green, and moments later it was in the center of the cup for a birdie two. That moved Jack to within a single shot of Watson, who had watched the birdie stroke from the twelfth tee, where he was waiting to play his next shot.

Nicklaus got his birdie four at the thirteenth hole and momentarily was tied for the lead with Watson at ten under par. But Watson had yet to play the hole and had his own chance to make the birdie that would match Jack's. Tom was on No. 13 comfortably in two and came close to the eagle three that really would have set him up in front, but, most importantly, had gone one stroke ahead of Jack again. Watson was eleven under par, Nicklaus ten under.

Then, to add to the drama, what did Watson do but three-putt the fourteenth and once more fall back into a tie with Jack at ten under. He had put his second into the "Valley of Sin" at the front of the green, a spot from which few golfers escape without a three-putt. His first putt, up the hill, was four feet to the side of the hole and the second not even close.

Nicklaus was heading down the fifteenth, already anticipating a birdie at the pond-guarded five-par. By the time he was ready to putt, after two prodigious shots—a drive and a towering high four iron to the back edge of the green—the roar of the crowd and the nearby scoreboard told him that Watson had lost his precious lead stroke at the fourteenth.

Watson did not weaken, though. He came right back with his own birdie at No. 15, on the green in two strokes and two putts for the four. Watson and Nicklaus were again tied, at eleven under par.

Both players got their threes at the sixteenth. Jack had an anxious moment when he had to take a drop without penalty when

Linda Watson proudly adds a kiss to husband Tom's $40,000 first-place winnings.

his ball landed on a spectator's blanket. Jack had to tackle the seventeenth hole first, of course. He played it beautifully with a long drive to the left center of the fairway and a marvelously controlled eight iron to twenty feet from the flag. The putt would not drop. Jack headed for the last hole as Watson's second shot at the seventeenth landed on the green about the same distance from the hole as Jack's had moments before.

The green was icy; the putt was "impossible" to make. But Watson putted that ball into the center of the cup and did a delighted war dance when it went in. Watson was now a stroke ahead with one hole to play.

Nicklaus was on the eighteenth fairway, debating his shot to the green, when he heard the cheers from Watson's gallery at the seventeenth hole. At first, Nicklaus was going to try to make a safe par by placing his ball slightly above the pin. He would try for a tie and a play-off. But the roar that told him of Watson's birdie changed his mind. He had to get his own birdie or lose out. Jack played a poor shot and caught the bunker in front of the green, and, although he blasted out well to only twelve feet from the hole, he could not hole the putt to save his par.

With a two-stroke lead now, Watson played a safe par, a three wood to the center of the fairway and a seven iron to twenty feet from the hole. He could afford to three-putt and win. He two-putted and had a two-stroke winning margin in the forty-first Masters. The victory was worth $40,000 to Watson. Second place paid $30,000 to Nicklaus, while Kite and Massengale shared $35,000, $17,500 each, tying for third. For the second time, Watson had decisively beaten Jack Nicklaus in a head-to-head confrontation down the stretch in a major championship. It was very reminiscent of the similar battle they had at Turnberry in the British Open of 1975.

48
THE MASTERS OF 1978

Gary Player	72	72	69	64	277
Hubert Green	72	69	65	72	278
Tom Watson	73	68	68	69	278
Rod Funseth	73	66	70	69	278
Bill Kratzert	70	74	67	69	280
Wally Armstrong	72	70	70	68	280
Jack Nicklaus	72	73	68	67	280
Hale Irwin	72	67	71	71	281
Joe Inman	69	73	71	69	282
David Graham	75	69	67	72	283

The Masters Tournament of 1978 again produced a most dramatic finish. It saw Gary Player, already twice a Masters champion, blaze through his last round and tie the course record of 64 with a final beautifully stroked fifteen-foot downhill birdie putt at the seventy-second hole, which allowed him to post an eleven-under-par score of 277. Not until that crucial putt dropped into the cup was Player in the lead during the tournament. Furthermore, he had not even tied for the lead until the sixteenth hole of the last round, where he carded a birdie.

No fewer than three formidable players could have made par fours or birdie threes at the eighteenth hole and tied Gary. But one by one—first Tom Watson, then Rod Funseth, and finally Hubert Green—after valiant tries, they failed to hole the crucial stroke. Thereby, Gary Player captured his third Masters Tournament win and put himself into the special niche in golf history occupied by Ben Hogan, who also was the winner of nine major championships in his illustrious career. Jack Nicklaus made a serious attempt to catch the front-runners on the last day. He cashed four birdies in a row on the thirteenth, fourteenth, fifteenth, and sixteenth holes and electrified the gallery, though he eventually fell short of the winning score by four strokes.

The weather was magnificent during all four days, and the greens were, if anything, a little slow. Lee Trevino was heard to say, "It is not the Augusta of old. You can take a run at a cup. Before you had to lag it up."

When the firing on the first day had finished, John Schlee, with a score of 68, found himself in the lead by one stroke over Joe Inman with 69. Schlee was two strokes ahead of Lee Trevino and Bill Kratzert, both of whom checked in with 70s. A veritable army of nineteen players was at 72 or better, so it was evident that if the weather remained favorable the scoring might be expected to be low. Among the 72-shooters were Hubert Green and Gary Player, while Rod Funseth at 73 was a stroke farther back in the pack.

On the second day Rod Funseth played the greatest golf game of his life. Rod, then forty-five years of age, had not made much of a name for himself in the golf world thus far. Colorless, plodding, workmanlike, he had had only two finishes in the top ten players in the tournaments of 1977. He had won only $25,400 in 1977. In 1977 he had had a few moments of Masters glory when he found himself at 139 strokes after two rounds and tied with Tom Watson, the eventual winner. But in that tournament Rod had ended weakly with 74 and 73, ten strokes behind Watson. Perhaps this was the year Rod would finish as strongly as he started.

Seven birdies and one lone bogey brought Funseth in at 66 and into a tie with Trevino for the halfway lead. Two of Rod's birdies, at the fourth and eleventh holes, were what he called "tap-ins" of fifty and forty feet. His first red figure on the scoreboard came at the second hole when he chipped over the bunker to within nine feet and sank the putt. He birdied the eighth hole with a delicate chip to within a foot of the hole. His birdie at the thirteenth was accomplished with a three wood to the green and two putts. At the fourteenth his eight iron was only ten feet from the hole for yet another birdie, and the sixteenth hole surrendered to his six iron and a fourteen-foot putt. Rod's only bogey came at the tenth hole when he overshot the green and failed to save his four there.

Saturday morning, the third day of the tournament, found Funseth and Trevino tied and leading the field at 139 strokes apiece, with Hale Irwin and Gene Littler one stroke behind at 140 while Tom Watson and Hubert Green were at 141. In the meantime, Gary Player was lurking in the background, having had two successive, far-from-threatening 72s.

Now it was Hubert Green's turn to provide the fireworks, and he did. Once again the day was bright and sunny with only light winds. Hubert seized what appeared to be a commanding three-stroke lead with a slashing 65 that included seven birdies. Putting with his ancient, rusty, wooden-shafted putter—and in his awkward crouched-over stance with the ball far out in front of him, hands low on the putter shaft, right forefinger down its side—he worked his magic this day as putts of eighteen, twenty, two, five, and twelve feet fell for five of his seven birdies. The other two were mere tap-ins as his long game brought him two of the five-pars in two strokes for two-putt birdies.

Tom Watson was playing with Hubert Green on the third day and he too sprang into the thick of things with a 68 that "could have been better." Tom three-putted both the third and fourth holes and took three strokes to get down from the edge of the sixth hole. Things looked bad at that time for him but Watson roared back with six birdies and six pars in his last twelve holes.

Here was the scoreboard as the last round began:

Hubert Green	72	69	65	206
Tom Watson	73	68	68	209
Rod Funseth	73	66	70	209
Gary Player	72	72	69	213

On the last day of play Gary Player was paired with the new foreign star golfer, Severiano Ballesteros. They started at 1:04 P.M., about forty minutes ahead of the front-runners. Watson teed off with Gene Littler at 1:36 P.M., while Green and Funseth constituted the day's final twosome at 1:44 P.M.

As Gary Player stepped onto the first tee that afternoon, he knew his work was cut out for him. He was seven strokes behind with one round to play. After all, wasn't Jack Burke eight strokes behind Ken Venturi in 1956? And didn't Burke catch Ken by one stroke at the end? He would see what he could do. He had to count on two things happening. First, he had to accomplish a subpar round himself, as many strokes under par as he could possibly get. Second,

After starting the final round seven strokes behind the leader, Gary Player shows justifiable satisfaction as he sinks a birdie putt on the eighteenth to win.

Green, Funseth, and Watson, the leaders, had to do no better than hold steady or even fall back.

After starting the day with a three-stroke lead over Watson and Funseth, Hubert Green played raggedly on the outgoing nine. However, he managed to one-putt both par fives, the second and the eighth, and reached the turn at even par for the round, still ten under par for the tournament. By that time, both Watson and Funseth had picked up a stroke on Green. Funseth and Watson were then eight under par to Green's ten under par. Funseth birdied the tenth hole on a six-foot putt and found himself tied with Green for the lead at nine under when Hubert lost a stroke at eleven. Green's drive on the eleventh found the left rough. He hooked his second shot into the water and was fortunate to score no more than a bogey five there.

In the meantime, Player, five or six holes ahead of the Watson-Green-Funseth groups, was starting to make his presence known. The thousands of spectators could see from the omnipresent leader boards that Gary had moved to five under par by the time he reached the tenth tee. Then the screams of the crowd started coming at regular intervals as Gary proceeded down into and through the Amen Corner.

Here's what Gary was doing:

No. 10: A five iron to twenty-five feet to the right of the hole.
One putt, birdie three.
Six under par.

No. 11: A four-iron second missed the green to the left.
His wedge pitch almost holed but rimmed the cup.
One putt, par four.
Still six under par.

No. 12: A seven iron to fifteen feet from

Previous year's winner, Tom Watson, presents Gary Player with his third Masters green jacket.

the cup.
One putt, birdie two.
Seven under par.

No. 13: A four-iron second to twelve feet from the hole.
His eagle putt grazed the cup but did not drop, birdie four.
Eight under par.

No. 14: An eight iron to six feet from the cup.
Two putts, par four.
Still eight under par.

No. 15: On the green in two shots with a three-wood second, fifty feet from the hole.
Two putts, birdie four.
Nine under par.

No. 16: A five iron to fifteen feet from the hole.
One putt, birdie two.
Ten under par.

No. 17: An eight-iron second to twenty feet from the hole.

Two putts, par four.
Still ten under par.

No. 18: A three wood from the tee, a six iron to fifteen feet above the cup.
One putt, birdie three.
Eleven under par!

Gary Player knew that he was tied for the lead when he made his birdie at the sixteenth hole. He knew, as well, that one more birdie would possibly, even probably, win the tournament for him. He played the seventeenth hole well, but his twenty-foot putt did not sink. He had to get that deciding birdie on the eighteenth. The fact was that if he made three at the last hole he would have a score of 64 and tie the course record and maybe just win himself the tournament.

His tee shot at the last hole was played carefully with a three wood to the center of the fairway. He struck a perfectly played six iron and the ball sailed over the flagstick but quickly skidded to a stop fifteen feet above the cup. Gary said later that he had had the identical putt earlier in his career at the Augusta National and that he had misjudged the roll by several inches. This time he did not. The putt, beautifully stroked, went down the hill at perfect pace and dead into the center of the cup. Player leaped in joy as the crowd roared its appreciation of the great champion and world competitor in golf.

In the meantime, playing well behind Player, Tom Watson had been producing a steady but unspectacular round with ten straight pars. Watson had suddenly sprung into the lead at ten under par when he cracked a two iron to within twenty feet of the hole on the five-par thirteenth, and he promptly sank the putt for a sensational eagle three. Tom quickly gave back his advantage by three-putting the fourteenth hole to slip to nine under par. But, champion golfer that he is, he came right back and birdied the five-par fifteenth by getting home in two shots and two-putting for his four.

Playing directly behind Watson, both Funseth and Green had birdied No. 13 to go back to ten under par and into the lead. Unfortunately, Rod Funseth three-putted the No. 14 hole, and, as it turned out, the missed putt was costly to him in the long run.

Green urgently needed a birdie at No. 15. Hubert hit two mighty blows to reach the green safely. He had an eagle in his sights but had to settle for a birdie four and moved to eleven under par. Ominously, there was a loud scream from No. 16 as Watson birdied that hole to go eleven under par. Another scream roared in the distance from the eighteenth hole. Gary Player had sunk his fifteen-foot putt there for his last birdie and had posted a final eleven-under-par score of 277.

Then Funseth added to the growing excitement by sinking a ten-footer at No. 15 for his birdie. He had played short of the water and had put a beautiful pitch close to the flagstick. Funseth was now ten under par, Watson eleven under par. Hubert

Green next faced the three-par sixteenth—the water hole. His iron shot was bold and straight for the flag in its usual difficult spot on the far left back edge of the green. His ball came to rest a difficult slippery fifteen feet above the cup. Green putted with great caution, yet nothing he could do other than holing the putt decisively against the back of the cup could keep the ball from racing three feet beyond the hole. Sadly, Hubert missed his second putt and once again had slipped to ten under par, one stroke behind Player.

Tom Watson came to the eighteenth needing a par four there to tie Player for the championship. Watson tried to play his tee shot safe with a three wood, but he hooked badly into the trees on the left side of the fairway. From there he had a most difficult angle to the green. Watson was unable to reach the green, pulled the shot again, and missed to the left down among the crowd of spectators below the green. Faced with a tricky chip up the hill to a cup cut close to the edge nearest him, Tom elected to putt the ball. His stroke was executed magnificently, an "impossible" shot that came up the hill, over the crest, and then settled not eight feet beyond the cup. But sadly, needing to hole that putt to tie Player, he misjudged the break and missed to the right. One contender down and two to go. Green and Funseth were now coming down the eighteenth fairway, each needing a birdie three to tie Player.

Funseth's drive was safely in the fairway, but his lofted second flew over the flagstick and finally stopped some twenty feet above the cup. The flag that day was on the left-hand side of the green in a most difficult spot, almost inaccessible to the golfer from below the green. Funseth's putt down the hill was brave, but he never had a chance of holing it. He settled for his par four, a score of 278, one stroke behind Player.

In the meantime, Hubert Green had hit a perfectly placed three wood on his drive into the fairway. After his usual fidgeting many times over the ball, he hit a perfectly aimed crisp six iron that skidded to a stop not three feet from the cup, slightly beyond it.

The tying putt for Hubert would be downhill, curving slightly to the left, but certainly makable for Green, who was well known as as excellent putter. Certainly there would be a tie and a play-off for the title.

The crowd hushed in almost perfect silence as Hubert bent over his putt. Then, in the sudden stillness, Hubert could hear distinctly the voice of a CBS radio announcer saying, "He has to make this putt to tie Player." Green was distracted by the sound and backed away from his stance. Soon he resumed his familiar crouch and bent over the ball once more. Everyone seemed to sense in advance that he would miss the putt. And miss it he did with a push to the right, an ineffectual stroke not typical of Hubert Green.

So, for the second time, Gary Player had gone through the suspenseful experience of watching a competitor miss a short putt on the eighteenth hole to allow him to take the championship alone.

Green was philosophical about losing the tournament and said later, "I did not play well enough to win. If I had shot a score of two under par, I would have won. I made some mistakes, and I paid for it."

Thus Player won his third Masters, his ninth major championship. At the age of forty-two, he was the oldest winner of this prestigious event.

49
THE MASTERS OF 1979

Fuzzy Zoeller	70	71	69	70	280
Play-off 4,3					
Ed Sneed	68	67	69	76	280
Play-off 4,4					
Tom Watson	68	71	70	71	280
Play-off 4,4					
Jack Nicklaus	69	71	72	69	281
Tom Kite	71	72	68	72	283
Bruce Lietzke	67	75	68	74	284
Leonard Thompson	68	70	73	74	285
Lanny Wadkins	73	69	70	73	285
Craig Stadler	69	66	74	76	285
Hubert Green	74	69	72	71	286

In the second Masters to end in a triple tie, Frank U. Zoeller, Jr., who is nicknamed "Fuzzy" from the combination of his initials, won by defeating Tom Watson and Ed Sneed on the second hole of a sudden-death play-off. The three players had tied at 280 strokes at the seventy-second hole.

Just as the 1956 Masters Tournament is remembered as the one Ken Venturi lost to Jack Burke, and the 1961 tournament the one Arnold Palmer lost to Gary Player, the 1979 tournament will be remembered for the man who lost it, Ed Sneed, as it will be for the man who won it, Fuzzy Zoeller. In 1962 Arnold Palmer, Gary Player, and Dow Finsterwald finished in a tie at 280. Subsequently, Palmer won an eighteen-hole play-off, scoring a 68 to Player's 71 and Finsterwald's 77. Because of increasing demands on the professionals' schedule, the Masters Committee decided in 1979 that thenceforth a tie for the Masters Championship would be settled at once in a sudden-death play-off.

Ed Sneed, thirty-four years of age, had been on the professional tour for five years with only moderate success. He had won only three minor tournaments in his short career, the Kaiser International in 1979, the Milwaukee Open in 1974, and the Tallahassee Open in 1977. He had never been a contender in any major championship. Tall and slim at six feet, two inches, handsome, and possessed of a sweet, rhythmic swing that was working beautifully, Sneed opened with a 68. He was two strokes behind Craig Stadler, who had 66, a remarkable score because it had been played in a steady rain that began just as Sneed finished his round.

Scoring was very low on the first day with twenty-three players under par and ten at par 72.

On Friday, the second day, a most frightening situation developed. The skies had been darkening and ominous all morning, with sporadic light and heavy rainstorms that struck suddenly and unexpectedly. Then came word that a tornado watch had been put into effect in the Augusta area. Soon the warning of impending danger was passed on to the tremendous crowds. Thousands began to leave the course and take refuge in their cars in the jammed parking lots. When lightning began to strike nearby, the Masters Committee wisely called a temporary halt in the play.

Fortunately, the threat abated after torrential rains that lasted more than two hours. By 3:20 P.M. the storm had passed, and at 3:45 P.M. the players were able to return to the course and complete their rounds. Only superhuman effort on the part of the greens crews kept the round from being irrevocably washed out.

Interestingly, one of the finest rounds ever played at the Augusta National was under way without much fanfare or attention. Miller Barber was forced to stop his round after he had played only the first hole and then later continued it on the rain-drenched course. By the time Miller reached the fifteenth hole, he was five under par on his round, having birdied the first, second, third, fifth, ninth, and tenth holes. (He had bogeyed the thirteenth to offset one birdie.) As darkness fell, Miller chipped in from eighty feet for an eagle three and was then seven under par for the day. With five other twosomes, he had to wait until Saturday morning to complete his round. When he did, he parred the sixteenth, birdied the seventeenth on an eighteen-foot putt, and parred the eighteenth for a score of 64 to become the sixth coholder of the course record. It was an amazing accomplishment considering the difficulty of the sodden course and the two interruptions of play that undoubtedly broke his concentration.

Sneed was fortunate enough to finish his second round before the storm struck. He

Fuzzy Zoeller, winner of the 1979 Masters.

Ed Sneed, along with Tom Watson, parred the tenth and eleventh holes of the sudden-death play-off while Fuzzy Zoeller scored a par four and a birdie three to win.

Miller Barber's round of 64 (a course record tie) was interrupted twice, once by a storm alert and again by darkness. He had to finish the round the following day and birdie one of the three remaining holes. He birdied the seventeenth and parred the other two.

had a gorgeous 67 to go with his first-round 68 and shared the lead at the midway point with Craig Stadler, who had a 66—most of which was played in the annoying rain. On Saturday Sneed moved out ahead of Stadler into the undisputed lead. Sneed had not gone over par on a single hole in his first two rounds.

This year's thirty-six-hole cutoff occurred at 145, three strokes under the previous low mark of 148. Forty-five players were at 145 or under. A notable casualty was Arnold Palmer, who hung on the edge of qualifying overnight and did not know until Saturday morning whether or not he had made it. Scott Hoch (an amateur who had qualified for the Masters by reason of his being a quarterfinalist in the National Amateur), playing with Miller Barber in their rain-delayed twosome, blasted from the front bunker at No. 17 and holed out for a birdie three. This enabled him to be the last player

in at 145 and squeeze Palmer out of the field.

On the third day, in beautiful weather at last, Sneed made his first bogey of the tournament when he went over the back of the fifth green and could not get down in two strokes. He was out in 35 strokes on the front nine and took a four-stroke lead on the field after he hit a six iron to four feet from the hole on No. 12. He then followed up with a birdie four at the thirteenth as well. At the eighteenth hole he showed remarkable skill with a save from one of the fairway bunkers about 175 yards below the elevated green. He picked a four iron cleanly out of the sand, put the ball eighteen feet from the hole, made his par there to end the round strongly, and found that he had increased his lead to five shots—only one more day to go.

Here was the scoreboard as the last round began:

Sneed	68	67	69	204
Stadler	69	66	74	209
Watson	68	71	70	209
Zoeller	70	71	69	210
Lietzke	67	75	68	210
Nicklaus	69	71	72	212

On Sunday the winds rose in continual fury, gusting and swirling, especially in the areas guarded partially by the trees on the north edge of the course. Sneed started to make some mistakes. His swing became more hurried, and he appeared to be a little less certain about his game. He three-putted the second hole and hit a poor tee shot at the fourth. He missed an explosion shot in the bunker at the sixth and left the ball in the sand. He took three shots to get down from the edge of the tenth hole. Suddenly, his lead had evaporated to a single stroke over Watson and Zoeller, who were playing in the group ahead of him. Sneed himself was in a head-to-head confrontation with Stadler and brought up the rear of the field. Stadler was playing badly alongside Sneed and stumbled around in 76 shots to finish well down the list.

Sneed seemed to settle down when he saved par at the twelfth hole, playing a delicate sand shot from the rear bunker. Into the wind at No. 13, he played safe and laid up short of Rae's Creek. From there he pitched close to the flagstick and made a birdie four that seemed to give him renewed confidence, for he parred the fourteenth and then collected a natural birdie at the fifteenth—on in two strokes and down in two putts. With only three holes to play, he was three shots ahead of Watson and four ahead of Nicklaus and Zoeller.

Jack Nicklaus had not become a serious contender until the very end of the round, after being eight strokes behind the leader when he started his round. Jack came within one shot of making it a foursome in the play-off that would commence on the tenth tee. He went into the water at the fifteenth hole, but was able to save his par there with a beautifully controlled wedge shot over the pond and made the important short par putt for his five. When Jack birdied the sixteenth, it looked as if it would be Nicklaus again as champion, but he ended his chances when he struck a mediocre second shot at the seventeenth. His ball ran over the back edge of the green into a most difficult spot with the green sloping down and away from him. Unable to get down in two, he knew the tournament was over for him, right then.

In the meantime, Zoeller was pouring it on in the stretch. Feeling that he and Watson were playing for second place, he birdied three of the last six holes, got on both the five-pars, the thirteenth and the fifteenth, in two strokes with his tremendous driving power, and cashed a final crucial tie-for-the-lead birdie at the seventeenth hole on a sweet little eight-footer after a high eight iron zeroed in on the flagstick all the way. Watson had bogeyed the fourteenth to fall behind momentarily but was able to birdie No. 16 to bring himself back to eight under par as well. Watson continued to play steadily on the way in and made unspectacular pars, but simply could not drop that birdie putt he needed to take the lead alone. They both finished at 280, Watson with a 71 and Zoeller with a 70, and then sat down to await Sneed, who was finishing behind them.

With the tournament clearly in his grasp after his birdie at No. 15, Sneed now played three shaky holes in succession. At the sixteenth he left his tee shot forty feet from the hole, much too far away, and the ensuing three-putt was a foregone conclusion. At the seventeenth, just as Nicklaus had done, his second shot carried too far and ran to the back edge of the green. Again he failed to get down in par, and another stroke of his lead was gone. He could still par the eighteenth and win, but could he do it? He struck a seven-iron second shot on the eighteenth hole, and the ball splashed into the edge of the right-hand front bunker but did not become buried there as it might well have done. His explosion shot, in absolute desperation, was a good one and a brave one. His ball rose out of the bunker well and came to rest only five feet from the cup. The putt was not a difficult one. It would take, he thought, a subtle break of less than an inch. He played the slight curl only to watch the ball go perfectly straight after all and come to a halt on the very edge of the cup, where it refused to fall. Sneed had given back three strokes to par in the last three holes and backed into a tie with Zoeller and Watson.

Soon the golfers proceeded to the tenth tee for the play-off. Thousands of spectators hurried down the slope into the Amen Corner to surround the tenth green, eleventh tee, and eleventh green in expectation of the exciting event they were about to witness. All three players drove beautifully on the tenth hole, down the hill, slightly hooking their tee shots to the left in order to pick up the extra yardage needed on the long, extremely difficult four-par beneath the lengthening shadows in the lower reaches of the course. Sneed, slightly away on his second shot, put a six iron to ten feet from the cup. Watson, a little farther left than Sneed on his drive, 170 yards from the hole, put his ball on the green inside Sneed's. Zoeller, the long driver, as usual, then put his on the green so close that later there had to be a measurement to see which ball was farther from the cup, Watson's or his. Sneed putted first and barely missed. His putt was only an inch from holing, and

Fuzzy Zoeller jumps for joy after sinking his birdie putt on the second hole of the first sudden-death play-off in Masters history.

now he was confronted with the possibility that either of the other players would hole and shut him out. It was not to be. First Zoeller missed; and then Watson pushed his putt to the right—he never came close to holing.

The drama continued. Sneed was still alive and could hope yet to win. Again all

Defending champion Gary Player helps Fuzzy slip into the green jacket.

three drives were magnificent under the circumstances, truly of championship quality. Zoeller was the long hitter and drove the ball 300 yards down the eleventh fairway, which drops fifty feet from the tee to the green guarded on the front and left by a frightening pond of water. Sneed hit first to the green and, dodging the water, overshot the hole, putting his ball into a shallow green-side bunker behind the flagstick. Watson played a fine iron shot to fifteen feet, and then Zoeller, with the whole tournament now clearly in his hands, put his ball only eight feet from the hole.

Sneed had a difficult and dangerous shot from the bunker. The green sloped away from him, and the surface was extremely slick. He played the shot with courage and nearly holed out, the ball coming to rest only inches away for a sure four for Sneed, but not the birdie he so sorely needed.

Now Watson putted—short and two inches to the right of the cup, not the bold stroke for which Watson ordinarily was famous in the clutch. Zoeller did not waste any time. He putts in an exaggerated crouched stance with the ball far in front of him, his head bent behind the ball, not over it. But he is a good putter; he sank that eight-footer for the Masters Championship of 1979.

50
THE MASTERS OF 1980

Severiano Ballesteros	66	69	68	72	275
Gibby Gilbert	70	74	68	67	279
Jack Newton	68	74	69	68	279
Hubert Green	68	74	71	67	280
David Graham	66	73	72	70	281
Ben Crenshaw	76	70	68	69	283
Ed Fiori	71	70	69	73	283
Tom Kite	69	71	74	69	283
Larry Nelson	69	72	73	69	283
Jerry Pate	72	68	76	67	283
Gary Player	71	71	71	70	283

At the age of twenty-three years and four days, Severiano Ballesteros, of Spain, became the youngest Masters champion of all time, three months younger than Jack Nicklaus was when he won in 1963. Ballesteros, a handsome and exciting player, first broke into the world golf scene at the age of nineteen, when he nearly won the British Open of 1977. In 1979 he won the British Open outright at Royal Lytham and St. Anne's. Ballesteros won this Masters by four strokes, 275 to 279, over Jack Newton, of Australia, and Gibby Gilbert, who finished in a tie for second. This tournament promised to be almost as unsuspenseful as that of 1976, when Raymond Floyd ran away with the title. But midway in the last round, there was the usual heart-pounding drama and excitement as Ballesteros's two closest competitors, Gilbert and Newton, drew within a few strokes of a suddenly weakening Ballesteros.

On opening day, in balmy Georgia spring weather, with temperatures in the low seventies, and in a light breeze that died in mid-afternoon, the field was off to one of the fastest starts the Masters had ever seen. There were three 66s—the first by Ballesteros, who began to take command of the tournament at once. The other two were recorded by Jeff Mitchell and by David Graham of Australia, the current P.G.A. champion.

Ballesteros is noted for a slashing game and monstrous drives that often go astray. His recoveries are equally spectacular and his putting stroke so delicate that potential bogeys are more often than not turned into startling birdies. Ballesteros was uncharacteristically straight and orthodox on the first day; he missed only two fairways off the tee and only one green in the regulation stroke.

On the second day, Ballesteros suffered from occasional wildness off the tee, but luck as usual was with him. When he did get into possible trouble, the ball would bounce fairly for him, as it did out of the woods on the second hole, or else he capitalized on his great power and exploded out of trouble, over trees, over scoreboards, and made his birdies and pars for a bright 69 to go with his opening 66 and a 135 total. On the seventeenth hole, for instance, where a large tree guards the left side of the fairway, about 175 yards from the tee, Ballesteros hooked wildly on his tee shot. The ball ran through the left-hand rough onto the seventh green, which lies adjacent to the seventeenth hole. There his angle to the green was blocked by another tree and partially obscured by the huge scoreboard that keeps the crowd up to date on the current standings of the leaders. Undaunted, Ballesteros took a seven iron up over the tree and scoreboard. Result: the ball on the green fifteen feet from the cup and, moments later, his fifth birdie of the round.

On Saturday, the weather changed for the worse, and, while threatening thunderstorms failed to materialize, there was a steady, light rain throughout much of the day.

Tom Watson, one of the few golfers who was believed capable of mounting a challenge to Ballesteros, started to catch fire, it appeared. He successively birdied the sixth, seventh, and eighth holes to put himself at four under par and, at that time, only four strokes behind Ballesteros, who was playing a few holes behind him. "Seve" had just gotten his first birdie of the day at the seventh hole to go eight under par. Then the crowds erupted with a sustained roar of approval that, at the Masters, connotes only two things—either a hole-in-one or an eagle. It was Ballesteros at the five-par eighth. A three iron 245 yards long, straight through the narrow opening of the green, with the ball finally nestling a mere five feet away

Seve Ballesteros lines up a putt on his way to winning the 1980 Masters Tournament.

from the hole. The smooth stroke, and it was an eagle three for Ballesteros.

Watson knew what Ballesteros had done by looking at the scoreboard at the tenth hole. Then, instead of continuing his run at Ballesteros, Watson ruined his chances by bogeying the eleventh hole and by letting the little twelfth hole frighten him into submission. There he blocked out his tee shot to the right and put his seven iron into the water. He took a horrendous triple-bogey six there, and from then on he never got back into contention in the tournament. The entire tenor of the tournament changed with the almost simultaneous events of Ballesteros's eagle at No. 8 and Watson's six at No. 12. Watson finished with 71, 71, and 284, nine strokes behind the winner.

On Sunday the storms had passed through at last, and the weather turned

The youngest Masters Champion in history, Seve Ballesteros is congratulated by his caddy on No. 18 of Augusta National.

1979 winner Fuzzy Zoeller does the honors as the young Spaniard Severiano Ballesteros dons his champion's green coat.

bright and beautiful. Ballesteros was paired with Jack Newton, who was nine strokes behind him, 203 to 212. One stroke behind Newton was Gibby Gilbert at 213, who would play in front of the final twosome.

Ballesteros showed no early signs of weakening as he maneuvered delicate wedge shots to birdie putting positions on the first and third holes. No one seemed capable of closing the race at that time. Scoreboards showed Ballesteros at sixteen under par at the tenth tee after a first-nine score of 33, now ten strokes ahead of the field with only nine to play.

Suddenly there was a change in the mood of the tournament. Ballesteros lost a stroke at the tenth on a three-putt and another stroke at No. 11, when Newton birdied and he did not. Ballesteros was still eight strokes ahead, fourteen under par.

The wicked twelfth next took its toll. Ballesteros's iron shot struck the bank and fell back into the water. A drop, a penalty stroke, and he had a double-bogey five. Newton, in the meantime, had put a perfect shot near the hole and scored a two. A three-shot swing, and the lead was down to five strokes. The crowd started to murmur and wonder whether Ballesteros was blowing up.

The pressure started to increase as the two played the thirteenth hole. Ballesteros had only an iron shot to the green after an excellent drive. But his second shot was not as crisp as usual; it did not have its usual power. The ball fell short of the creek in front of the green. Before the horrified eyes of the crowded thousands, the ball ran on and on, irrevocably into the rock-strewn water. A penalty stroke, a drop, a wedge shot, and two putts later, Seve had a bogey six, another shot gone.

Ballesteros later said that at this point in the round he was extremely upset with himself. "I was very angry with myself after the thirteenth hole. I told myself I was stupid. I could lose the tournament. I had to work hard."

Although his tee shot at the fourteenth strayed left again, he managed to accomplish another sensational recovery shot up over the same familiar tree to the green and make his par there. Now he began to breathe a little easier. Gilbert in front of him had just sunk his fourth birdie in a row to move to ten under par and only two strokes behind Ballesteros. But Seve had the eminently birdieable fifteenth fairway. Then, recovering his equanimity, he played a magnificent four iron to a spot only twenty feet from the flagstick. An eagle would have been nice, but he settled for the birdie four. His final holes were anticlimactic as he played them in flawless par. Gilbert lost another stroke on a poorly played eighteenth. Newton never got any closer, either, and Severiano Ballesteros won the Masters of 1980.

51
THE MASTERS OF 1981

Tom Watson	71	68	70	71	280
Johnny Miller	69	72	73	68	282
Jack Nicklaus	70	65	75	72	282
Greg Norman	69	70	72	72	283
Jerry Pate	71	72	71	70	284
Tom Kite	74	72	70	68	284
David Graham	70	70	74	71	285
Raymond Floyd	75	71	71	69	286
Ben Crenshaw	71	72	70	73	286
John Mahaffey	72	71	69	74	286

Tom Watson, with a score of 282, won his second Masters championship by a two-stroke margin over Johnny Miller and Jack Nicklaus and by three strokes over Greg Norman, the new international star from Australia. This was a particularly satisfying victory for Watson because once again he defeated Nicklaus in a showdown reminiscent of their classic final eighteen holes in the British Open of 1977 at Turnberry, Scotland, where the two players shot 65 and 66 respectively to finish one stroke apart, with Watson the winner.

Nightfall of Thursday found four players—Lon Hinkle, Curtis Strange, Johnny Miller, and Greg Norman—in the lead with three-under-par rounds of 69. Nicklaus and Watson were close behind on rounds of 70 and 71. Watson had only one poor shot in his round, a thinly hit two iron that caught Rae's Creek at the thirteenth hole. He took a bogey there.

On Friday there were some better scores—three 68s, one by Watson holding his position close to the top of the field, and a sensational 65 by Jack Nicklaus. Nicklaus's game is worth reviewing inasmuch as it was only one stroke off the course record of 64.

Jack was truly on his game this day. His surge began at the three-par fourth hole with a three iron only a foot from the hole. He got that two, of course, and followed with three more birdies in a row. He should have made it five in a row, because he put his second shot onto the eighth green only to three-putt. He was out in 32 strokes. Jack was a little erratic on the second nine, missing some of the greens with his second shots. But he chipped miraculously well five times and sank short putts to save pars. So Jack stormed into the lead at the end of the second round with a 135 total. Four players were tied at 139, Watson and Norman among them.

On the third day, Watson began his move to the top. He had two bogeys in the early holes but then settled down and cashed six birdies through the first fifteen holes. He was then four under par for his round.

In the meantime, Nicklaus had run into all sorts of trouble. He pulled a couple of tee shots into the trees and took bogeys. He took a double-bogey five at the short twelfth when his tee shot struck the bank in front of the green and then rolled back into Rae's Creek. Then he proceeded to bogey the five-par thirteenth, usually a Nicklaus birdie hole, with his length and ability to reach the green on his second shot. This day, however, Jack's two-iron second hit the right side of the green and plunged into the water.

The startling fact was that there had been a swing of eight strokes between Nicklaus and Watson. Watson was now in the lead by four. Then Jack came back to birdie the fifteenth and sixteenth holes. Watson was playing ahead of Nicklaus, and just as Jack made his birdie two at the sixteenth, Watson's score at the seventeenth was posted on the tremendous scoreboard at the sixteenth green: double-bogey six for Watson. He had buried his second shot in the front bunker at No. 17, exploded out, and then three-putted. His four-stroke advantage had disappeared.

Then came another twist of fate. Jack Nicklaus missed a thirty-inch putt on the eighteenth hole to bogey the hole and fall a stroke behind Watson.

Nicklaus played with John Mahaffey on the final day, one twosome ahead of Watson, who was in the last group, paired with Greg Norman.

The news soon flashed across the course that Johnny Miller was hot. He was playing a good hour ahead of the leaders and cashing birdies left and right. He birdied three of the last four holes to finish with a 68 for 282 and the hope that he might back into victory if the front-runners should stumble.

The Watson–Nicklaus confrontation, though truly not head to head, was almost so

Tom Watson holds onto the lead at thirteen and goes on to win the 1980 Masters.

as each player knew what the other was doing in clear view on the greens and fairways nearby.

At one time Watson was on the eleventh green fifty feet away from the hole. He needed to two-putt to keep himself at even par and seven under par for the tournament. Nicklaus, at the same moment, was only a hundred yards away on the twelfth green, needing to sink a seven-footer to save his par and keep within three shots of Watson. Nicklaus sank his putt first so as to put the pressure on Tom. Watson was up to the challenge and two-putted safely for his par.

Jack birdied the thirteenth after reaching the green with his second but then lost a stroke at the fourteenth when he chipped badly from the fringe and missed his putt. Once again he came back vigorously with a birdie at No. 15 and a remarkable twenty-five-foot curving hole-out for a birdie two at No. 16. But Jack was running out of holes, and Tom was not weakening.

Watson had a scare at the thirteenth, a hole that might have cost him dearly if it had not been for his sensational chipping ability. His second shot to the green went irrevocably into Rae's Creek. He chose the most favorable drop area of several choices and chipped over the creek to five feet from the cup. He sank the putt for his par.

Tom parred the fourteenth and went after an insurance birdie at No. 15. His high four-wood second floated beautifully onto the green and stopped forty feet from the hole. When he two-putted for his birdie four, Tom was at eight under par, while Nicklaus was six under, still two strokes behind.

At the seventeenth tee, Tom needed two pars to win. He remembered his horrible double bogey there the day before. An excellent drive in the middle of the fairway left him the same shot for the second day in a row. Again, he selected his wedge. Again, he put the ball into the front bunker, missing the far edge by no more than an inch or two. Fortunately for Tom, the ball did not bury itself in the sand. His lie was clean, and this time his blast was sure and true. The ball stopped four feet from the cup, and, although the putt was a ticklish one, he stroked it home safely for his par-saving four. The eighteenth hole was an anticlimax. Tom hit a good safe drive, a six iron hole-high thirty feet from the hole.

Two putts gave Tom Watson a 71 for a 280 total. He was Masters champion again by two strokes over Nicklaus and by three over Greg Norman.

Tom Watson, a master at getting up and down.

52
THE MASTERS OF 1982

Craig Stadler	75	69	67	73	284
Dan Pohl	75	75	67	67	284
Severiano Ballesteros	73	73	68	71	285
Jerry Pate	74	73	67	71	285
Tom Kite	77	69	70	71	287
Larry Nelson	79	71	70	69	289
Curtis Strange	74	70	73	72	289
Ray Floyd	74	72	69	74	289
Andy Bean	75	72	73	70	290
Mark Hayes	74	73	73	70	290
Fuzzy Zoeller	72	76	70	72	290
Tom Weiskopf	75	72	68	75	290

Craig Stadler won his first Masters championship in a hair-raising finish that did not end until the completion of a one-hole play-off, the eighth play-off in Masters history.

Dan Pohl, whole full name is Danny Joe Pohl, twenty-seven years old and a professional golfer since 1977, almost beat Stadler out of the victory by posting a closing round of 67 against a shaky 73 by Stadler. Craig is familiarly known as "The Walrus" because of his bushy mustache and bulky body. He is a powerful man and a long driver of the golf ball. But Pohl, slim wiry, five feet, eleven inches in height, drives the ball even farther than Stadler, truly prodigious distances, averaging more than 270 yards per tee shot. In the P.G.A. earnings list for 1982, Pohl stood at thirty-ninth, while Stadler became the leading money-winner that year, taking home nearly a half million dollars.

This was the year the Masters Committee had decided to install bent grass greens. Normally, bent does not survive well in the southern climate, but the agronomists had finally developed some heat-resistant strains of grass. The result of their installation was a series of screams that could be heard from the players all the way to downtown Augusta. Sometimes a well-placed pitch to the green would land on the putting surface and spin backward, completely off the front of the green. At one point in the second round, Mark Hayes putted from eight feet slightly above the cup at the eighteenth hole. His putt ran past the hole, nearly stopped three feet away, and then

184

When Craig Stadler hits a shot he doesn't like, he lets you know it, like here at the ninth green.

made the first of three birdies he got on opening day. He was too bold again on the third hole and was required to sink a six-foot second putt for par. He did. His only error was a hooked second on the eighth hole. His ball found the left rough about seventy-five yards from the green. However, he had to clear or go under a clump of pines that were in his line of play. He chose to go over them, and his shot was most successful, ending only a few feet from the hole. He saved his par.

Jack Nicklaus and Tom Watson were both two strokes behind the leaders, Curtis Strange and Craig Stadler. Strange and Stadler had played together as teammates on the 1975 Walker Cup team, which was victorious at St. Andrews Old Course in Scotland.

There was so much complaining about the incredible speed of the greens that, on the third day, the committee members had mercy on the players and placed the flagsticks in more accessible locations on the greens. The result was that scores were better. The winds that had been moderately strong the first two days diminished to a mere breeze. The greens held the approach shots better on Saturday, and more birdie putts were going into the hole.

In the first two days, only four scores were under the 70 mark, not one under 69. On Saturday, however, with the more favorable pin positions, there were ten scores in the 60s. Bob Gilder was low with a 66 but fell off from then on, not to be heard of again.

The field was so logjammed in mid-afternoon of Saturday that it appeared probable that the third round would start with a dozen or more of the players within a stroke or two of the lead. Then, as the afternoon wore on, the picture changed. Craig Stadler had come into the tournament on a hot streak. He had finished in the top ten in seven of the tournaments he had entered.

Craig was two under par and in a tie for the lead at the fifteenth hole. Then he proceeded to birdie the last three holes in a row. A fifteen-footer fell for him at the sixteenth; a monstrous forty-footer dropped at No. 17;

started to move again. It came to rest forty feet below the cup. Hayes putted up the slope again, his second putt. The ball neared the cup, stopped short of it, and then reversed itself and once more rolled back forty feet away. Hayes took four putts and staggered off the green with a 74 that might have easily been a 71.

This four-putt by Hayes was undoubtedly in the mind of Craig Stadler as he faced the necessity of taking no more than two putts on the eighteenth green to win the tournament on Sunday, the last day.

Now, to the dramatics of the tournament. Tom Watson was the odds-on favorite to win this year. He started out in blazing fashion with a birdie two on the second hole, having made the edge of the five-par green with his second shot. Tom chipped strongly, some five feet past the hole. He sank the putt and

and on the eighteenth, from a distance of at least thirty-five feet above the cup and to the golfer's right, he trickled a curving putt down the slope to the very front edge of the cup. The ball hesitated a fraction of a second and then toppled in. Craig had scored a 67 for a total of 211 and found himself with a three-shot lead with only one round to go.

Severiano Ballesteros, the handsome and dashing Spaniard, was in with a 214 total, as was Jerry Pate. Pate's third round was a 67, while Seve's was a 68. In the meantime, Dan Pohl had started with a pair of 75s (150) and lay six strokes behind Craig Stadler's 144. Stadler and Pohl, as well as Pate, shot 67s on their third rounds.

Filling out the scoreboard as the final day began were Tom Weiskopf and Raymond Floyd, both at 215. Watson had fallen off to 216.

Dan Pohl's 67 featured an amazing streak of subpar golf. He went no fewer than six strokes under par on four holes in succession. He eagled the thirteenth and fourteenth and birdied the fifteenth and sixteenth. Tremendous roars were rising from the southwest lower part of the course, and the crowds around the monstrous scoreboards were getting more and more excited each time a new red number was placed on the line for Pohl.

On the last day, conditions for good scoring were ideal. There was not much wind, and once more the pins were not in unusually difficult places.

No one seemed ready to challenge Stadler. Craig, who started with a three-shot lead over the field, widened his lead to six strokes by shooting six pars and three birdies for a 33 first nine. Now he led Pohl, who clearly was turning out to be his most serious rival, by six strokes.

Then Craig started to run into trouble. On the pesky short twelfth hole his tee shot ran off the left edge of the green nearly hole-high in the short fringe. The shot from there to the flagstick was a difficult one—down a slight incline, then up an eighteen-inch rise, then down again to the cup. Craig putted the ball. It rolled past the hole about eight feet, a good shot under the conditions, but

One of the game's strongest hitters, Craig Stadler powers this shot down the middle.

when he missed the putt, one stroke of his lead was gone.

In the meantime, Dan Pohl, playing three twosomes ahead of Stadler, had birdied the five-par thirteenth with a sensational long-iron second shot that stopped no more than ten feet beyond the hole. His eagle putt barely missed holing, curling around behind the cup. Pohl had gained another stroke on Craig and was then three strokes behind Stadler.

Dan could sense the possibility of winning as he came to the lake-protected three-par sixteenth. As usual on the last day, the hole was cut in a difficult place near the back of the green on its plateau. It took a courageous golfer to attack that hole, but Pohl continued his rush with a six iron to about fifteen feet from the hole. He sank the putt for his birdie two, and now he was within two strokes of Stadler.

Craig "The Walrus" Stadler won the 1982 Masters and scored an impressive 33 on the front nine because of his great touch on and around the greens. Here he pitches up close to the flag on No. 8.

Craig did not make what is considered the normal birdie four at the par-five fifteenth, his second shot over the water having ended in the right bunker. His blast from there was too strong to permit a one-putt.

Craig came to the sixteenth and, seeing his lead slipping hole by hole, tried to guard against having his shot hook into the water on the left. But he overcompensated and was once more dismayed when he saw the ball fly into the bunker on the right, hole-high with the flagstick. He now had a most frightening shot to contemplate. He had to get the ball near the hole and try to make par. An ounce too much of power might send the ball hurrying past the hole with the possibility that it would run all the way across the green into the water. He did not dare think of that eventuality.

Craig's delicate blast, if a blast can ever be called delicate, popped the ball just out of the bunker onto the edge of the green. It ran slowly on a perfect line for the hole. Would it go in? No, it touched the right rim of the cup without hitting the flagstick, which would most certainly have stopped it dead alongside the hole or even allowed it to drop in the hole. Craig was horror-stricken as he stood helplessly in the bunker and watched the ball roll and roll and roll slowly down the hill to about forty feet away from the cup, where it finally came to rest on the green.

Craig made a valiant effort to hole that forty-footer but had to settle for a four, a bogey. His lead was down to only one stroke. Two holes now to go, and pars on them would win the tournament for him.

On the seventeenth, Craig had a monstrous drive and a comfortable wedge to the green above the cup. He made his two-putt, and now all he had to do was get his par at the eighteenth.

Stadler drove with his three wood to avoid the fairway bunker on the left of the fairway. He was safely in the fairway with a five iron to the green. His second shot was a good one, a little shorter than he might have wanted, but on the green thirty feet below the hole. He was glad to be below the hole, for he remembered the awful four-putt of Mark Hayes when Hayes got above the cup earlier.

Craig said later, "I don't know what happened!" His first putt was woefully short of the cup, in the six- to eight-foot range. His second was pushed off to the side of the cup, and his six-stroke advantage had completely evaporated. He had backed into a tie with Dan Pohl.

One would think, under the circumstances—the rush of birdies by Dan Pohl on his last nine and the weakening of Craig Stadler, particularly on the eighteenth hole with his three-putt—that Pohl would continue his pressure in the play-off and win.

Craig Stadler seemed to gather new strength and resolve. He smashed a perfect drive down the tenth fairway so far that it caught the downslope and rolled on, stopping about 150 yards from the green. Pohl was not intimidated by Craig's mighty blow and matched it yard for yard. Stadler was slightly away, so he struck an eight iron beautifully straight at the flagstick. The ball came down and stopped about twenty feet below the hole, leaving Craig a desirable uphill putt at the cup.

Pohl came off his short-iron second shot, pushing it to the right, and left it about eight feet off the edge of the green in the short-cut grass. He now had a most difficult putt or pitch for his par. There was a tremendous right-to-left slope on the green, one that would require a borrow above the cup of about ten feet. Pohl elected to putt the ball rather than chip it. The result was not good, a weak effort that left his ball ten feet below the cup, not quite on Stadler's line to the hole.

Craig putted first and struck a firm putt to about eighteen inches from the cup. Even at that distance, the putt was not a certain hole-out. Craig stepped up and, having the option to do so, sank his putt for the four.

Then it was up to Dan Pohl to tie him with his nasty ten-foot side-hiller. Unfortunately, he could not do it. Craig Stadler was the new Masters champion of 1982. His victory was a very popular one because Craig is truly one of the strong characters of modern-day golf, one who shows his emotions at a bad shot and at a good shot. The Walrus had won his first major championship. He went on that year to win nearly a half million dollars and to be named the number one golfer of the P.G.A. Tour. He was also the leader in putting with a 28.63 average per round and number one in breaking par. Altogether, it might be said that 1982 was Stadler's year.

53
THE MASTERS OF 1983

Severiano Ballesteros	68	70	73	69	280
Ben Crenshaw	76	70	70	68	284
Tom Kite	70	72	73	69	284
Tom Watson	70	71	71	73	285
Raymond Floyd	67	72	71	75	285
Craig Stadler	69	72	69	76	286
Hale Irwin	72	73	72	69	286
Lanny Wadkins	73	70	73	71	287
Dan Pohl	74	72	70	71	287
Gil Morgan	67	70	76	74	287

Seve Ballesteros, an international superstar of golf, wins the 1983 Masters.

Severiano Ballesteros, who had won the 1980 Masters at the age of twenty-three, won his second championship in a decisive manner by four strokes over a strong field. Playing conditions were horrible but moderated to fair on the final day. Torrential rains that swept the course caused extensive delays and lengthened the tournament by a day, with the finish coming on Monday in improved weather. That was only a preview of troubles yet to come for the ragged tournament. Another storm early Friday morning dumped so much water on the course that at 8:25 A.M. play was cancelled for the day. All day long the rain fell as greens

189

crews strove mightily to drain the course and clear the greens.

The second round finally got under way at eleven o'clock on Saturday. The field went out in threesomes, with the low forty-two scorers starting on the first tee and the remaining thirty-nine players starting on the tenth. Play was terribly slow because the golfers frequently had to stand aside to allow workers to mop the greens and fairways, which continued to gather water in the hollows.

Only a third of the field completed their second rounds, so it was impossible for the tournament committee to determine a thirty-six-hole cut.

The decision was this: Let those who had not finished so far complete their Saturday rounds on Sunday morning, and then the whole field would play their third rounds immediately afterward. The fourth round would be played on Monday.

Fortunately, the weather moderated somewhat, but the course was not the slick, fast Masters course it usually was. Not until Sunday were the greens near top speed.

Jack Nicklaus shot a respectable 73 on his first round, but he experienced some back pain during his play. Jack had had problems with a pinched nerve in the past. This time, perhaps aggravated by the cold rain and wind, his back tightened up so badly that he found himself unable to bend down to pick up his ball on a practice putt on Saturday morning. He had not yet started his second round, so, realizing he simply could not play, he withdrew from the tournament. It was only the second time in his career Jack had had to withdraw, the other time being the World Series of Golf in 1980, when he had similar back trouble.

The last two rounds were truly contested by only four players—Severiano Ballesteros, Tom Watson, Raymond Floyd, and Craig Stadler. Each of these players had won the Masters previously, so there was no question of experience versus inexperience in the final analysis.

At the end of the third round, Floyd and Stadler were tied for the lead at 210, six under par. Ballesteros was one stroke be-

After a long drive on No. 2, Seve reaches the green with his second shot and sinks his putt for an eagle.

hind at 211, Watson two strokes behind at 212.

On the last day, Ballesteros and Watson were paired together, and they played immediately in front of Stadler and Floyd, the final pair of the day.

Ballesteros immediately seized the lead with a brilliant start of birdie, eagle, par, birdie, which took him two shots in front of Floyd and three shots ahead of Stadler and Watson.

Seve birdied the first hole by hitting his seven-iron second to eight feet from the hole. He made the putt, birdie three. On the second hole, both Watson and he hit long drives and were able to reach the green with their second shots. The flagstick was set in the far back corner of the green, in a very difficult position behind the right bunker. Both players hit magnificent second shots onto the green, Tom nearly hitting the flagpole as the ball rolled by to finish sixteen feet from the cup. Seve's was equally beautiful, to fifteen feet away. Tom missed his eagle putt; Seve made his. Seve was then in the lead, two strokes ahead of Floyd and three ahead of Watson.

Seve parred the third hole, barely missing a twenty-footer for his birdie three. That day the cup had been placed only fifteen feet beyond the front bunker on the fourth green. It would take a magician to get close to the hole. Seve hit a two iron into the headwind absolutely perfectly, and the ball stopped two feet from the hole. Of course, he made his two.

Seve was three strokes in the lead now, and he played solid golf all the rest of the way to win. Tom Watson got within two strokes by eagling the eighth, but then he three-putted the ninth, which Ballesteros birdied. Neither Floyd nor Stadler was able to make any sort of move, and the result was that they fell back to let Ben Crenshaw and Tom Kite finish strongly and tie for second.

Ballesteros went on to win his second British Open championship in 1984 at St. Andrews, Scotland, in a classic showdown in the stretch with Tom Watson and Bernhard Langer. He had won his first Open in 1979 at Royal Lytham in England.

It was clear that Severiano Ballesteros had established himself as a true international superstar of golf.

54
THE MASTERS OF 1984

Ben Crenshaw	67	72	70	68	277
Tom Watson	74	67	69	69	279
David Edwards	71	70	72	67	280
Gil Morgan	73	71	68	67	280
Larry Nelson	76	69	66	70	281
Ronnie Black	71	74	69	68	282
Tom Kite	70	68	69	75	282
Mark Lye	69	66	73	74	282
David Graham	69	70	70	73	282
Fred Couples	71	73	67	72	282

At last, "Gentle Ben" Crenshaw broke through to win his first major championship. Ben had had a distinguished career as an amateur, and once he became a professional it was believed he might be the new dominating force on the professional scene.

Alas, he had several tragic finishes in tournaments he might have expected to win. He lost to David Graham at Oakland Hills on the third hole of a play-off for the P.G.A. Championship in 1979. Another time, with the 1975 U.S. Open title in clear view at Medinah, he dumped his seventy-first tee shot into the water to lose. He double-bogeyed the frightening seventeenth hole at St. Andrews when he had a chance to win there in 1978.

So this year, when Ben opened his Masters with a sparkling 34-33-67, the heads nodded and the experts said, "Wait until the seventy-second hole is finished, and we'll see where Crenshaw finishes."

At the end of the first day, played in sunny but sweater weather, there were five players within a stroke of Ben. Lee Trevino had 68 to stand alone in second place but then finished sadly with scores in the mid-70s for a 294 total, well down the list. Close behind Crenshaw there were four players tied for third place with 69, Masters rookie Mark Lye, Japan's Isao Aoki, David Graham, the Australian, and 1984 Phoenix Open winner, Tom Purtzer. Tom Watson recovered from a shaky 39 first nine with a more satisfactory second nine of 35 strokes for a 74 to remain in contention. There were eighteen players at 72 or better, so the tournament shaped up as one that would be hotly contested.

Ben's second round was a solid 72. In the meantime, Tom Kite and newcomer Mark

Lye were making their presence heard.

Mark Lye stands two inches over six feet in height. His appearance is quite a contrast to that of Ben Crenshaw, who is slightly built and a good five inches shorter. With his loping stride and long legs, Lye could be recognized from afar. He had a serious demeanor, too, never smiling as he galloped down the fairways of the Augusta National course. As we shall see, Lye was a serious contender for this title, and but for a remarkable final nine holes by Crenshaw he might well have captured this Masters title, a feat a first-time player rarely accomplishes.

In his second round, Lye shot the first nine in 31 strokes, just one stroke off the course record for the nine, and then proceeded to birdie No. 10. When his second shot at the eleventh stopped only ten feet from the cup, it appeared that the course record of 64 might be in jeopardy. But Mark mised the ten-footer and then unfortunately bogeyed the thirteenth. He was in at 138 after two rounds, leading the field by one stroke, Crenshaw's opening 67 having been followed by a 72 for 139.

Weather had been ideal for the first two rounds, but on Saturday in the third round there were two driving thunderstorms along with dangerously close lightning strikes, and the course was flooded. Play was halted for an hour while crews worked frantically in an attempt to mop up the greens and fairways. Then a second storm materialized and closed the play for the day with the last few groups of golfers still on the course.

Starting early the next morning, Lye and Kite went back to the twelfth hole, where they had been interrupted on Saturday. Lye proceeded to three-putt the ball, while Kite parred it, and, at that moment, Kite went into a tie for the tournament lead. Tom went on to birdie the eighteenth hole and took a one-stroke lead over Mark Lye, who double-bogeyed the sixteenth and finished with a 73.

Here is the way the scoreboard looked at the start of the final round:

Tom Kite	70	68	69	207
Mark Lye	69	66	73	208
Ben Crenshaw	67	72	70	209
David Graham	69	70	70	209
Tom Watson	74	67	69	210

There was no stopping Crenshaw that day after he put himself in a position to win with a birdie barrage in the early part of his last round. Ben was one stroke behind Tom Kite after seven holes, holes that Ben had done in one under par with a birdie on No. 2 and six pars. Then a brilliant third shot to within eight feet of the eighth hole helped him cash a birdie four and brought him into a tie for the lead. The ninth hole was especially difficult on the final day, with the flagstick placed in the lower third of the green, where shot after shot would arch high and land near the cup and then roll backward and downward off the front edge of the green. Ben's lofted pitch to the hole had considerable spin, but fortunately the ball held the green and came to rest only eight feet away. Down went the birdie three, his fourth birdie of the nine, and Ben had the lead by a stroke.

The tenth hole, always difficult with its demand for a perfect long draw down the hill into the start of Amen Corner, appeared to be a potential problem for Ben. His drive was long and was drawn properly, to the left, but his second shot was less than aggressive. He left the ball on the front right edge of the green and faced a difficult sixty-foot putt uphill and side-hill with a right-to-left break of about three feet. It was clear to everyone watching that the outcome of the tournament hung on Ben's ability to get down in two putts.

The gallery was hushed. Ben stepped up to the putt and made his customary pair of accelerating practice strokes as he viewed the hole, cocking his head sideways a couple of times. His stroke, well known for its smoothness and fluidity, could not have been better. On and on the ball tracked toward the hole. The gallery started to cheer in anticipation that it might go into the hole. Bang, right in the hole for the birdie three, and Ben Crenshaw had a lead he would never relinquish.

Kite and Lye were playing immediately behind Crenshaw on the final day. So they were in the tenth fairway, waiting for Ben to putt his horrendous sixty-foot snake on the tenth green. From their own experience with that green, they knew he had about an even chance of three-putting from that distance. When they saw the stroke and they heard the tremendous roar from the crowd, they knew he had his birdie three.

Later, Mark Lye said: "When we saw that putt go in, it just turned the lights out. You could see, too, that Tom was hurt as well." Kite was badly shaken by that putt and by the undoubtedly great pressure that only a golfer in contention can understand.

Kite bogeyed the tenth and met absolute disaster at No. 12 when his tee shot hit the water. He took a six there, closing with a 75 and sixth place in the tournament.

Crenshaw showed some weakness after his remarkable three at No. 10 when he bogeyed the eleventh. But, in spite of that momentary lapse, he went most courageously for the flagstick at the vicious par-three twelfth. The hole was cut in the far right corner near the back of the green and, of course, close to the water in the pond created out of Rae's Creek. He cut a six iron to within twelve feet of the hole and, most confidently, with his usual silken putting stroke, wafted the ball into the center of the hole. Birdie two for Ben Crenshaw!

The tournament was over right then. All Ben had to do then was preserve his lead. He played safe on both five-pars—the thirteenth and fifteenth holes—with their dangerous water hazards guarding the front of the greens. He made his birdie four at No. 15 anyway, with a delicate pitch over the pond to within fifteen feet of the hole. He stroked that putt in, too, right in the middle of the cup, gauging perfectly a ten-inch break from right to left.

When Ben got his four at the fifteenth, he was four strokes ahead of the field. Watson narrowed the gap to two strokes with a late rush, but Ben came to the eighteenth still two strokes ahead. Both Crenshaw and Watson parred the last hole in conventional style, and Gentle Ben had at last won his first major tournament.

After the presentation ceremony, he said, "This is really a sweet, sweet win. I don't think there will ever be a sweeter moment."

There was never a more popular victory in the Masters than that of Ben Crenshaw. Gentle Ben had at last won the major title that had eluded him so long.

55
THE MASTERS OF 1985

Bernhard Langer	72	74	68	68	282
Curtis Strange	80	65	68	71	284
Severiano Ballesteros	72	71	71	70	284
Raymond Floyd	70	73	69	72	284
Jay Haas	73	73	72	67	285
Craig Stadler	73	67	76	70	286
Gary Hallberg	68	73	75	70	286
Bruce Lietzke	72	71	73	70	286
Jack Nicklaus	71	74	72	69	286
Lee Trevino	70	73	72	72	287
David Graham	74	71	71	71	287
Tom Watson	69	71	75	72	287
Fred Couples	75	73	69	70	287

Bernhard Langer, twenty-seven-year-old German international star golfer, broke through to win his first major title when he captured the 1985 Masters Championship.

The first round was played in ideal weather, but diabolical pin positions took their usual toll at Augusta National. Only three players were able to break 70—Gary Hallberg with a 68, which featured two-putt birdies on the five-pars, the thirteenth and fifteenth, and a birdie on No. 17; Payne Stewart, in Scottish plus-fours with 69; and

Tom Watson, also with 69. Hallberg is the young player who wears a fedora with a wide brim to protect his skin from sunburn.

The first round was highlighted by an eagle two by Raymond Floyd at the seventeenth hole. He had struck a tremendous drive on the 400-yard-long hole and had only 117 yards to the hole. He figured he had to hit his second shot 122 yards and let it draw back toward the hole. The shot came off as planned. The ball hit, bit, and drew back into the hole fifteen feet away to the accompaniment of the screams of the tremendous gallery surrounding the green.

Another tournament oddity occurred when Jack Nicklaus had his first four-putt green at Augusta. It happened on the 205-yard fourth hole, also in the first round. Jack used a two iron. His tee shot carried to the front edge of the green. He had an uphill, side-hill putt about thirty feet long, and, trying not to go over a ridge near the ball, he left his first putt four feet short. He putted again and to his horror saw the ball slide five feet past the hole. Then, putting for a bogey, he missed once more, running four feet past the hole. At last he sank the

Bernhard Langer, the "Red Baron," breaks through to win his first major title—the 1985 Masters.

fourth putt, another dangerous twister for a double-bogey five.

Jack took his misfortune in stride, though, and played well on the rest of the round for a 73, six shots behind first-round leader Ben Crenshaw.

Raymond Floyd took the lead at the end of the third round on a fine 69, which included three birdies and an eagle against two bogeys.

Curtis Strange, who had shot an 80 on opening day and then promptly made reservations to fly home early, certain he would not make the cut, roared back into contention with a 65 second round and a 68 third round to lie just one stroke out of the lead held by Floyd at 212 strokes.

Also very much in contention were Bernhard Langer and Severiano Ballesteros, the foreign threats. Ballesteros, of course, had won the Masters in 1980 and in 1983, while Langer had almost won the British Open title from Ballesteros in 1984 at St. Andrews in a famous shootout that included Tom Watson as well. Langer had had some remarkably good luck on his third round. He was cruising along on the second nine six shots out of the lead when he pushed his tee shot into trouble in the right rough on the thirteenth hole. Facing the possibility of a bogey, or worse, he smashed a low one iron that amazingly jumped the creek in front of the green. His putt for an eagle was successful, and Bernhard was back in the hunt.

Bernhard had a similar good break on Sunday at the treacherous eleventh hole. He hooked his drive into trouble on the left, but this time his ball struck a tree and bounced to the right, back into the fairway. He was faced with a frightening 205-yard second shot to a green that usually requires no more than a five or six iron. He managed to put the ball on the back edge of the green and two-putt for a par that kept him in the chase with Curtis Strange at that time.

Let's go back to the dramatic scene that was about to develop on the final holes of the course. Curtis Strange was seven under par as he came to the tenth hole. Bernhard Langer was ahead of him at the eleventh and had just enjoyed the lucky break of escaping the woods on the left. Curtis's second shot was not as crisp as usual. His ball came to rest a good forty-five feet away from the hole, and he had a difficult uphill putt. Raymond Floyd, his playing partner, had hit an excellent second shot at No. 10, about seven feet from the hole. Raymond sank his putt and went to three under par. Strange, about four feet from the cup, missed his par to show his first weakness in two days. His last previous bogey had occurred on the first hole of the third round.

In the meantime, Langer at the twelfth hole was preparing to putt for a birdie two from about twelve feet away from the cup. He heard the groans from the Strange-

Floyd gallery but did not know immediately that the gap between Strange and him had narrowed to three strokes.

Strange proceeded to play the eleventh hole in conventional style but continued to show weakness. His first putt from a twenty-five foot distance was four feet short of the cup. Courageously, he holed the second putt and settled for his par four.

At that very moment, Langer dropped his twelve-footer for his birdie two at the twelfth. Strange's lead over Langer had dropped one more stroke. It was now Strange six under par, Langer four under par.

Langer played the thirteenth hole boldly and brilliantly with a long drive that curved around the dangerous corner near Rae's Creek. A crisp two iron took his second shot to the green on a perfect line for the flag. Another two feet of carry would have put him within a foot or two of the cup. His ball rolled back down a slope, about twenty feet away from the hole.

Strange played the vicious short twelfth with a shot to the back edge of the green.

As Langer was putting for an eagle three on the par-five thirteenth, Strange sank his twenty-foot birdie putt from the edge of the twelfth green. Strange was now seven under par.

A tremendous roar went up from the crowd around the twelfth green, easily heard by Langer on the thirteenth green, 500 yards away. But Langer was apparently not disturbed by it. He did not hole his eagle putt but made a successful two-putt for a birdie four. So he headed for the fourteenth hole five under par, two strokes behind Strange.

Strange drove well at the treacherous thirteenth, no doubt encouraged by his two at twelve. He was safely in the middle of the fairway at a point 225 yards from the green. He took the head cover off his metal five wood, and the crowd screamed in delight, knowing that Curtis was going for the green in two.

As a matter of historical interest, Ben Hogan, in the same situation when he won the Masters in 1953, did not attempt to make the green on his second shot. He laid up in front of the creek, pitched on, and made his four. Hogan played the fifteenth with the dangerous lake in front of the green the same way, cautiously but safely.

In 1954, once more in a similar tactical situation, Billy Joe Patton, leading the tournament at the time, went for the thirteenth green and came to a disastrous end in the water, eventually losing the tournament to Sam Snead.

The crowd lining the side of the thirteenth fairway was absolutely still as Strange made his swing. Sadly, he came off the shot at impact, a fault that caused a loss of potential distance. The result was that the ball landed short of Rae's Creek and tumbled in, but with enough speed so that it ended on the far edge of the creek in water no more than an inch deep. Strange would have a chance to play the ball out of the water. He decided to do so rather than take the penalty shot and play for the green on his fourth stroke. He would try to splash the ball out with his sand wedge in much the same way a bunker shot is played, with his right foot in six inches of water and his left foot on the grassy bank. Strange blasted at the ball. It popped six feet in the air, but not high enough or far enough to escape the deep bank of vindictive Rae's Creek. Horror-stricken again and helpless to do anything about it, he watched the ball come rolling back down the slope, fortunately not all the way back into the water, but down near the water's edge only inches from true disaster, an unplayable lie in water too deep for him to consider playing it. He could try to pitch out again.

This time Curtis pitched out safely onto the green, but the ball rolled far from the hole. Two putts later, he was down in a bogey six and had fallen to six under par and was now only one stroke ahead of Langer, who was then parring the fourteenth in normal fashion, on the green above the hole with his second shot and down in two putts for his four.

Langer drove so far on the par-five fif-

Bernhard Langer tees off at No. 14, five under par and two strokes behind the leader, Curtis Strange.

teenth hole that he had only a four iron to the green. He lofted a high shot, which settled down on the back edge of the green. His putt was a tricky one with a great deal of break to the right. Nicklaus, faced with the identical putt a few minutes ahead of Bernhard, had three-putted the green to end any chance Jack had of closing in on the leaders. Langer's putt, cross-handed, was a beautiful one nearly holed. He made his short second putt and went to six under par to pull into a tie at that mark with Strange, who had just parred the fourteenth to remain at six under par.

Langer's tee shot on the water-filled sixteenth drifted just over the back of the green down the slope a few feet. He had a most difficult shot, a putt or chip to the hole only twenty feet away but downhill on a glassy surface. It was doubtful that he could stop the ball anywhere near the hole. Bern-

hard elected to putt the ball and, with just a tiny tap, was able to get the ball onto the green, and slowly, under no more than the momentum of gravity alone, the ball drifted down the slope and stopped very close to the hole. It was truly a magnificent example of touch. He made his three to remain six under par.

Strange, now on the fifteenth hole, hit a fine drive that split the fairway in the middle. Once more he was faced with the decision of whether or not to try to carry the water in front of the green. He knew from the roar of the crowd that Langer had birdied the hole.

Curtis decided not to lay up. He struck a four iron and again came off the ball slightly. He missed carrying the water by no more than a foot or two. The ball struck the far bank and rolled back into a watery grave.

His pitch to the green was a weak one, and another run-up shot was fair, but Strange bogeyed the hole to fall five under par and one stroke behind Langer.

Langer played the seventeenth hole aggressively, with a long drive and a pitch to fourteen feet from the hole. His cross-handed putt found the hole.

Bernhard, normally a stoic Teuton, rarely showing emotion, gestured in triumph as his ball disappeared into the hole for the birdie he needed so desperately. He was now seven under par, two strokes ahead of Strange. Bernhard appeared to be the winner unless Strange could pull a miracle or two out of his bag.

Langer struggled home on the eighteenth. His drive was safe, but his second went into the right-hand bunker. He blasted out well but could not hole the six-foot putt that resulted. His score was 68, four under par for a total of 282.

Curtis parred the sixteenth but played No. 17 weakly, having to chip from the right edge and save his par with a four-foot putt. Needing a birdie to tie, Strange stumbled in on the last hole, his second shot short of the green and his run-up chip too long. His putt from six feet away never had a chance to go in. Bernhard Langer, the "Red Baron," had at last won his first major championship.

LANGER'S FINAL ROUND—1985

Here is a stroke-by-stroke, hole-by-hole analysis of Bernhard Langer's final round of 69 that swept him past Curtis Strange to victory:

No. 1—400 yards, par four: Driver, eight iron to twenty feet. Two putts for par four.

No. 2—555 yards, par five: Driver, seven iron, sand wedge into front bunker, blast to thirty feet from hole on fringe, two putts, bogey six.

No. 3—360 yards, par four: Drive with one iron, pitching wedge to fourteen feet. One putt for birdie three.

No. 4—205 yards, par three: Four iron to twenty-five feet. Two putts for par three.

No. 5—435 yards, par four: Driver, eight iron to eighteen feet. One putt for birdie three.

No. 6—180 yards, par three: Six iron to fifteen feet. Two putts for par three.

No. 7—360 yards, par four: One iron, nine iron to twelve feet, two putts for par four.

No. 8—535 yards, par five: Driver, driver on second to forty yards short of green, sand wedge to twenty feet, two putts for par five.

No. 9—435 yards, par four: Driver, seven iron to eighteen feet, two putts for par four.

Par out: 4, 5, 4,   3, 4, 3,   4, 5, 4—36
Langer out: 4, 6, 3,   3, 3, 3,   4, 5, 4—35

No. 10—485 yards, par four: Driver, four iron to front edge, chip to three feet, one putt for par four.

No. 11—455 yards, par four: Driver, five iron to twenty-eight feet, two putts for par four.

No. 12—155 yards, par three: Eight iron to thirteen feet, one putt for birdie two.

No. 13—465 yards, par five: Driver, five iron to twenty-two feet, two putts for birdie.

No. 14—405 yards, par four: Driver, eight iron to twenty-five feet, two putts for par four.

No. 15—500 yards, par five: Driver, five iron to thirty feet, two putts for birdie four.

No. 16—170 yards, par three: Six iron to twenty-four feet, down back fringe, chip to three feet, one putt for par three.

No. 17—400 yards, par four: Driver, eight iron to fourteen feet, one putt for birdie three.

No. 18—405 yards, par four: Driver, four iron to right bunker, blast to ten feet, two putts for bogey five.

Par in: 4, 4, 3,   5, 4, 5,   3, 4, 4—36
Langer in: 4, 4, 2,   4, 4, 4,   3, 3, 5—33

56
THE MASTERS OF 1986

Jack Nicklaus	74	71	69	65	279
Greg Norman	70	72	68	70	280
Tom Kite	70	74	68	68	280
Seve Ballesteros	71	68	72	70	281
Nick Price	79	69	63	71	282
Jay Haas	76	69	71	67	283
Tom Watson	70	74	68	71	283
Tsuneyuki Nakajima	70	71	71	72	284
Payne Stewart	75	71	69	69	284
Bob Tway	70	73	71	70	284

In one of the most thrilling and dramatic finishes in all of Masters history, Jack Nicklaus captured a record sixth Masters title and, at last, won his twentieth major championship, a personal goal he had been seeking unsuccessfully since his last major victory in the U.S. Open Championship of 1980 at Baltusrol.

The weather this year was clear but cool, and for the first two days gusty winds up to twenty miles per hour swept the course. The greens were truly frighteningly fast, doubly cut by the mowers, and the cups were situated in devilish positions.

The first day saw only four scores under 70, including two by relatively unknown players—Ken Green, who had qualified by reason of his winning the Buick Open, a minor P.G.A. meet held opposite the British Open; and Bill Kratzert, a journeyman professional who had won four P.G.A. events in ten years and who had fallen at one time to 166th on the P.G.A. list. Sadly, both early leaders fell off in later rounds to finish well down the list.

Close pursuers on the first day were Gary Koch and T. C. Chen with 69s, while not far behind at 70 were Tom Kite, Tom Watson, and Greg Norman. Severiano Ballesteros was at 71, while Jack Nicklaus was in at 74. Jack complained about the slickness of the greens. He claimed that there was no possibility of putting offensively and said that every putt of six-foot length or more had to be struck cautiously so as not to three-putt. There were, in fact, several greens four-putted by established players. The players were truly running scared of the Augusta greens. Gary Player was observed practicing fifteen-foot putts on the practice green. Someone asked him, "What are you doing?"

He replied "Practicing one-inch putts." For, in fact, the power to carry the ball one inch would cause it to roll ten to fifteen feet on the greens, which were like polished marble.

On the second day the weather continued to be cool and windy. The cups were in friendlier places on the greens, as if the course had spoken and said, "Now that you know how difficult these greens can be, we'll give you a better chance today to hole a few putts."

The colorful, handsome Spaniard Severiano Ballesteros, Masters champion in 1980 and 1983 and international champion as well, is recognized as probably the greatest golfer of the modern day. He showed his formidable skill as he added a 68 to his first-round 71. His total of 139 put him in the lead ahead of a mixed batch of ten golfers who were in at 142. The only "names" were Greg Norman, the Australian star at 70-72, 142, and 1985 Masters champion Bernhard Langer, who followed up a weak first-round 74 with a strong second-round 68 on Friday. Jack Nicklaus made a move toward the top with a 71, still complaining that he could not hole a putt of reasonable length. At 145 Nicklaus was six strokes behind Ballesteros as the third round began.

Greg Norman seized the lead on Saturday with a sparkling 68 for a 210 total, which put him one stroke ahead of a strong group of four golfers: Bernhard Langer with 69 for 211; Seve Ballesteros with 72 for 211; Nick Price, who skyrocketed from nine strokes off the pace to 211, only one stroke behind, while posting a new course record score of 63, which included no fewer than ten birdies and one bogey.

Jack Nicklaus had not yet given up hope of winning this, his sixth Masters, as he scored a strong 69 for 214 on his third round to be four strokes behind the leader. Norman was at 210 and one behind Ballesteros, who was at 211. Tom Kite also moved into contention with an excellent 68 on his third round. At 212, Tom was only two strokes out of the lead. As we shall see, Kite, Norman, and Ballesteros all contributed to the dramatic fireworks of the final day, the incred-

Jack Nicklaus gets a congratulatory hug from son and caddie, Jackie, as "The Bear" completes his miraculous come-from-behind round.

ible race of Nicklaus past the front-running field.

Many of the experts were now practically conceding the tournament to Severiano Ballesteros, though they were not discounting the chances of the long-driving Norman, who was, in fact, one stroke in the lead as the day began.

On the final day, Jack Nicklaus was playing steady, even-par golf on the front nine. Jack had made a remarkable save of his par five at the uphill eighth hole when he smashed a second shot out of the woods through an opening between the trees "no bigger than this," as he later said, demonstrating with his hands held a few inches apart.

Jack had reached the par-four ninth green with his second shot. His ball lay in a favorable position on the green in a fairly level spot about twelve feet from the hole, with a slight break from right to left. Kite and Ballesteros were at that moment approaching the five-par eighth hole, Kite 125 yards away, Seve about 75 yards away from the flagstick. Suddenly a tremendous roar went up from the eighth green. Kite had holed his third shot for an eagle three to go to five under par. Jack Nicklaus backed away from his putt.

Then another roar went up from No. 8. Seve had holed his wedge shot for an eagle three, too. He was now in the lead at eight under par, one stroke ahead of Greg Norman.

Jack knew he had to make that birdie at the ninth so as not to lose any more ground to Ballesteros or Norman.

Jack's son, Jackie, was caddying for his father that day, helping him to "read the greens." They both intensely studied the line of the putt at the ninth hole. Then, after the customary Nicklaus stare at the hole, as if he dared it not to receive his putt, there was the slow backswing of his new, extremely wide-bladed, even awkward-looking putter. The results were good, no matter what the putter looked like. The ball dropped into the center of the cup, and Jack was only four strokes behind the leader. He was off and running.

Down to the tenth hole now. A tremendous drive 275 yards long, a sweet iron to twenty-five feet below the cup, not close enough in Jack's opinion. Yet once again the putt found the hole for a birdie three. The roar of the crowd was almost a hole-in-one yell, sustained and reverberating out of the Amen Corner back to the ninth hole, where Seve Ballesteros heard it and took a bogey on the hole. He had driven into the woods, chipped out in front of the green, and pitched much too far onto the green to be able to save his par. Ballesteros now was seven under par through the ninth hole, tied with Greg Norman at that figure.

Jack surged on with another birdie at the eleventh hole after a long sweet drive and a

crisply struck iron to twenty feet from the hole. When that putt went in, Jack was only two strokes behind Ballesteros.

Now it was on to the three-par twelfth hole, always treacherous with its shifting winds and dangerous water surrounding the front and right side of the green. Overly cautious now, Jack pulled his short-iron tee shot to the front left side of the green. His situation was a nasty one as the hole had been cut at the bottom of a slope near the back of the green, a good forty paces away. Jack could not execute that chip successfully. Perhaps no one could have done it. The result was a bogey four for Nicklaus. Perhaps here he felt he had lost his momentum and, with it, the tournament.

In the meantime, Tom Kite began to move toward the top. He birdied the tenth hole after a marvelous second shot on the long four-par to within ten feet of the hole. As Tom did this, Greg Norman, his playing partner, got into serious trouble. His drive bounced safely out of the left woods, but he pulled a long iron to the green, made a trip into the left bunker, and it was a double-bogey six on the hole for Greg. Norman thus fell to five under par, two behind Ballesteros.

Now Jack Nicklaus was confronted with the dogleg five-par thirteenth with its dangerous water hazard in front of the green. Jack thundered an extremely long drive, just barely missing the meandering rocky creek on the left. His lie in the fairway was a flat one, which is unusual on that normally severely tilted fairway. A strong three iron took him to the green, and two putts later he had his fourth birdie in five holes and was then five under par.

Jack played the fourteenth wisely, placing his second shot past the hole, where it had to be for utmost safety. He nearly holed his putt but settled for par.

At the fifteenth hole, I'm sure he recalled how he had driven the eighteenth hole at St. Andrews to win the Open there in 1970. Jack put every ounce of power he had into his tee shot. Straight down the fairway, the ball landed and rolled and rolled past the 300-yard mark. He said to Jackie, "Do you

An emotional Jack Nicklaus gets his unprecedented sixth Masters jacket from defending champion, Bernhard Langer.

think a three [an eagle] might do some good here?" Jack's answer to his own question was an almost perfect three-iron second.

The ball soared high and dropped softly on the hard green no more than fifteen feet away from the hole. Again, it seemed to be foreordained that he would sink that eagle putt, for that is just what he did, right in the center of the cup. Jack crouched over the ball for twenty seconds before he drew back his putter head on that most satisfying eagle three. He was now seven under par, while Ballesteros, coming down the fifteenth fairway, was riding at nine under par. Ballesteros would certainly be expected to birdie or even eagle the fifteenth hole himself.

When Jack Nicklaus hit his tee shot at the sixteenth hole, Seve Ballesteros was several hundred yards away on the fifteenth fairway, about to hit his second shot to the fifteenth green. Seve's drive had been a tremendous one, slightly more than 300 yards. He had 205 yards to the flagstick,

only an iron shot for this very strong player.

At that moment Nicklaus's ball landed on the sixteenth green about twenty feet to the right of the flag, checked a little, and then began to drift down the slope directly toward the hole. Closer and closer it crept as the screams from the spectators reached new highs not only in intensity but also in duration.

Ballesteros knew that Jack had made another marvelous shot—whether a hole-in-one or merely a leaner on the flagstick he could not tell.

There is no doubt that Ballesteros was disturbed by the monstrous roars of the crowd, which seemed to be unending, one after the other, as Jack made his eagle at No. 15 and now his tee shot at No. 16.

Jack's ball nearly did go into the hole for an ace but then, just barely missing the cup, continued at a slow pace, stopping about three feet from the hole. Jack said later, "It was a nasty putt," but he did sink it for a

Still a Master at age 46.

birdie two and went to the seventeenth tee only one stroke behind Ballesteros, who had yet to finish play at the fifteenth.

Back in the fairway, Seve debated between a four iron and a five iron. Later he said he should have taken the five. Perhaps the four iron was a more cautious selection, a club he thought would surely enable him to carry the pond in front of the green. The gallery was pin-drop quiet as he made his swing. They knew, of course, that he would hit a high soft iron straight at the flagstick. He would get his own eagle three or, at the worst, a birdie four.

Sadly, Ballesteros made a bad golf swing, a rare occurrence for him. He came across the ball and hooked it far short of the green, and the ball went kerplunk into the pond.

As the ripples spread, one could see the dismay on Ballesteros's face. He couldn't believe what he had done. He still had a chance to save his par with a good pitch to the pin. He suffered a penalty stroke, of course, and then, after dropping his ball short of the pond, pitched his fourth shot over the water onto the green. Seve is an expert at that pitch shot, but this shot was not one of his best. The ball rolled a good twenty feet beyond the hole. Almost in a daze, Seve two-putted for a bogey six. He had fallen to eight under par.

Now Jack Nicklaus was attacking the seventeenth hole. Groans went up from his gallery as his tee shot darted to the left of the fairway. The television commentators admitted that they did not know where Jack's ball had gone. He was in trouble, no doubt.

Fortunately, his lie, although in the left rough, was not a bad one. Jack gave a mighty swing from about 125 yards away and once again showed his skill as the ball came to rest only fifteen feet to the left of the hole. He would have a slippery putt, slightly downhill, but there was no severe break to complicate matters. It was one of those fifteen-foot putts that Jack has holed so many times under pressure over his lifetime of championship golf. I think Jack knew he would make the putt because he approached it with his usual cautious study, helped by his son with the slope analysis. Jack stroked the ball smoothly, and it never had a chance to miss the cup. Perfect speed, perfect direction. Jack gave a yell of delight and brandished his putter in the air as he sprang away from the hole.

When Jack made his three at No. 17, he went to nine under par and into sole leadership of the tournament. Ballesteros and Kite were both at eight under par after finishing the sixteenth hole with mutually difficult pars. Seve saved his with a delicate improvised stroke with his putter, using an awkward stance with one foot in the left bunker, one foot on the edge of the green. Kite flew his tee shot over the green and putted back up the fringe of the green and let the ball roll down to about eight feet from the hole. He sank the nerve-wracking putt for his three.

In the meantime, Greg Norman, still reeling from the effects of his double-bogey at No. 10, was fighting back valiantly. He birdied the five-par thirteenth, on in two and two putts, and had only a 190-yard second shot to No. 15. He counted a birdie four there and then nearly duplicated Jack Nicklaus's "almost ace" at No. 16 with a curling tee shot that ended only three feet from the hole.

Nicklaus was now playing the eighteenth hole. His drive was a beautiful one, cut slightly to the right of the mid-fairway bunker. His second shot with a six iron, however, was not long to reach the hole, which was cut on the far back right side of the green. Jack faced an extremely difficult fifty-foot uphill putt, about forty feet up the slope and then to the hole on a level plateau.

If Jack Nicklaus ever needed a two-putt in his life, he needed it now. Calling on all his putting skill and the memories of many long putts he had made on slippery greens in the past, Jack stroked that putt firmly and well. On and on it came up the slope, and then it broke slightly to the right as if it

Seve Ballesteros takes time out for an official ruling.

would actually go into the hole. It stopped a mere six inches short of the cup, but Jack Nicklaus knew he had his final par and his final nine-under-par score of 279.

As Jack Nicklaus made his final par at the eighteenth, Ballesteros was attempting to putt on the seventeenth hole. He had hit a poor second shot to the green, leaving himself above the hole and to the left with a huge left-to-right break in the green. He tried to jam the ball into the cup for a desperate birdie that would tie him with Nicklaus. His ball missed the cup and rolled ten feet beyond. The three-putt that resulted ended Ballesteros's last chance for his third Masters championship.

Jack would win this tournament if Kite and Norman, still on the course, did not tie or beat him.

A bad tee shot to the left at the seventeenth left Norman under a tree in the rough. He improvised a magical run-up shot to about twelve feet from the hole. Norman sank that birdie three and was then tied with Nicklaus. A par at No. 18 would bring a play-off; a birdie would yet win for Norman.

Kite, too, had a chance. He had held his eight-under-par position since his own birdie at the fifteenth. If he could birdie the eighteenth, he, too, might tie Nicklaus and force a play-off.

Both players drove well into the fairway at No. 18. Kite struck a magnificent iron to about twelve feet to the right of the hole. Sadly, Greg Norman made a poor shot, his ball tailing to the right into the crowd around the green. His chip to the hole was impossible, but he did the best he could, stopping the ball about fifteen feet away from the hole and above it.

First Norman missed his putt, and then Kite failed, too, by a mere inch or two. Nicklaus had scored a record-tying 30 on the second nine, a 65 on his round, and had sprung past a host of players to capture his sixth Masters championship, his twentieth major championship.

The sight and sound of the crowd cheering Nicklaus in his last hundred yards up the hill to the eighteenth green will be long remembered. Jack admitted that there were tears in his eyes as he realized he might be the winner. No one, either, will ever forget the warm, spontaneous hug of Jack Nicklaus and his son, Jackie, on the eighteenth green after the last putt had been holed.

Without doubt, this was the greatest Master Tournament in history and in years to come may well be determined to have been the greatest golf tournament of all time.

57
THE RECORD IS FINALLY BROKEN

Twenty-nine-year-old Nick Price, of South Africa, playing in only his second Masters, had little idea that his second round at the 1986 Masters would turn out to be of historic Masters significance, that he would break the course record score of 64 that had stood for forty-six years since it was originally set by Lloyd Mangrum in 1940. That score had been tied five times since—by Jack Nicklaus in 1965, Maurice Bembridge in 1974, Hale Irwin in 1975, Gary Player in 1976, and Miller Barber in 1979.

Price was playing early on Tuesday morning after an opening round of 79 that included six three-putt greens. His drive at the first hole did not carry the bunker on the right. He splashed out well short of the green, wedged to about twenty-five feet, and two-putted for a bogey five. Then the fireworks began. He cashed a birdie four at the second hole with a pitching wedge to six feet from the hole and sank the putt. At that point Nick was four over par for the tournament.

At the third hole he hit his second shot over the shallow elevated green but pitched back within three feet of the hole and got his par four. He parred the fourth hole with a three iron to twenty feet away and took two putts for his three. At the difficult 435-yard fifth hole he drove well and then drilled a five iron to within twelve feet of the hole. He cashed his second birdie and was then three over par for the tournament.

At the three-par sixth Nick hit a six iron, which stopped on the fringe of the green twenty feet from the hole. Down went the putt, his third birdie of the round, and he was now two over par for the tournament. He parred the seventh in normal fashion, driving so far that he had no more than a pitching wedge to the green. He two-putted from twenty-five feet.

Nick birdied the eighth hole with a drive, a three wood short of the green, and a wedge to six feet—birdie number four.

He had a routine par at the ninth, so he turned in 33 strokes, still one over par for the tournament.

Although he was aware that the course record was 64, it had not yet entered his

Nick Price goes down in the history books with his remarkable course record 63 (Was it fate that his caddie happened to be wearing the number 63 on his white coveralls?)

mind that he might have a chance to equal it until he had finished the first four holes of the second nine. The tenth hole yielded a birdie three when he placed his six-iron shot only four feet from the hole. Then the eleventh hole fell, too, to his birdie barrage when his five-iron second stopped only fifteen feet away. He conquered the pesky twelfth hole with a seven iron to twenty feet from the hole. He drained that putt, too, for his third birdie in a row. Now he was two under par for the tournament.

The scoreboards were now showing Price's remarkable charge at the record in one red number after another. From green numbers showing him over par to red figures showing him now well under par, Price's march down and through the Amen Corner was being greeted by tremendous roars from the crowds as a red 1 and a red 2 were inserted in the score line on the scoreboards alongside Price's name.

Nick said later than when he got his two on the twelfth he started thinking about his chances of tying or even breaking the record. He was then six under par and would need three more birdies to break the record. He felt that with his long-driving ability he might be able to make birdie fours at the five-par thirteenth and fifteenth holes. He did just that, but he did it the hard way, laying up in front of the troublesome water at both holes and wedging to six feet at No. 13, to only four feet at No. 15.

Nick was now eight under par for the round, five strokes under for the tournament. He needed par on the sixteenth, seventeenth, and eighteenth holes to tie the record; one birdie and two pars to break the record.

The cup was cut on the left side of the sixteenth hole, and there was a raised portion of the green to the right of the hole.

Nick struck a five-iron shot that drew

Hole	1	2	3	4	5	6	7	8	9	Out	10	11	12	13	14	15	16	17	18	In	Totals
Yardage	400	555	360	205	435	180	360	535	435	3465	485	455	155	465	405	500	170	400	405	3440	6905
Par	4	5	4	3	4	3	4	5	4	36	4	4	3	5	4	5	3	4	4	36	72
Player	5	4	4	3	3	2	4	4	4	33	3	3	2	4	4	4	2	4	4	30	63

OFFICIAL SCORECARD   Saturday, April 12, 1986

ATTEST _Bruce Lietzke_

I HAVE CHECKED MY SCORE HOLE BY HOLE.
PLAYER SIGNATURE _Nick Price_

Nick Price (South Africa)

This is the actual score card of Nick Price when he shot his record score of 63, breaking the 46-year-old record originally set by Lloyd Mangrum. Note the circled birdies.

gently from right to left. He gauged the effect of the slope of the mound almost perfectly. His ball landed to the right, took the slope, and ran slowly but surely right for the hole.

The crowd screamed in delight, hoping for a hole-in-one. The ball grazed the cup and rolled a mere two feet beyond. Price sank the birdie two and was now on the track of a new record.

The seventeenth hole nearly brought him another birdie as his fifteen-foot putt barely failed to hole. Then, to the eighteenth and a little show of nerves.

Nick's drive was long but hooked to the left, fortunately missing the fairway bunkers. His second shot to the elevated green, normally no more than 160 to 165 yards, was 192 yards long. The flagstick was well back on the green.

Nick struck a marvelous four iron that came to rest to the right of the hole, thirty feet above the cup. The putt was downhill on green ice, and, if he missed hitting the cup, his ball would most certainly roll six to ten feet beyond it and jeopardize his chances at the record.

He putted boldly, and, though he did not hole the putt, he did touch the cup edge. The ball spun around the edge of the hole and then decided not to drop, ending inches away in front of the cup.

Nick, of course, tapped in that short putt and was now the sole possessor of the course record score of 63 at Augusta National Golf Club.

An oddity about Nick Price's record score of 63 is that his caddie, David McNeilly, was wearing the number 63 on his white coveralls, a number assigned at random.

Coincidence or fate, we'll never know.

58
THE MAJOR TOURNAMENTS: RECORDS OF THE MASTERS CHAMPIONS

BEN HOGAN: Masters 1951, 1953; U.S. Open 1948, 1950, 1951, 1953; P.G.A. 1946, 1948; British Open 1953. Total major championships, nine.

JACK NICKLAUS: Masters 1963, 1965, 1966, 1972, 1975, 1986; U.S. Open 1962, 1967, 1972, 1980; P.G.A. 1963, 1971, 1973, 1975, 1980; British Open 1966, 1970, 1978. Total major championships, eighteen. U.S. Amateur 1959, 1961.

ARNOLD PALMER: Masters 1958, 1960, 1962, 1964; U.S. Open 1960; British Open 1961, 1962. Total major championships, seven. U.S. Amateur 1954.

GENE SARAZEN: Masters 1935; U.S. Open 1922, 1932; P.G.A. 1922, 1923, 1933; British Open 1932. Total major championships, seven.

SAM SNEAD: Masters 1949, 1952, 1954; P.G.A. 1942, 1949, 1951; British Open 1946. Total major championships, seven.

BYRON NELSON: Masters 1937, 1942; U.S. Open 1939; P.G.A. 1940, 1945. Total major championships, five.

GARY PLAYER: Masters 1961, 1974, 1978; U.S. Open 1965; P.G.A. 1962, 1972; British Open 1959, 1968, 1974. Total major championships, nine.

BILLY CASPER, JR.: Masters 1970; U.S. Open 1959, 1966. Total major championships, three.

RALPH GULDAHL: Masters 1939; U.S. Open 1937, 1938. Total major championships, three.

CARY MIDDLECOFF: Masters 1955; U.S. Open 1949, 1956. Total major championships, three.

JACK BURKE: Masters 1956; P.G.A. 1956. Total major championships, two.

DOUG FORD: Masters 1957; P.G.A. 1955. Total major championships, two.

HENRY PICARD: Masters 1938; P.G.A. 1939. Total major championships, two.

CRAIG WOOD: Masters 1941; U.S. Open 1941. Total major championships, two.

TOM WATSON: Masters 1977; British Open 1975, 1977, 1980. Total major championships, four.

SEVERIANO BALLESTEROS: Masters 1980, 1983; British Open 1979, 1984. Total major championships, four.

Sam Snead chips to the pin at No. 13.

59
HOW TO BREAK 90
AT AUGUSTA NATIONAL

A Hole-by-Hole Experiment in Imaginary Golf

With a carefully arranged scenario, I staged a round of golf at Augusta National that would show the average golfer how he might break 90 (averaging fives on each hole) on that wonderful golf course. I was even assigned top Masters caddy Leon McClattey, who wore a "Taylor" nameplate on his back, just like those for the champion players in the Masters itself.

Through the use of what I call "subjective photography," the reader is put into the person of the participant, as much as it is possible to do so through the camera lens, and views exactly what the golfer is seeing as he performs the athletic movement of striking the golf ball. In some of the photographs, the ball is actually caught in the act

of moving away from the clubhead in the shot. I believe that this adds to the ability of the reader to experience vicariously the thrill of playing golf at Augusta National Golf Club, the home of the famous Masters Tournament.

Join me now in a highly involving round of imaginary golf that I trust will be pleasurable, informative, and provocative reading.

Hole No. 1, 400 Yards, Par Four
White Pine
375 Yards from Your Tee

You are on the high first tee at Augusta National Golf Club. You have the feeling that you are almost suspended in space, looking out over the valley extending northward toward the first green. You are surprised to find that the teeing area is quite small. As you tee your ball up, you wonder whether you are about to swing from the exact spot that Arnold Palmer or Ben Hogan used in some past Masters Tournament.

Ahead of you is an awesome sight, a

*Portions of the following descriptions (not including the notes on each hole) are based on or quoted from commentaries by Robert Tyre Jones, Jr., and are used with the kind permission of Augusta National Golf Course and Doubleday and Company, coming from materials supplied to the press and public, *Spectators Suggestions for the Masters Tournament* by Robert Tyre Jones, Jr., and Augusta National Golf Clubs.

213

difficult par four of 375 yards. You will drive, or attempt to drive, to a flat plateau fairway some twelve-and-a-half feet above the level of your teeing ground. On the right side of the fairway is a monstrous yawning trap that appears to be twenty-five yards long by ten yards wide. It has been known to catch half-hit tee shots, driven against a heavy wind. It has a high forward bank sloping outward toward the green, so you resolve to avoid that bunker by staying to the left of it with your tee shot.

On the left side of the fairway and the right as well (to the right side of the bunker) are moderately dense woods. You do not want to go either far left or far right, or your second shot to the green will be completely blocked out.

You drive from the tee. Hands trembling a bit at being in this historic spot, but you hit a fine drive, curving slightly to the right, but on the fairway. You almost carry the valley and reach the plateau. From the tee it appears that, although your ball is short of the crest of the hill, you should be able to see the green as you make your second shot.

Your second shot now is toward a very small green on a still slightly rising fairway level. On the left of the green there is another moderate-sized bunker. The flagstick is on the left center of the green, so you resolve to head for the right side of the green or right side of the fairway, if you cannot reach the green.

Your shot is from an uphill position, so your stance must be taken carefully so as to avoid losing balance in the swing. Your caddy, Leon McClattey, advises that you can hit everything you've got, so you take your three wood. You are approximately 200 yards away from the hole. The ball is lying on very closely cropped grass. You swing and hit an excellent straight wood shot to a few yards short of the bunker on the left.

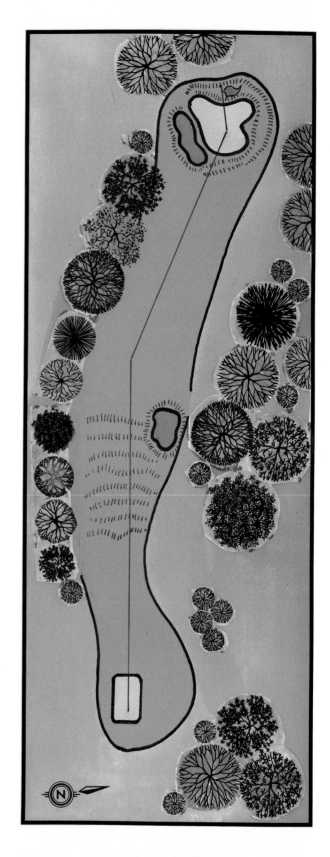

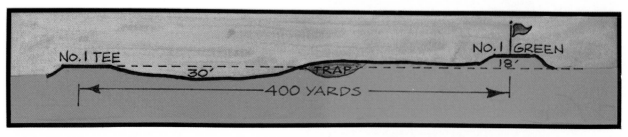

The drive from the first tee.

The chip-shot to the first green.

With a prayer of thanksgiving that you didn't go into that bunker, you prepare for a chip shot to the pin, about thirty-five yards away.

The green is also plateaued, and it is obvious that if you fly the ball onto the flat part of the green it is unlikely that you will be able to stop the ball near the pin. The only shot left is a chip onto the green into the lower area so that the ball can run up the slope to the pin.

You take an eight iron and pick out a spot on the lower level to land the ball so that it can run to the hole. The fairway lie again is a tight one, the grass very short under the ball.

You chip successfully, and the ball hits the green about where you planned that it should go and runs fifteen feet beyond the hole. All in all, a good shot under the circumstances. You realize at once that this green and probably all the others are very fast and resolve to chip more delicately on subsequent occasions.

Your putt seems to be straight into the cup. Leon advises you that the ball may break an inch or two right to left. You putt the ball and miss on the left. The ball rolls another eighteen inches beyond the hole. Rather shaken, you putt again and hole the ball for a successful opening five on the first hole of the Masters.

Hole	Par	Your Score	±5s
1	4	5	Even

Notes on Hole No. 1   Sunday, April 14, 1968, was Roberto de Vicenzo's forty-fifth birthday, and when he holed his second shot for an eagle two at the start of his last round of 1968, the entire gallery sang, "Happy birthday, Roberto, happy birthday to you!" This was the round that tied him for the lead, but Roberto lost because of an incorrectly totaled scorecard.

In 1970, Takaaki Kono scored an eagle two on his second round. He ended with 68 on the round and finished in a tie for thirteenth in the tournament, a fine showing on his first appearance in the Masters.

Hole No. 2, 555 Yards, Par Five
Red Dogwood
475 Yards from Your Tee

Professional Strategy: Place drive to left of bunker at right center of fairway 230 yards away so as to catch forward kick off left center of fairway beyond bunker and have a chance to hit the second green on the second shot. Although this is the longest hole of the course, it still follows one of the guiding principles of Augusta National's builders—that even the par fives should be reachable in two excellent shots.

Keep your drive left and short of the same bunker, aim right on second shot so as to leave a 75- to 100-yard pitch over the green side bunkers for a possible par five.

Your Strategy: Leon points out to you the best and shortest line for you to take on the second hole, the line to the left of the fairway bunker looming ominously straight ahead. He assures you that you cannot reach

The drive from the second tee. The bunker is 230 yards away; the carry is 255 yards.

the bunker with your drive, and you breathe a little more easily.

You drive, and your tee shot is straight, 220 yards down the left-hand side of the fairway. For an awful second as the ball left your driver's face you thought you might catch some of the overhanging limbs on the left side of the tee directly down the chute into which you were driving.

Your ball lies just short of the bunker in the center of the fairway, and you have a left-hand side-hill shot with your feet below the ball. Using your three wood and attempting not to hook off the feet-below-the-ball lie, you aim well right on the green toward right rough. You can see the green ahead on your left tucked behind the two large bunkers. Your second shot is well struck, curves slightly left, and comes to rest about seventy yards from the green directly in front of the right-hand bunker. The wind is slightly behind you so you hit a nine iron fairly flush, attempting to carry the bunker in front of the green.

Too bad! You fall short by about five

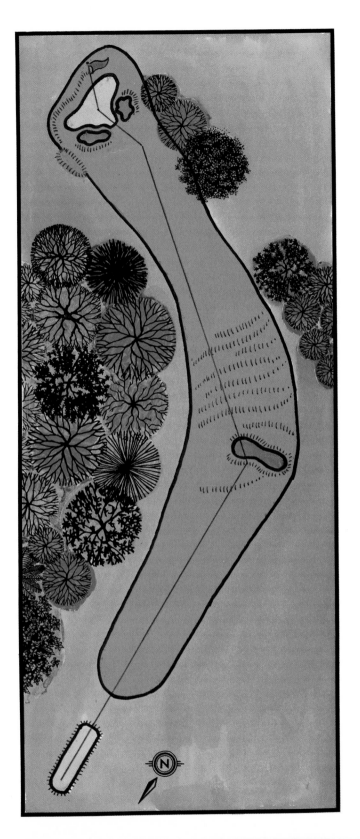

yards, and now you wish you had taken your eight iron so as to be sure to get over the bunkers. You lie three strokes in the bunker. The lie is good, the sand very white and fluffy underfoot. You blast hard two inches behind the ball, being careful to stay behind the ball with your head, and delightedly you look up after the stroke has been taken to see the ball gently settling down about fifteen feet beyond the flagstick. You still have a chance to hole the putt and save your par five.

The green is very slippery. Your putt is downhill. Leon advises a three-inch left-to-right break. You putt carefully, even gently, and the ball rolls down toward the hole, almost going into the hole but not doing so, and then rolls about two feet beyond the hole. You are surprised and a little shaken since you thought you had made it. You line up your two-foot putt carefully and knock it right into the middle of the cup. You have a bogey six on No. 2 and you are on target for your 89 at Augusta National!

Hole	Par	Your Score	±5s
1	4	5	Even
2	5	6	1 over 5s

Notes on Hole No. 2   In Jack Nicklaus's record-tying score of 64 in the 1965 Masters, he drove into the right-hand pine trees on his tee shot, came out through an opening in the pines 105 yards from the green, pitched to twenty-two feet from the hole, and then sank his putt for a birdie four on the hole, the first of eight birdies in that round.

Hole No. 3, 355 Yards, Par Four
Flowering Peach
330 Yards from Your Tee

Professional Strategy: This is a little trickster of a golf hole. Best strategy is to hit

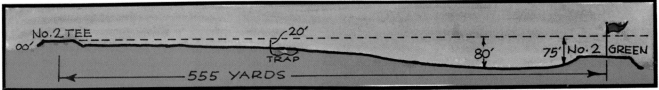

The second shot to the elevated third green.

a three or four wood off the tee to a spot just below the bunker in the center of the fairway. From there the shot is a delicate six, seven, or eight iron onto the very small raised crowned green that slopes down the hill from right to left. The main problem presented by the second shot is to gauge the distance precisely. By all means, it must be up onto the green, as the slightest shortness of the second shot will cause the ball to hit on the front slope and roll backward down the slope from where a pitch close to the pin is very delicate if not well-nigh impossible.

Your Strategy: Leon assures you that your drive will not carry into the fairway bunker. The wind is in your face. You will be hitting a four or five iron from short of the bunker, and with a club of such low trajectory it may be difficult to hold the small green. This may be another bogey hole.

Your drive is a good one just short of the bunker in the center of the fairway.

The lie for your second shot is good. Leon says that the distance to the green is about 150 yards, but that he would recommend a strong five iron favoring the right side of

The sunk putt, hole No. 3.

the green because of the right-to-left slope.

You strike the five iron but hit it a little fat and pull it as well. The ball heads for the green directly on line for the left bunker but fortunately stops about six feet from going into the sand.

Your pitch now is to the elevated plateau green, and, as promised, it is a delicate one. You decide on your nine iron because there isn't much grass under the ball. The pin is about thirty feet away from the front edge of the green, so you want the ball to land right at the edge and roll to the cup.

You pitch the ball exactly where you want the ball to land, and the shot is a good one. A putt of about eight feet is left from the down

or left side of the green. Leon warns you that you are putting a bit uphill and into the grain of the grass, that there should be a break of about one inch left to right. You stroke the ball smoothly, and it trickles up to the hole, catches the top side, and topples in. You have made a great par four on a very difficult hole at Augusta National.

Hole	Par	Your Score	±5s
1	4	5	Even 5s
2	5	6	1 over 5s
3	4	4	Even 5s

Notes on Hole No. 3   In the final round of the 1940 Masters, Olin Dutra, National Open champion of 1934, dubbed four straight shots on this hole, and scored a six on the way to an outgoing nine-hole score of 42. He came back in 1935 on the back nine for a 74 and third place in the tournament.

Hole No. 4, 220 Yards, Par Three
Palm
170 Yards from Your Tee

Professional Strategy: Proper club selection is difficult here, especially when the wind is gusty. Wind at the green is usually greater than that encountered on the tee, so chances are great that underclubbing will result in falling short in either of the two front bunkers. Too long a club will bring about a tough downhill, or downhill–sidehill chip to a slippery green. The professionals hope to hit the ball close enough to the flagstick so they will not three-putt. This is a hole to be played defensively.

Your Strategy: You can probably hit your best fairway wood without being afraid of going over the green. You may even make the green. Leon suggests a three wood and says, "Hit it!"

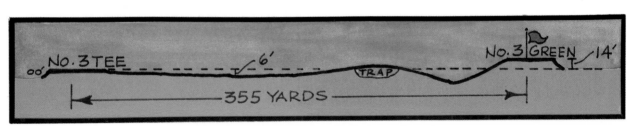

The wind is quartering from the northwest and now you are hitting almost directly into it. You swing well and hit a fine three-wood shot a little right of center of the green. Unfortunately, it is not quite long enough, and you find yourself in the right front bunker, ten feet in from the edge and twenty feet from the shallow upslope of the bunker.

The flagstick is about forty feet away in the center of the green, which rises from the edge of the bunker to the top back edge of the green. Your lie in the sand is good, not buried. You blast strongly, but because the pin seemed so far away, you have taken slightly too little sand, and the ball, while safely out of the bunker, skims right by the hole and comes to rest fifteen feet beyond the green on the upslope.

Now you have a very difficult shot to make. Your lie is close, so close that if you attempt to chip the ball you may blade it

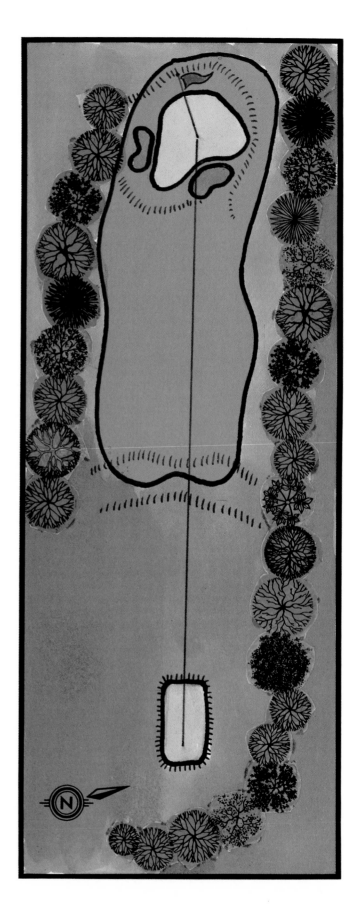

A view of the fourth green showing the steep slope from front to rear and the blast out of the bunker.

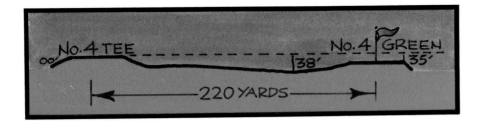

NO. 4 TEE - - - - - - - - - - - - - - - - - NO. 4 GREEN
38' 35'
|← 220 YARDS →|

Putt rolling into cup on No. 4.

few feet, you noticed that it broke slightly left to right. Leon advises a small right-to-left correction on your six-foot uphill putt. But he says, "Don't give the hole away." You are facing a double bogey that will neutralize your fine par at No. 3. Your putt goes squarely into the center of the hole. You have saved your bogey under demanding conditions on a green so large that more often than not even the professionals take a bogey there. You can be proud that you remain on target for your goal of breaking 90.

Hole	Par	Your Score	±5s
1	4	5	Even 5s
2	5	6	1 over 5s
3	4	4	Even 5s
4	3	4	1 under 5s

Notes on Hole No. 4   This quotation, taken from the *2nd Annual Invitation Tournament Year Book of April 4, 5, 6, 7, 1935 of Augusta National Golf Club*, gives these comments of architect Dr. Alister MacKenzie concerning the fourth hole:

This is a very similar hole to the famous Eleventh (Eden) at St. Andrews. There have been scores of attempted copies of this famous hole, but there is none that has the charm and thrills of the original. Most copies are failures because of the absence of the subtle and severe slopes that create the excitement of the original hole, and also because the turf is usually so soft that any kind of a sloppy pitch will stop. Previous failures, followed by, comparatively speaking, increasing successes may have given us sufficient experience to warrant us in hoping that here at last we may have constructed a hole that will compare favorably with the original.

and put it back in the bunker again. Remember that this green is shallow, though wide, and there is not much room between the hole and the front bunker. You decide to putt the ball and hope to come close to the pin. You feel safer in putting but not confident of getting the ball close to the hole.

You putt successfully, to about six feet past the hole. As the ball traveled the last

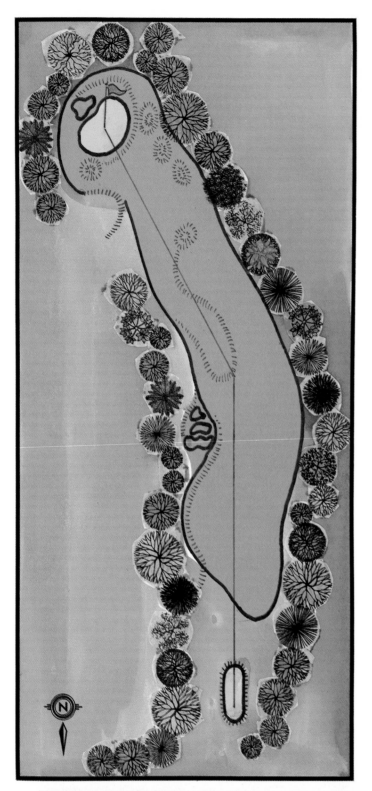

Hole No. 5, 450 Yards, Par Four
Magnolia
420 Yards from Your Tee

Professional Strategy: Attempt to make par! This is one of the most difficult four-pars at Augusta. The drive must be very long and favor the right side of the fairway. Driving down the left is a more proper—but more dangerous—line to take. A long iron or even five wood will be used to play for the green. Because the green is large and the pin usually in an inaccessible spot on top of the plateau, it is most urgent that the second shot be close to the pin. If the second shot is short or wanders, a very difficult run-up shot going up the front slope of the green results—very hard to hold at the flagstick.

Your Strategy: Leon says this hole is too long for you to hope to make in two shots. Play your drive safely to the right; hit a good fairway wood and hope your ball will run up onto the green.

Your drive is pulled to the left and lands in a bunker in the left rough at about 180 yards. You may have a buried lie.

As you approach the ball, however, it can be seen lying cleanly but far up on the upslope of the bunker. You are dismayed and wonder whether you can even get the ball out. Your stance is below the ball. You take a seven iron and hope to hit it cleanly, to get the ball out by any means and forgetting distance on the shot.

Your second shot comes off successfully. You hit the seven iron cleanly, and the trajectory carries the ball high over another bunker ahead but out onto the right fairway.

You are still 200 to 210 yards from the green, which can barely be seen at a little lower level than you are now playing from. There are a number of good sized hillocks in the right-hand side of the fairway. Leon tells you to stay to the left of them.

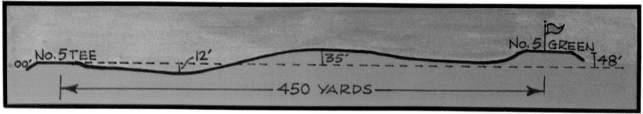

The long second shot into the par-4 fifth hole. Notice the Scottish style mounds which add to the difficulty of the hole.

The difficult and delicate run-up shot from the front of the fifth green.

You swing your four wood from another close lie. The shot is good. It heads left of the mounds and may even have run up onto the front edge of the green. You are elated. You have hopes of saving this bogey.

The ball, however, is about fifteen feet short of the green, and you are faced with that difficult Scotch-type run-up shot. No wedge or nine iron could ever stop the ball fast enough at the edge of the plateau on which the hole is cut, so you wisely take a four iron and try to pick out your line to the pin up the sharp incline at the front of the green.

You chip, and your line is good. The chip is a good one, and the ball stops six feet beyond the hole. Leon coaches you again on your putt. "Straight in!" After your good putt on No. 4, you feel more relaxed about this putt. You stroke it well, and down it goes. Bogey five, but again a masterful one for you.

Hole	Par	Your Score	±5s
1	4	5	Even 5s
2	5	6	1 over 5s
3	4	4	Even 5s
4	3	4	1 under 5s
5	4	5	Even 5s

Notes on Hole No. 5   In 1956, when Cary Middlecoff, defending champion, lost by two strokes to Jack Burke, Jr., it might be said that he lost it on this hole by taking four putts.

Hole No. 6, 190 Yards, Par 3
Juniper
170 Yards from Your Tee

Professional Strategy: This short hole is one of the easiest on the course and one of the most popular spectator spots during the Masters. It comes from an elevated tee, and since the tree line on the left tapers away left to leave the green more exposed than the tee, club selection here is difficult because the effect of the wind is difficult to gauge from the tee. The green itself is about fifteen feet below the tee level, so the shot is

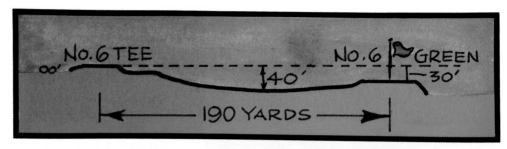

The tee shot toward the sixth green.

A bunker shot at the sixth green.

essentially downhill. There are several difficult pin positions, and it is extremely necessary that the tee shot be placed as close as possible to the flagstick, or a three-putt will result. The professional will also avoid hooking to the left, down a steep slope from where the chip to the pin is difficult or impossible if the hole is cut on the left side of the green. Make par—carefully!

Your Strategy: Almost the same as the professional's. Leon advises you to be up onto the top part of the green because, if you are short and must chip up or blast from

either of the two bunkers, you will have a hard time making a three.

The wind now is from the left, quartering, so rather than taking a four iron, Leon suggests a three and says: "Hit it!" Your swing is good, and for a moment you believe the ball is going to cover the pin all the way to the hole. Then the wind begins to have its effect on the ball, and it falls into the left-hand bunker in front of the green.

The walk down the hill is a steep one, and then you come up the hill to the raised green. Your ball is in a good lie in the

bunker, and you are about thirty-five feet from the flagstick.

You blast successfully to a position six feet above the hole. The green is very slick, and your putt is downhill. Leon suggests putting two inches to the right of the hole. You do. The ball hits the left edge of the hole, circles it completely, and drops in the front side. You are elated. You have saved your par on this short, beautiful, but very tricky three-par hole.

Not only that, but you have gained a precious two strokes in your battle to stay even fives.

Hole	Par	Your Score	±5s
1	4	5	Even 5s
2	5	6	1 over 5s
3	4	4	Even 5s
4	3	4	1 under 5s
5	4	5	1 under 5s
6	3	3	3 under 5s

Notes on Hole No. 6   The program of the Augusta National Golf Club "First Annual Invitation Tournament" made the claim that hole No. 15 (now hole No. 6) "surpasses the original 'Redan' at North Berwick, Scotland." Bernard Darwin, in his famous book *The Golf Courses of the British Isles*, had this to say about the "Redan." "The 'Redan' is a beautiful one-shot hole on the top of a plateau, with a bunker short of the green to the left and another farther on to the right, and we must vary our mode of attack according to the wind, playing a shot to come in from the front or making a direct frontal attack."

Aces have been scored on this hole by Leland Gibson in the first round of the 1954 Masters, by Billy Joe Patton in the fourth round of the same tournament, and by Charles Coody in the first round of the 1972 Masters.

Hole No. 7, 365 Yards, Par four
Pampas
315 Yards from Your Tee

Professional Strategy: This is one of the few birdie holes for the professionals. It is slightly downhill and then uphill to an elevated, well-bunkered green. A long, straight drive will result in a wedge or nine-iron that should sit down quickly on the rather small green. Make a birdie here, but be careful to hit a straight tee shot, as the trees right and left may interfere with a wandering drive. Those trees, in fact, make the tee shot tighter year by year, as their branches continue to spread.

Your Strategy: Leon advises you to stay to the right side of the fairway if possible. Your drive is a fine one about 230 yards as it catches the downhill slope, and it comes to rest on the right side of the fairway.

You wish you could have driven the ball another twenty-five yards, for it is evident that then you would have had a much more level lie at the bottom of the valley in front of the green.

Your lie is moderately downhill. The wind is crossing from the left and a little behind you. (This hole heads almost due east, dog-legging slightly to the left or northeast at the end.) Although your ball is only 130 yards away from the green, your club selection is difficult because of the elevation of the green and the fact that you have a close downhill lie.

Leon suggests that you use your seven iron. You swing and catch a little of the grass behind the ball and lose some of the power of the clubhead. The ball soars straight for the flag but falls short, into the front bunker only three feet from safety on the front edge of the green. You long for those extra three feet of carry because if you had been able to get over the bunker your ball would have been close to the hole for a possible birdie. Now you are fighting to save a bogey.

This time you are not so fortunate with your bunker lie. You have a fried-egg lie and an uphill shot as well. The hole is only twenty-five feet away but you are afraid you may not get the ball out of the bad lie with your first attempt. You close the face of your sand wedge and make a good hard swing, hitting a spot two-and-a-half inches behind the ball. Out it pops, to rest only four feet from the hole. You think, "Maybe I can save the four!"

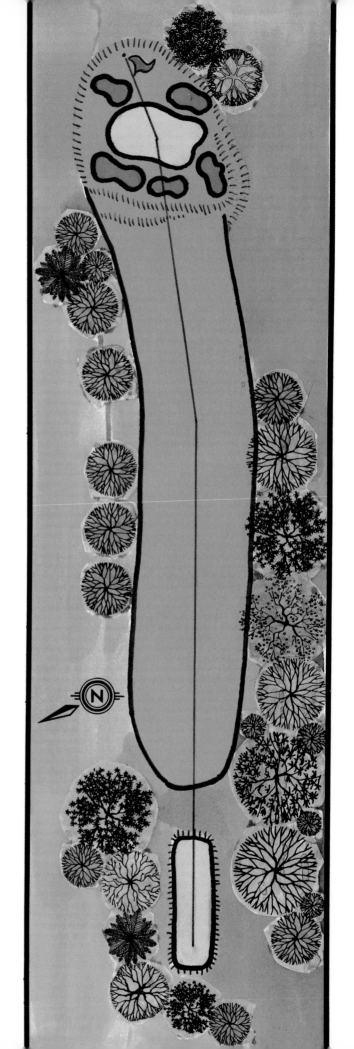

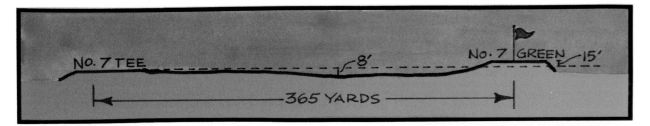

The tee shot at the seventh hole.

This green is like green ice to your view. Although you are only four feet away from the cup, you have a left side-hill putt that you think will break at least four inches. Leon tells you that the break is even more than that and advises six inches break from left to right.

You putt and don't even come close to the hole. Leon scolds you and says, "That wasn't a very good stroke." Rather shakily, you manage to hole the eighteen-inch putt you have left yourself and settle gladly for your bogey five. At least you haven't lost any more strokes to fives, and your score remains three under fives.

The pitch to the elevated seventh green.

Hole	Par	Your Score	±5s
1	4	5	Even 5s
2	5	6	1 over 5s
3	4	4	Even 5s
4	3	4	1 under 5s
5	4	5	1 under 5s
6	3	3	3 under 5s
7	4	5	3 under 5s

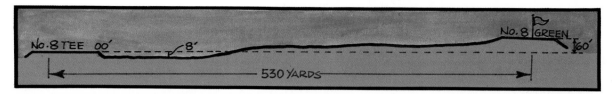

The chip shot to the eighth hole.

Notes on Hole No. 7   When Byron Nelson won the Masters in 1937, he set a new course record of 66 on opening day. In that round he drove the seventh green, 340 yards away. At that time the green was lower than it is today, and the entrance or tongue was wider. The hole now plays at 365 yards.

Hole No. 8, 530 yards, Par five
Yellow Jasmine
500 Yards from Your Tee

Professional Strategy: Drive as long as possible, favoring the area to the left of the fairway bunker so that a long second wood shot can make the green or the area just short of it. Advice: Stay out of the left woods. There is nothing but trouble there.

Your Strategy: Leon tells you that you don't have to worry about the fairway

bunker on the right that troubles all the professionals. The wind is still in your face as you head northwestward. You swing away confidently, but instinctively you quit a little bit on your drive and end up in the right rough just short of the bunker. Leon was right about your not being able to drive into it. Leon points out a large mound well up the fairway and tells you to hit your next shot right over it. The shot to the green is a blind one, and not until you have walked three-fourths of the distance up the hillside toward the green will the green and flagstick come into view.

Your lie for your second shot is only a fair one, and, using your four wood, you swing through the light rough and send the ball about 170 yards on a line to the left of the strategic mound. You remain nearly 200 yards from the green, and now you can just

barely make out the contours of the green up on the flat area adjacent to No. 1 green (Level 18 feet).

You have some hope now that a good fairway wood may get you to the green. But mounds in front on the left side, the uphill stance, and the long shot all upset your swing, and you find, to your horror, that you have pulled your third shot to the left and down the left slope of the rough into the pine trees. Your three-under-fives position seems to be threatened. Like the otherwise good rounds of many Masters participants, yours could be spoiled by this encounter with the trees on No. 8.

Leon finds your ball on the side hill about twenty-five feet down to the left of the fairway seventy-five yards from the green. There are several trees interfering with a shot of normal trajectory, and several thick tree trunks are staggered about twenty to thirty yards ahead. Any one of them may stop a low run-up shot through the trees. The ball lies on some pine chips and you don't dare move any of them for fear that the ball will move off its axis and cause you to incur a penalty stroke for moving the ball. In deep trouble, your chances of saving even a bogey on this long, hard hole are slim.

You choose a four iron for your run-up shot of about seventy-five yards. You think to yourself: Is it seventy-five yards or is it ninety? How hard shall I hit this four iron? You must stay to the right as well since the left mound may catch your ball if you hit it to the left. The green is slightly uphill from you.

You chip sharply with the four iron and catch a few of the pine chips with your clubface before it hits the ball. The ball miraculously goes toward the green, misses the trunk of the closest tree at twenty yards and runs up the fairway, stopping about twenty-five feet in front of the green in a small dip in the fairway. All in all, a good shot under the circumstances, but you now have taken four strokes on this five-par and are not on the green yet.

The flagstick is about forty-five feet away, and the green seems to slope from left to right from your approach position. Leon agrees with your analysis and suggests a chip on a line three feet to the left of the hole. The green level is slightly raised, about eighteen inches higher than your pitching positon. You choose a certain ball mark on the green about twenty feet from the hole and try to land your nine-iron chip on it, thinking that from there the ball will roll close to the cup.

Your chip-shot lie is tight, with little grass under it, and you are afraid you might chili-dip the shot and bring about complete disaster. You chip with your nine iron, and the shot comes off well. The ball rolls to a spot ten feet from the cup. The roll from left to right was miscalculated. The ball broke a little to the left instead of to the right. You pray you can get down in two strokes from ten feet. Your confidence is badly shaken, and you can see that you have lost two strokes (at least) of your precious under-five position.

You must save this hole by no more than a two-putt. Your putt is short of the cup by six inches, and you easily hole the next putt. Your score is seven, and you have lost two strokes to fives.

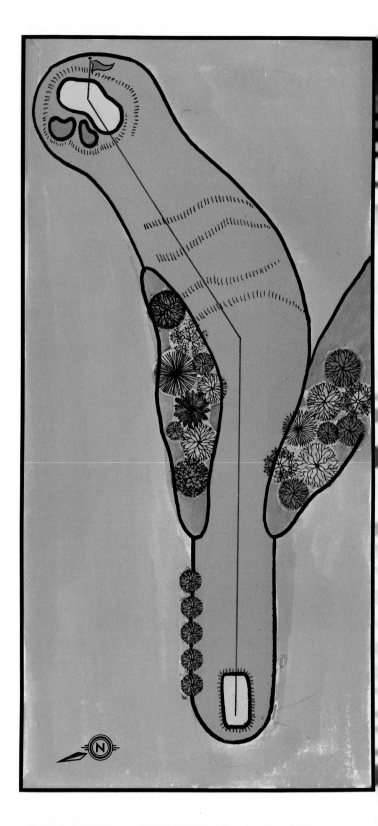

Hole	Par	Your Score	±5s
1	4	5	Even 5s
2	5	6	1 over 5s
3	4	4	Even 5s
4	3	4	1 under 5s
5	4	5	1 under 5s
6	3	3	3 under 5s
7	4	5	3 under 5s
8	5	7	1 under 5s

Notes on Hole No. 8   The second double eagle in Masters history was scored by Australian Bruce Devlin on the first day of the 1967 tournament. Bruce hit a 290-yard-long

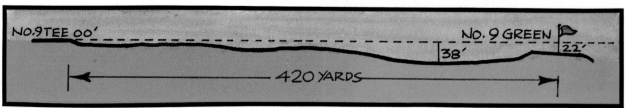

NO.9 TEE 00'   NO. 9 GREEN
                        38'   22'
|←————————————— 420 YARDS —————————————→|

drive and then used a four wood. He could not see the green from his position in the fairway. The ball hit just in front of the green, took a big bounce onto it, rolled toward the cup, hesitated on the front lip, and then dropped in. His score on the round was 74, and he eventually finished at 290, tying for tenth place, on scores of 74, 70, 75, and 71.

Hole No. 9, 420 Yards, Par Four
Carolina Cherry
395 Yards from Your Tee

Professional Strategy: A very long straight drive is required on this short dogleg to the left in order to reach the lower slope of the valley in front of the green. A short drive will end up on the downslope and will require a difficult shot in order to hold the small green. There is danger in a pulled shot since trees on the left will interfere with a shot to the green. A pushed shot to the right will find rough from which it is very difficult to stop the ball on the green. The player is called on to make use of local knowledge and good judgment and to resist the temptation to play close to the corner simply because the dogleg is presented. A good birdie hole for the professionals, but one that can cause trouble if the approach should find the front bunkers or be long on the green, making a three-putt a real possibility.

Your Strategy: Leon advises you to favor the right-hand side of the fairway with your drive. You swing well and drive precisely where he advised you to aim.

Because of the wind at your back and the downhill bounce, your drive ends up 250 yards from the tee. However, you do not reach the lower, flatter slope of the valley, and you have another hanging lie to a small, elevated green guarded closely by two bunkers in front and to the left side.

The wind is now quartering from the left and behind you. Although your shot is only 140 yards, you determine to take enough club so that you won't fall short of the green, as you did on the seventh hole.

You swing a seven iron, and, although you

The tee shot on the ninth hole.

hit the ball far enough, a slight pull left has put the ball into the farther left bunker.

Your lie is good in the sand, and your blast is aimed about four feet to the left of the flagstick, which is about thirty feet away. Your explosion shot is successful, and the ball comes to rest four feet from the hole. Perhaps you can make this putt and gain another valuable stroke under fives.

This green tilts at a great angle from back to front, and it is apparent that even though you are only four feet away you must borrow about four inches from the left if you hope to hole the putt. You tell Leon that you think the roll is "four inches, left to right" and he says, "You'd better give it more than that and hit it *easy*!"

Your putt is a good one, gently curving the six inches of break you gave it, but the ball rims the cup from the left side and squirts around it to stay out on the right side. A good try, and it's a shame to waste the fine bunker shot. But you haven't lost any more strokes to fives. Your first nine-hole score is a commendable 44. If you can stay even fives on the last nine, you will make your 89!

Hole	Par	Your Score	±5s
1	4	5	Even 5s
2	5	6	1 over 5s
3	4	4	Even 5s
4	3	4	1 under 5s
5	4	5	1 under 5s
6	3	3	3 under 5s
7	4	5	3 under 5s
8	5	7	1 under 5s
9	4	5	1 under 5s
Total	36	44	

Notes on Hole No. 9   Henry Picard, Masters champion of 1938, tells this anecdote: "Bob Jones played in the Masters Tournaments until 1948. For many years it was customary for him to play with the previous year's winner. So I played with him in the 1939 Masters. His second shot on the ninth hole went just over the back edge of the green, a couple of feet onto the short fringe. I said to him, 'I'll bet you the clubhouse you can't keep your chip shot on the green!' He scoffed at me. His chip rolled down the green and right off the front of it. The next year the green was flattened out."

Hole No. 10, 470 Yards, Par Four
Camellia
445 Yards from Your Tee

Professional Strategy: A very difficult four-par, the start of the Amen Corner, the stretch of holes from No. 10 through No. 13 where so many good scores have been ruined in the history of the Masters. From the level of the clubhouse this hole heads southeast downhill sharply, doglegging slightly left. The hill is so steep that it is impossible to see the green from the teeing area. Bobby Jones called it one of the most beautiful holes he had ever seen. A drive in the center of the fairway or slightly left center for the professional will catch a left side-hill kick and bring his ball down to the 270- to 290-yard mark from where a long

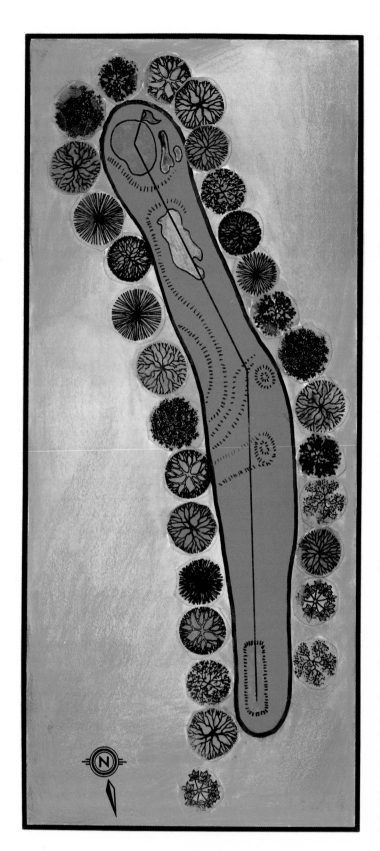

Some of the "trouble" on the right side of the tenth hole.

iron will put him on the slightly elevated green. Since the green is in deep shadow much of the time, the grass is thinner than on many of the other greens, and it is a very hard green to putt. A hole to be played defensively even by the professionals, by staying out of the woods to the right and left, and by being close to the pin on the second shot to avoid the chance for a three-putt.

Your Strategy: Try to make a bogey five. Leon tells you about the left side-hill bounce if you can drive the ball far enough down the hill. However, the prospect of hooking into the woods causes you to steer the ball to the right side of the fairway about 200 yards away.

As you approach your second shot, Leon points out the few more yards you needed to your left to catch the downslope of a deep swale to the left side of the fairway. The difference would be forty yards, but nothing can be done about it. You are faced with a downhill wood shot of 250 yards. You know that you cannot hit the ball that far, so you attempt to hit it as well as you can with your three wood. Your lie is downhill, and you come off the ball slightly, opening the face of the club. The ball curves to the right, and to your dismay you see it heading for a

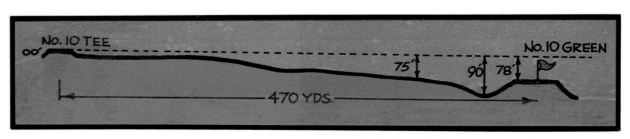

Studying a long putt at the tenth hole.

clump of trees to the right of the fairway, thirty yards short of the green. You are in trouble again.

You find your ball on a slight rise in right rough, but your shot to the flagstick and most of the green is blocked by some low branches of a tree on the hillside and by the side hill itself. Your only shot is a run-up shot with a three, four, or five iron, which should take your ball under the low branches into the bunker in front of the green and, if you are skillful, run the ball through the sand onto the green. Fortunately, there is no overhanging lip on the right front bunker, so you have a chance to accomplish this shot. You decide on a four iron and strike the ball well. The ball rises enough to clear the slightly raised terrain, goes under the threatening branches, runs through the bunker, and at last jumps out of the sand onto the very front of the green. You have pulled off a remarkable save, and now, if you can just manage to two-putt, you will have your bogey five on this hard hole and will be holding your own on your 89 score.

The putt from the front of the green to the flagstick, which is two-thirds of the way back in the right center of the green, totals fifty feet as you pace it off carefully. It is mostly uphill with only a slight break to the right. Leon advises you to allow one foot of left-to-right break. He reminds you that you are going uphill but that the green is very fast.

You putt firmly and well. The ball rolls beautifully and stops one-and-a-half feet from the hole. Confidently now, after the fine approach putt, you sink your second putt and get your five. Hole No. 1 of the Amen Corner is conquered safely!

Hole	Par	Your Score	±5s
10	4	5	1 under 5s

Notes on Hole No. 10   In the 1940 Masters, a three-putt here was the only error Lloyd Mangrum committed in a nine-birdie round of 64, the course record that stood until 1965, when Jack Nicklaus tied it.

In the Snead-Hogan play-off of 1954, which Snead won (70–71), this hole was the scene of a dramatic exchange of scores when Snead apparently headed for a bogey to go one stroke behind but holed a sixty-five-foot chip shot from the back of the green to go one stroke ahead.

Hole No. 11, 445 Yards, Par Four
White Dogwood
390 Yards from Your Tee

Professional Strategy: Now heading due south, here is another defensive hole. Make par at any cost. Drive safely downhill and as far as possible out of a very narrow chute of trees. It is a blind tee shot, in that the ball lands on ground not visible from the tee. Keep to the right on the second shot so as to avoid going into the water to the left and short of the wide green. Since the pin is very often cut into the far left side of this green, it takes a great deal of courage to go for the pin rather than play it safe to the right-hand side of the fairway or green. Playing safe may force a long putt and possible three-putt situation.

Your Strategy: Leon advises you to keep your drive to the right and to play this hole

safe. Your swing is a good one, and your drive carries 210 yards out onto the right fairway.

Your second shot is now 180 yards long. Your lie is fairly level, but you are afraid of hooking into the water hazard to the left. Your second shot is well hit but goes straight to the right-hand side of the green, coming to rest about ten yards to the right and almost hole-high. Now you wish that you had had the courage to go for the pin, for if you had you would have been close to the hole.

You are now faced with a very hard chip shot to a crowned green. The green level is several feet above the level of your lie on the ground. Leon advises an eight-iron chip and "gently—the green is hard and fast."

You miss this shot almost completely, catching the ball on the bottom of the blade, and clip it past the pin where, to your continued horror, it runs across the green and off downward on the left side of the green where it finally stops almost as far away from the hole as it was when you made your third shot. That sinking feeling comes again, and you are afraid that you are starting to blow your chances for a good score.

Again you chip with your eight iron, this time quite fearfully. The shot comes off well, though, and the ball rolls to ten feet from the hole. The green is like pure velvet in the sunlight. You know you can save this bogey and, now, confident again, stroke the ball well, straight into the back of the cup. Good score! Another tough hole behind you. You're still on the track of your goal.

Hole	Par	Your Score	±5s
10	4	5	1 under 5s
11	4	5	1 under 5s

Notes on Hole No. 11   This green was originally to the right of its present position.

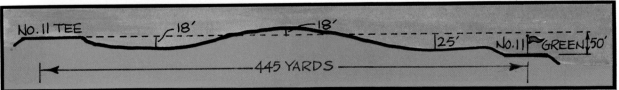

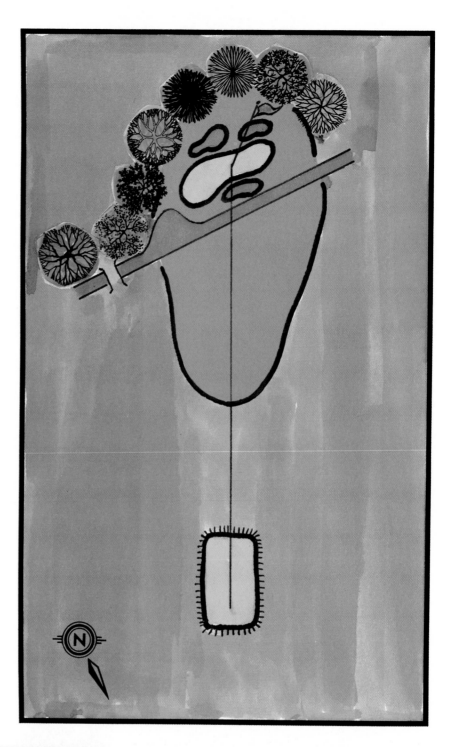

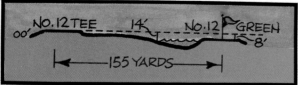

However, in the opinion of Henry Picard, 1938 Masters champion, the hole was just as difficult then as it is today.

Hole No. 12, 155 Yards, Par Three
Golden Bell
130 Yards from Your Tee

Professional Strategy: Still heading south, here is another apparently simple

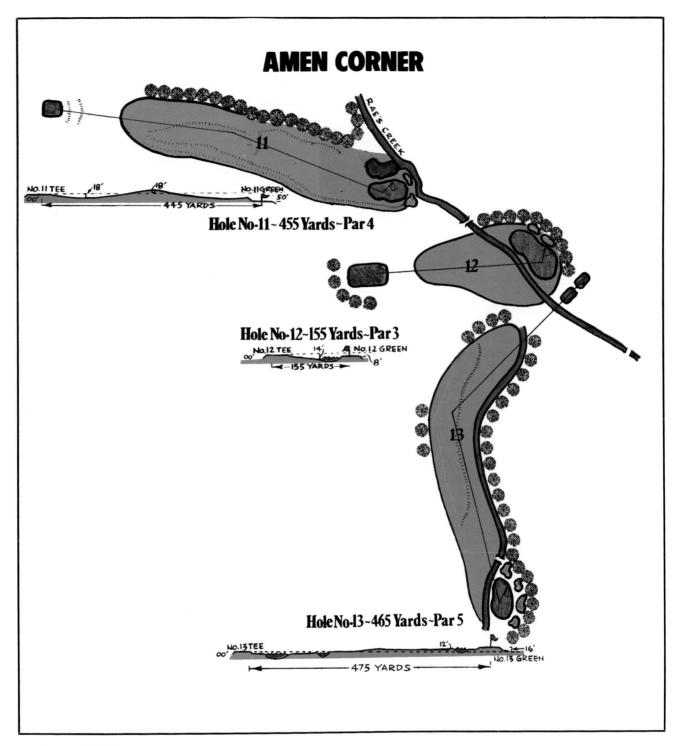

AMEN CORNER

Hole No·11~ 455 Yards~Par 4

Hole No·12~155 Yards~Par 3

Hole No·13~465 Yards~Par 5

AMEN CORNER

Hole No. 11, 455 Yards, Par 4   "White Dogwood": Player must hit a long second shot over a pond that guards the left front of the green. A trio of bunkers defends the right side of the green, with two traps covering the back. Behind the traps is Rae's Creek. Hole No. 11 has an undulating fairway which drops 18 feet from the tee, then rises 18 feet above the tee, dropping again 50 feet below the tee at the green.

Hole No. 12, 155 Yards, Par 3   "Golden Bell": A shallow green sitting on a narrow stage, it is set off at an angle to the tee. Guarded by Rae's Creek and a trap in front, the green has another trap behind it, followed by a sharply rising bank covered with floral thickets. Swirling winds are often a problem. The fairway drops 14 feet from the tee to Rae's Creek, lying in front of the green. There is an eight-foot drop behind the green.

Hole No. 13, 465 Yards, Par 5   "Azalea": The green is approached by a sharp dogleg to the left and requires three crossings of meandering Rae's Creek, which guards the front of the green. Just in front of Rae's Creek at the green are two bunkers. Four traps cover the left side of the green. The fairway has a 12-foot rise from the tee on the approach to the green, which sits 16 feet above the tee.

The twelfth green viewed from Hogan Bridge. A most frightening "little hole"!

little three-par hole, but one that often causes a great deal of trouble. Club selection is hard here because of swirling gusty winds customarily coming out of the thirteenth fairway to the northwest. Since the pin is very often placed close to the bank of the creek that guards the front of the green, the temptation of the professional is to attempt to cut the ball as close to the hole as possible and seize a birdie. This may result in a ball cut into the water instead. The rear bunkers, too, are extremely dangerous because a shot into either one may bury and leave the golfer with the frightening prospect of a downhill blast onto the green or possibly right over the green into the water. Get the ball onto this green and settle for par, if you can.

Your Strategy: Leon advises a six iron, and you wonder whether you can get up the courage to hit your six over that frightening water between you and the flagstick. You reconcile yourself to getting a shot into the water hazard and swing away, not very confidently. The ball flies very well but hits on the left side of the green and skips into the far left trap. Now you have a shot to get back onto the green safely. You may yet be in the water.

Your lie in the bunker is a good one, and you have only a slightly downhill shot to the hole some thirty feet away. You resolve to make as good a bunker shot as you can, keep your head down, and swing smoothly. The shot is acceptable. The ball pops up, just clears the trap's edge, and rolls beautifully down toward the hole, stopping seven feet from the pin.

You may even save your par, and if you do you will gain two precious strokes under five.

Here is another gorgeous green, perfectly true, and if you can only stroke the ball properly, you know you can make this putt. Leon advises a little break to the left, not more than one inch. You putt carefully, holding your head very steady, and watch the ball head for the hole on the right side and then at the last second slip into the hole for your three. Exaltation! Two more strokes under fives and a margin for the rough finishing holes. You calculate that if you can continue to play in even fives from this point on, you will score a great 87!

Hole	Par	Your Score	±5s
10	4	5	1 under 5s
11	4	5	1 under 5s
12	3	3	3 under 5s

Notes on Hole No. 12   Aces have been scored on this hole by William Hyndman III in 1959 and Claude Harmon in 1947.

Lloyd Mangrum is said to have called this hole "the meanest little hole in the world."

Hole No. 13, 475 Yards, Par Five
Azalea
455 Yards from Your Tee

Professional Strategy: The design of this hole is a splendid example of what can be done by taking advantage of natural features. It marks the end of the Amen Corner, a possible birdie hole or possible disaster. The drive should be long and favor the left center of the fairway from where a courageous second shot may carry Rae's Creek and find the green for a two-putt birdie. It is most important to guard against the quick hook to the left that will result in a penalty shot, a bogey, or worse.

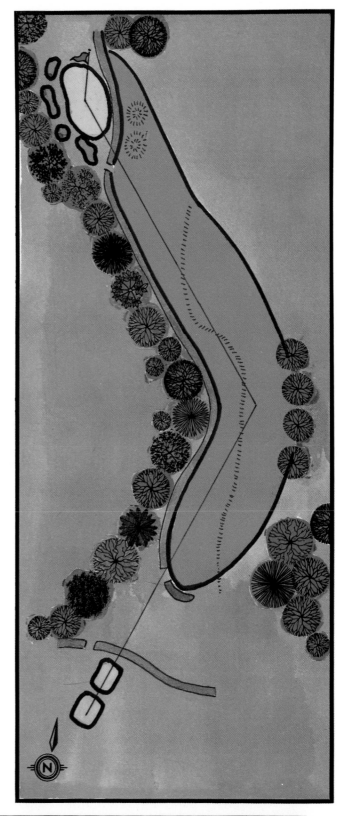

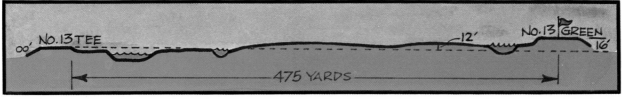

The tee shot at No. 13. Notice the slope of the fairway to the left which will cause a tee shot to "kick" left and into Rae's Creek.

Your Strategy: Leon advises you to keep your drive to the right center of the fairway to avoid at all costs going into Rae's Creek, which borders the left-hand side of this hole all the way along the fairway until it crosses in front of the green from left to right. Your drive is an excellent one, but because you are now heading back into the northwest and the hole is slightly uphill, your distance is cut down to 200 yards.

The lie for your second shot is a good one, and by leaping up into the air you can catch a glimpse of the thirteenth green and the slope down to Rae's Creek at the left-hand side of the fairway. You swing your three wood well, and the ball flies on a good line toward the thirteenth green. Leon is not too confident about the results of the shot, however, and warns you that your ball is "awful close to the trouble."

As you come over the rise in the fairway, however, you can see the little white dot lying safely on the fairway only ten to fifteen feet away from a point where Rae's Creek hairpins into the fairway unexpectedly. You are very pleased to find your ball in safety and have a great deal of admiration for Leon's knowledge of the course and its trouble spots.

Your third shot to the green is now only about eighty yards long. Now, however, the danger begins to be more apparent to you. The creek is wider than you thought it was and considerably deeper. You can see the rocky boulders in it and the rushing water. The hole is halfway back on the crowned green, and you begin to doubt that your approach shot with any club can hold the green.

You take a nine iron. Your lie is good.

In trouble in Rae's Creek.

The chip to the thirteenth green.

There is no reason why you shouldn't accomplish this pitch shot very well. But you don't; you cold-top the ball, pulling it to your left, and, now horror-stricken, you watch the ball roll on and on to the left, finally hopping into the creek. Again, you have the feeling that perhaps you have blown your chances at a good score. Perhaps you have. You now have taken four strokes. Three into the hazard, a penalty shot, four, and you are about to play your fifth shot. You still have a difficult pitch to the thirteenth green.

You drop a brand-new ball at arm's length two club lengths away from the hazard, Rae's Creek, on the line on which the ball entered the water. Fortunately for you, the drop is a good one, and the ball now sits up pertly, just waiting for you to chip it onto the green.

Now you feel a surge of renewed confidence. You determine to make a good swing at this chip and see whether you can still save the hole. Your stroke is good with your pitching wedge, and the ball floats up over the creek, strikes the front crowned edge of the green, killing part of its forward motion, and then dies marvelously close to the flagstick. You are sure you can get down in two strokes now.

Your putt is about fifteen feet long, slippery, and right side-hill. Leon coaches you again and tells you to allow two feet of break.

You can't believe him, but you trust his judgment and long experience. You stroke the ball gently on a line two feet to the right of the cup. It makes what appears to be a perfect parabola and heads for the cup. Then it curves around and stops just behind the cup only one inch from falling in. A great putt, but still a two-putt for a double-bogey seven. The margin for error has suddenly been cut to zero.

Hole	Par	Your Score	±5s
10	4	5	1 under 5s
11	4	5	1 under 5s
12	3	3	3 under 5s
13	5	7	1 under 5s

Notes on Hole No. 13   In the 1968 Masters, Don January hit his drive around the corner of the thirteenth hole and then put a three iron on the green near the back fringe, sixty feet away from the cup. He then putted off the green into the downslope of Rae's Creek. It was said that this was the first time in Masters history that anyone had done this. January chipped the ball back and scored a six.

Hole No. 14, 420 Yards, Par Four
Chinese Fir
400 Yards from Your Tee

Professional Strategy: A deceptively innocent-appearing, moderately difficult, uphill four-par doglegging slightly left. A birdie is hard to get because of the crown effect of the green. A straight drive is necessary because woods on the right offer trouble.

You are now in the stretch. The traditionally devastating Amen Corner is completed, and you know that you have played the last four difficult holes in even fives. Your margin of one under fives (44) on the first nine is holding up so far, and you are on the way to your coveted 89, provided you are able to keep at even fives for the next five holes.

Your Strategy: Leon points out a tree on the left side of the fairway at about 170 yards and advises you to avoid it. He also tells you not to go too far right for fear of going into the trees there. With these instructions in mind, you tighten up on your drive, and it falls quite short of your usual distance but finds the right side of the fairway.

Leon advises that you can hit everything you've got to attempt to reach the raised green 210 yards away. Your lie is a good one, and so is your swing with your three wood. The ball goes straight but on a line twenty yards to the right of the green and stops in a little hollow or swale about thirty yards from the flagstick.

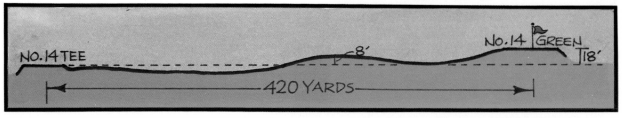

A pitch from the right to No. 14.

This hole appears to be cut into a devilish place, being at the very edge of a rise in the center of the green.

Fortunately, you have the best lie so far for a wedge shot out of the hollow. There is plenty of grass under your ball, so, quite confidently, you take the pitching wedge. Picking out a spot on the top edge of the upslope, you attempt to land the ball on the green about twenty feet from the hole. You hope that the upslope will kill the run of the ball and allow it to slow down quickly and stop near the hole.

Your pitch is almost exactly what you are trying to accomplish. The ball rises in the air and then strikes the spot you have picked out ahead of time. Then, with the brakes on as heavily as you hoped, it settles down and runs to the hole—and by it by about fifteen feet—a very good shot, and you have a possible chance to save your bogey five.

Leon coaches you on this putt and tells you that the grain is hidden, that it really runs uphill a little bit, and says that you'd better allow for three inches of right-to-left

break. You take a lot of time on this putt. You stroke it well, and it is beautifully on line. It rolls up to the cup and stops just one-quarter turn from falling into the center of the cup. You sigh and hope that this tiny tap-in does not prove to be your margin for breaking 90! Leon is disconsolate, but he encourages you by saying, "Here comes a nice five-par; let's see if you can pick up a stroke here."

Hole	Par	Your Score	±5s
10	4	5	1 under 5s
11	4	5	1 under 5s
12	3	3	3 under 5s
13	5	7	1 under 5s
14	4	5	1 under 5s

Notes on Hole No. 14   This hole is of the Scottish type often requiring a carefully placed run-up shot to hold the green. It is similar in character to the sixth hole at famous St. Andrews.

Hole No. 15, 520 Yards, Par Five
Fire Thorn
465 Yards from Your Tee

Professional Strategy: This is a must birdie hole for the professional golfer. The wind is an important factor in determining whether the player can attempt to carry the large pond directly in front of the green. The hole heads southwest, and with the wind against the golfer the best strategy is to lay up in front of the pond and attempt to wedge close enough to the hole to get a birdie. The drive must be a long one, avoiding some newly built mounds on the right of the fairway at the 250-yard mark. (These mounds were added in 1970 to increase the difficulty of the hole.) If a long-wood second is attempted, the shot may land on the crowned green and bounce over. The pitch back to the green sloping away from the player is a most difficult one. A second shot unusually long may catch more water to the left rear of the green.

Your Strategy: Leon says to do your best on your tee shot, to stay left of the mounds on the right. Your drive heads straight up the right side of the fairway directly for the mounds. Leon says, "Don't worry; maybe we'll get a good lie anyway."

As you approach the largest mound, you do not see your ball, so you begin to worry that you may have a downhill lie on the other side of it. However, as you come closer, you now see your ball almost exactly on the top of the mound. It appears that, while you will have a hard shot from that position, it is a makable one.

Leon suggests that you hit a three iron and tells you to watch for a pull from your lie, which has your feet several inches below the ball.

You swing the three iron, and the shot is struck well. The ball continues on a line down the right-hand side of the fairway and stops on the downslope well in front of the

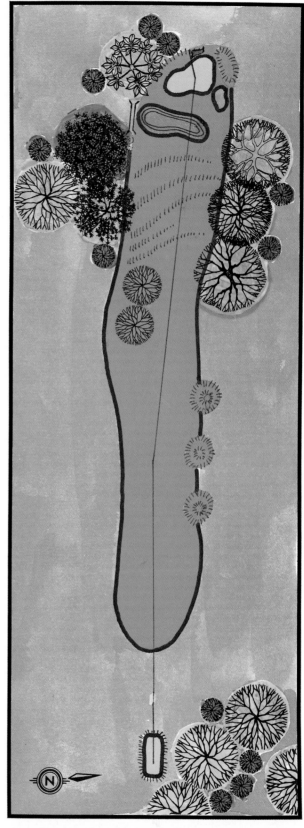

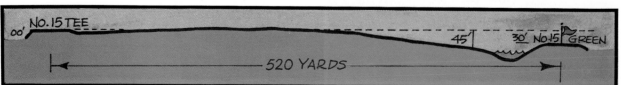

The pitch shot across the pond in front of No. 15 green, a frightening one indeed.

pond guarding the green. This was the water hazard that kept Billy Joe Patton, in 1954, from being the first amateur to come close to winning the Masters.

Your third shot is now a very delicate one over the pond to a flagstick fairly close to the water's edge in the center of the green. Your lie is on a downslope, and you are a little afraid that you might skull the shot into the pond. Leon suggests that you hit an eight iron, but you disobey him and take a seven iron for a greater margin of safety. The wind is a little against you, and you would rather be up or over than into the water. Furthermore, you remember falling short of No. 7 and No. 9 and don't want to duplicate either of those shots.

You swing the seven iron, and a beautiful shot results. However, although the ball flies directly for the pin, the shot is a little too long and, after hitting on the back edge of the green, rolls over the green up a slope and stops about twenty-five feet from the edge of the green.

While you are happy to have gotten over the water, you are now worried about a hard chip back onto the green.

You inspect your lie and find that it is a very close one. You feel that if you try a nine or pitching wedge chip you may blade the ball and end up in the lake after all. So you decide to chip with your five iron, attempt to land the ball on the top fringe of the green, and let it roll down the green gently toward the hole.

Your five-iron chip turns out well. The ball lands at the green's edge and trickles down to the hole, stopping about fifteen feet away—a very good shot from a bad place.

Regrettably, your chances of sinking this fifteen-foot putt are remote, and you know it. The green has a steep tilt from the back edge to the water's edge, and your fifteen-footer must break two feet from the right to the left.

Leon advises you to let the ball die above the cup, indicating a spot about two feet above it. You putt very gently, and the ball

Putting on the fifteenth green.

rolls on the line you want it to take. The ball curves around behind the hole and stops about eighteen inches away. Aware that if you miss this next short putt you will have a double-bogey seven, you study the eighteen-incher carefully and barely manage to sink it in the side of the hole. You breathe a sigh of relief at getting your bogey. You are a little upset at yourself for not getting your par after being in such a promising position short of the water on your second shot on No. 15.

Hole	Par	Your Score	±5s
10	4	5	1 under 5s
11	4	5	1 under 5s
12	3	3	3 under 5s
13	5	7	1 under 5s
14	4	5	1 under 5s
15	5	6	Even 5s

Notes on Hole No. 15   The spectator's view of this hole, either from behind the hole or from the rough along the right-hand side of the fairway, is one of the most exciting on the course for experiencing the drama of the players' decisions as to whether or not to go for the green with the second shot.

Hole No. 16, 190 Yards, Par Three
Red Bud
165 Yards from Your Tee

Professional Strategy: Stay out of the water. Make par. A very difficult three-par over water most of the way. Traps to the right hinder a safe shot, and the green itself is oriented with the left side sloping away from the golfer toward his left. Pin placement on the left or water side makes this hole a particularly hard one.

Your Strategy: Leon advises that you hit a four iron so as to be sure to get over the water hazard. Your heart is in your throat as you tee up most carefully on the left side of the sixteenth tee, knowing you are closing in on that cherished 89 at Augusta. You use a short tee and take a couple of extra practice swings with your iron club. You decide to firm up your left hand and left side so as to prevent a pull or a hook into trouble on the left. If only you can get the ball over the water, even in front of the green on the right.

You swing but hurry the hit after all. The ball heads toward the left side of the green, flying fairly well. You hope that it will clear the far embankment and make the green toward the rear. Then you know in your heart that the ball was not struck that well. The ball fails to carry the water by ten feet, and, as the splash occurs and the ripples spread out from the spot, you are sure that you no longer have any chance to finish with even bogeys or better on this tough golf course.

You are most upset for a moment, but then you decide that you can do nothing about your situation now and make up your mind to finish as well as you can no matter what the score.

You even laugh to yourself as you think, "Maybe I'll put another shot in the water." Since you think that the four iron you struck would have carried to the flagstick if you had hit it straight, you decide to use it again.

Once more you practice a couple of swings, and then, this time a little more relaxed, you strike the ball. To your pleasant surprise, you see it heading slightly to

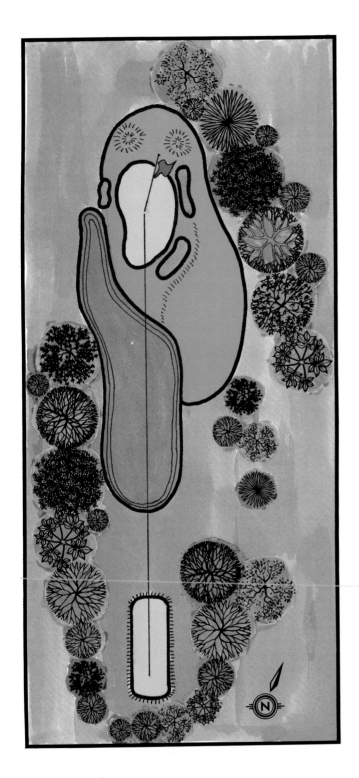

the right of the flag but on a line that should take it nicely onto the green.

You watch carefully as the ball hits on the green about twenty feet in front of the hole. It carries slightly left with the contour of the green and heads directly for the hole. The ball almost goes into the hole and ends up so close that from the tee it appears to be a leaner or close enough to fall into the hole any second. It doesn't, however.

You and Leon hurry to the green, and as you get nearer it is apparent that the ball is behind the hole, but still very close to it, perhaps only a foot or so away. Now you

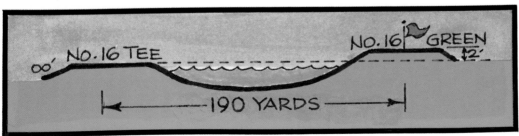

begin to recalculate your chances at the 89. Your third shot is lying only a foot away from the hole. Sink it, and the score is four and the bogey pace maintained. You have a chance yet to make your 90-breaking score!

On the green you measure the short putt with your hands. There are only three hand spans between your ball and the bottom of the hole and the bogey four you need so badly.

What if I should miss this little putt? goes through your mind. Then, without letting yourself dwell on the possibility any longer, you step up to the ball, go through your normal putting routine, and click the ball into the cup. You have your bogey four on the tough No. 16, and you now need only two more fives on the difficult No. 17 and No. 18 and you are home with an 89!

Hole	Par	Your Score	±5s
10	4	5	1 under 5s
11	4	5	1 under 5s
12	3	3	3 under 5s
13	5	7	1 under 5s
14	4	5	1 under 5s
15	5	6	Even 5s
16	3	4	1 under 5s

Notes on Hole No. 16   Ray Billows scored a hole-in-one on the fly on this hole in the Masters of 1940. The hole played at 145 yards at that time. He used a wedge for the shot. Willie Goggin also aced this hole in the tournament of 1934. Other aces were scored by Ross Somerville in 1934, John Dawson in 1949, and Clive Clark in 1968.

Bert Yancey made two on this hole eight times in nine consecutive rounds in 1967, 1968, and the first round of 1969.

Hole No. 17, 400 Yards, Par Four
Nandina
345 Yards from Your Tee

Professional Strategy: This hole demands a straight drive or, even better, one with a little draw on it, to miss two trees, one on the right at about 230 yards, the other somewhat closer on the left-hand side of the fairway. This green, trap-guarded in front,

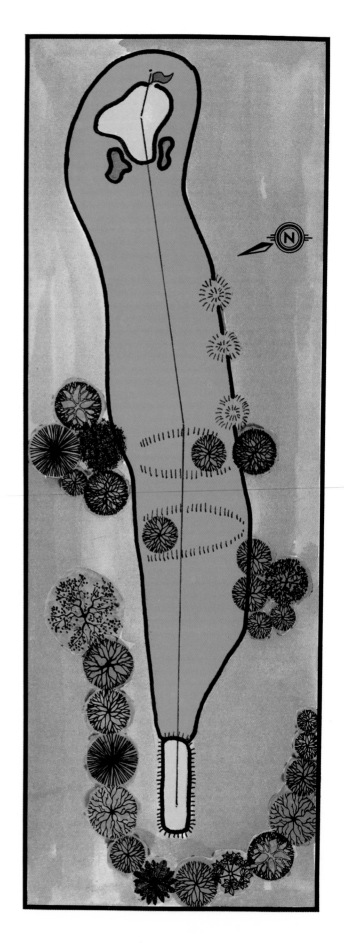

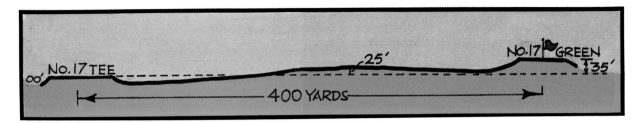

is somewhat uphill and has a crowned appearance with the pin usually up on the top of the crown. The second shot must be high with lots of bite on it or the green may be overshot. A difficult hole and one the professionals are happy to par.

Your Strategy: Leon tells you that the tree on the left at 170 yards is "General Ike's" tree. He hit it so often on his tee shot from here that he wanted that tree cut down. Leon says, "Miss that tree and you can have an open shot to the green. But don't go too far to the right either."

With these instructions swirling around in your head and getting more excited all the time now at your chances of breaking 90, you decide to aim directly at Ike's tree and slice the ball just a little bit by opening your clubface slightly clockwise. You swing a little too carefully, and your ball flies straight for the top branches of the tree, hits it hard, and drops directly downward, where it comes to rest under the tree. From the tee it is apparent that you will have swinging room under the tree, and the line to the green should be clear. Things could

be worse; at least you will have a shot for the distant green.

Your lie is a good one, and Leon hands you your three wood with the instructions to "hit it with everything you've got."

You can barely make out the green about 210 to 220 yards away with a wicked bunker in front of it. You swing and hit a beautiful rising three-wood shot, but on a line to the left of the green. You figured that you would slice this ball a little bit and the slice did not come off.

Your third shot to No. 17 green is from a very difficult downhill, side-hill position about forty yards away from the hole. There is a yawning bunker between you and the green, and you dare not even think of the possibility of leaving the ball in the bunker after this third shot is taken.

Your feet are above the ball, you lay open your pitching wedge, and you do a little praying that you can keep your head down and make this shot come off successfully—if you can just get the ball onto the green in three and down in two for your urgently needed five. You can visualize the arc of the

A difficult pitch from the left side of the seventeenth green.

ball over the bunker and up to the pin.

You swing, trying very hard to keep your balance. The shot comes off very well, carries the bunker, but stops very quickly once on the green. Again you have a problem making your five on the seventeenth hole. Visually you quickly calculate the distance between your ball and the hole. It must be all of eighty feet. You walk onto the green and pace off the space between your ball and the flagstick: thirty-one paces, uphill for the first thirty feet and then steadily rising until about twenty feet from the hole where the green's surface finally starts to slope downward to the hole. What a putt to save a bogey five! Uphill and then downhill. Being almost certain that you cannot accomplish the stroke, you resolve to do the best you can. You stroke the ball well and give it quite a rap. It's the longest putt of the day for you. The ball climbs the upslope rapidly, settles down on the flat terrain, and then starts to lose speed as it nears the hole. For a happy moment, you think, it may even go in to the hole, but then at the last second it switches off an inch or two and finally stops only one foot away from a magnificent one-putt. Even Leon shakes his head as you tap in the little twelve-incher for your five. You really have a chance. One more bogey, and your 89 is in your pocket.

Hole	Par	Your Score	±5s
10	4	5	1 under 5s
11	4	5	1 under 5s
12	3	3	3 under 5s
13	5	7	1 under 5s
14	4	5	1 under 5s
15	5	6	Even 5s
16	3	4	1 under 5s
17	4	5	1 under 5s

Notes on Hole No. 17   This hole has been both cruel and kind to Arnold Palmer. In 1959, when he was defending champion, he missed a two-footer here that cost him his chance to catch Art Wall, Jr. However, in 1960 he holed a thirty-five-footer for a birdie and then followed with a six-foot birdie on No. 18 to edge Ken Venturi out of first place.

Hole No. 18, 420 Yards, Par Four
Holly
395 Yards from Your tee

Professional Strategy: This difficult finishing hole finds the player coming out of a chute lined with trees on both sides of the fairway to the 180-yard mark on the left side and to 225 yards on the right. The hole doglegs uphill to an elevated plateau type of green hidden behind a small bunker in front. There is a flat bunker to the right-hand side. In the center of the fairway, waiting to catch a good drive, is a deep bunker at the 240-yard mark. Many professionals drive short of the fairway bunker with their three-woods, and then the shot to the green is a medium iron.

Now you have reached the moment of truth on your round. All you must do is get your bogey five here, and you have made your 89.

Your Strategy: Leon tells you that you need not worry about driving into the fairway bunker, that you can hit your best drive and will fall short of going into it. The wind is slightly against you, and, as you look out toward the northwest up over the valley in front of the tee, you can hardly believe that only one more hole remains to play. You know you have done well to save the last hole from disaster and still cannot believe your luck on No. 16, saving your four after going into the water.

You decide to swing away with this last drive, not steering the ball. The hill at the top of the valley looks unattainable, but Leon coaches you: "Just swing easy; you can do it."

Away she goes, a good swing, a satisfying crack, and the ball heads up the center of the fairway, as long a drive as you have had all day. For a moment, you are afraid that you have driven into the center of the fairway bunker but at the last moment the northwest wind seems to have some effect on the ball, and you can see it come to rest on the fairway just to the right of the bunker, very close to it but not in it. You breathe a sigh of relief at not being bunkered but start to worry about whether you will have any place for a stance for your second shot.

You and Leon hurry down into the valley in front of the tee and puff up the slope toward your second shot.

The ball has taken a good lie on the fairway grass just outside the right edge of the bunker. However, in order to make any kind of a swing at it, it will be necessary for you to stand in the sand of the bunker where your feet will be from eighteen inches to two feet below the level of the ball. And four strokes away from this shot is your 89!

You confer with Leon, and he says that the distance remaining to the elevated green is about 170 yards but all uphill. He asks whether you can swing your four wood. You take a practice swing but feel that the stance is so awkward that you would be better off to sacrifice distance for accuracy. Hit the ball up the hill to a spot in front of the green, chip on, and still you get your five.

You decide to use a three iron and go down on the shaft an inch or so. Keeping your balance very well and aiming fifteen degrees to the right of the green, because you know this shot will be pulled left on account of your stance, you swing away and hit an excellent low-lined shot up toward the right-hand side of the green. You know that you are going to miss the bunker guarding the left front of the green.

The ball raises a puff of dust as it comes to rest in the right-hand bunker. A little disappointed that it didn't end up on the putting surface, you are relieved that you are now close to the green with an excellent chance to save your score if you can only get this next shot out of the bunker and onto the green.

You remember that Arnold Palmer skimmed a shot out of the right-hand bunker in 1961 and eventually took a six on the hole to lose to Gary Player. The thought that you might do the same thing comes to

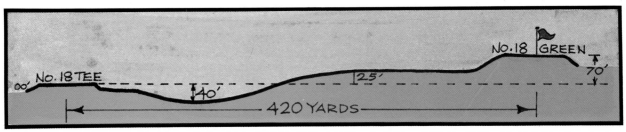

A difficult shot from the grass at the side of the bunker in the center of the eighteenth fairway. Notice how hard it is to determine where the flagstick is on the eighteenth green.

your mind as you and Leon make the last long climb up the hill to the eighteenth green at Augusta National.

The ball has a good lie on top of the sand in the far end of the right-hand bunker. Your shot is slightly downhill out of the bunker and then very much downhill once the ball gets onto the green. You are confronted with a very delicate shot. In order to be anywhere near the hole it will be necessary for you to pop the ball up out of the bunker and land on a spot on the very edge of the green no larger than a three-foot circle, from where the ball should trickle down to the hole.

You must get the ball out of the trap and down in two strokes to save your 89. You are afraid to hit the ball too hard for fear of going far past the flagstick and having a very long uphill putt to save your score.

Again, with a deep breath and a decision to play the best explosion shot you possibly can, you dig your feet into the sand solidly, keep your head down, and the result is an excellent blast out of the bunker. The ball, however, just barely clears the front edge of the bunker, catches the fringe of grass on the green edge, and stops abruptly just on the green.

You are elated at being on the green at last and now have a twenty-five-foot downhill slider to save your bogey five and your score.

Leon looks over the putt with you very carefully. He tells you, "Just touch it; don't hit it hard and aim about two feet above the cup."

Without taking too much time, you line up

your putt and tap it very gently. The ball rolls off the fringe straight along the line you intend and moves steadily on down the slope toward the hole. It comes to rest about ten inches below the cup, but now you feel that your task is successfully completed. You have your 89 if you can only tap in this tiny putt.

You line up the short putt, taking your time with your putting routine. You breathe deeply again and putt the ball squarely into the hole for your bogey five, your 45 on the back nine, and your 44–45 equals 89 strokes on Augusta National Golf Club! You have done it! You are Arnold Palmer, Ben Hogan, Jack Nicklaus, and Billy Casper all rolled into one! Remembering Gary Player, you throw your fist into the air in exultation. If there were a gallery, you would throw your ball to it. Leon is all smiles. "We did it, we did it!"

Notes on Hole No. 18   In 1957, when Doug Ford holed out his explosion shot for a birdie three from the front bunker, he exclaimed, "My God, that's the best shot I ever made."

It undoubtedly was. He won with 283 to Snead's 286.

Hole	Par	Your Score	±5s
1	4	5	Even 5s
2	5	6	1 over 5s
3	4	4	Even 5s
4	3	4	1 under 5s
5	4	5	1 under 5s
6	3	3	3 under 5s
7	4	5	3 under 5s
8	5	7	1 under 5s
9	4	5	1 under 5s
Total	36	44	
10	4	5	1 under 5s
11	4	5	1 under 5s
12	3	3	3 under 5s
13	5	6	1 under 5s
14	4	5	1 under 5s
15	5	6	Even 5s
16	3	4	1 under 5s
17	4	5	1 under 5s
18	4	5	1 under 5s
Total	36	45	
TOTAL SCORE	72	89	

60
A FINAL WORD

Overall, the Augusta National is not intended to be a punishing golf course. It is, however, a course that under tournament conditions (that is, with the green surfaces firm and keen), severely tests the player's temperament. The difficult greens demand fierce and unremitting concentration and determination. When the golf course is wet and the wind quiet, it is easy. We always hope it will not be that way during the first week in April.

ROBERT T. JONES, JR.

INDEX